Duties and Responsibilities for
Security
Officers in NYS

3RD EDITION

Terrance W. Hoffman, M.A.L.S.

Looseleaf
Law Publications, Inc.

43-08 162nd Street
Flushing, NY 11358
www.LooseleafLaw.com
800-647-5547

Library of Congress Cataloging-in-Publication Data

Hoffman, Terrance W.
  Duties and responsibilities for security officers in New York State / Terrance W. Hoffman. -- 3rd ed.
    p. cm.
  Includes bibliographical references and index.
  ISBN 978-1-60885-028-0
  1. Private security services--New York (State) 2. Police, Private--Training of--New York (State) I. Title.
  HV8291.U6H64 2011
  363.28'909747--dc22

                                                                                    2011003750

NOTIFICATION

This document is derived from the following material:

1- The eight hour pre-employment training course for security guards-course topics and objectives as copyrighted by the New York State Division of Criminal Justice Services.
2- The sixteen-hour on-the-job training course for security guards-course topics and objectives as copyrighted by the New York State Division of Criminal Justice Services.
3- The eight hour annual in service training course for security guards-course topics and objectives as copyrighted by the New York State Division of Criminal Justice Services.
4- New York State Division of Criminal Justice Services approved sixteen-hour on-the-job course submitted curriculum.
5- New York State Division of Criminal Justice Services authorized eight hour in-service course curriculum.

ABOUT THE AUTHOR

Terrance W. Hoffman is an award-winning, tenured faculty member in the Criminal Justice Department of Nassau Community College, Garden City, New York, where he instructs on law enforcement and security administration issues. He is the recipient of the prestigious State University of New York Chancellor's Award for Excellence in Teaching, the Nassau Community College Distinguished Faculty Award, the NCC's Sponsor an Educator Award and the Richard B. Lewis Award for Lifetime Dedication and Contributions to Criminal Justice Higher Education awarded by the Criminal Justice Educators' Association of New York State where he has served as both Vice President and Secretariat.

Throughout his 23-year career as a sworn member of the Suffolk County, New York Police Department, Mr. Hoffman served as a patrol officer, patrol supervisor, and investigator, retiring from active duty in 1991 as a detective-sergeant. During his on-duty tenure, he also served in the security industry at the operational level, as a consultant and in administration. As a New York State Certified Security Guard Instructor, Mr. Hoffman has developed curriculum and instructed for various Security Guard Training Schools.

Mr. Hoffman received a Master's Degree from the State University of New York at Stony Brook after completing undergraduate studies at Saint Joseph's College and Suffolk County Community College.

DEDICATED TO:

Peter, Joann, Mike, Rob,
Walter, Irene and Judith Anne

and they know why!

PREFACE

This volume contains eight chapters. Each, in turn, covers the knowledge-objectives the New York State Division of Criminal Justice Services require for completion of the various security guard courses. For the beginner, the first seven chapters include and exceed all of the course objectives required for the pre-employment education. These chapters include the ncw material added by the State late in 1995. A qualified instructor should be able to recognize the objectives and confine his or her instruction to those areas.

The objectives of the sixteen-hour on-the-job course are either included in an extension of the initial pre-employment course's objectives are clearly identified as add on objectives. The sixteen-hour course objectives follow the State's lesson plan and other New York State approved lesson plans.

Objectives for the annual eight hour in service course have been included. These objectives have been previously disseminated by the State. Some of the objectives have been incorporated into the appropriate areas of the pre-employment course because a review is required and the material has been expanded to meet the needs of this additional training. Other objectives are new and are identified at the beginning of that segment. In this course the State has allowed the addition of new objectives devised by the school. The results of a survey indicate that the following objectives shoud be included in this course: security history and current state of affairs, supervision, sexual harassment, narrative report writing and furthering security education. When trying to locate an objective the index should prove to be helpful.

This volume was designed with the student in mind. Similar subject matter is presented together. After completion of any aspect of security education, the student can refresh the memory or refer back to the book when handling situations.

No volume, large or small, can possibly cover the correct handling procedure of every situation involving human beings. This work presents guidelines based on developed curriculum, security guard input and some small measure of common sense. Company procedure, consideration of and adherence to law, both civil and criminal, the need to protect life and property and the respect of others' dignity should prevail when taking any course of action.

TABLE OF CONTENTS

Table of Contents (Continued)

CHAPTER 1

INTRODUCTION

1-1 INTRODUCTION

After taking a seat in this room, two reasonable questions should come to the would be security officer's mind. They are, *"Why am I in this classroom and what am I supposed to learn?"* The average answer to the first question is: because the State of New York wants me here. I am going to learn what being a security officer is all about is the usual answer to the second one.

The questions that remain unanswered are, *"Why does the State want security officers to become trained and regulated and exactly what is it that they will learn?"* This information will become clear as this chapter unfolds.

1-2 OVERVIEW OF THE LAW, WHY THE STATE WANTS POTENTIAL GUARDS HERE

Several years ago leaders in the security industry decided that all guards in New York State should be trained and registered. They approached an elected State official with this idea and he submitted a proposed law to the New York State Legislature. In 1992 the law, known as "The Security Guard Act of 1992," was passed. This law, now Article 7-A of the New York State General Business Law (G.B.L.) went into effect on or about January 1, 1994.

The law gave the State the power to regulate the "proper screening, hiring and training of security guards [based on] state concern and compelling state interest" (89-e, G.B.L.). State concern and compelling State interest means that the state has a duty to protect its residents from harm by passing laws that do just that. It was not by chance that this law was passed after a security guard shot and killed two young men outside of a Long Island high school. The guard was hired to protect the interests of the school district. He was not authorized to possess or use a handgun. The intentional killing of these two people is neither in the interest of the school board or in the interest of the residents of New York State. As a result of this horrendous incident, the guard was convicted of murder and society began to look into the identity and actions of security personnel more carefully.

The legislature also realized that the security industry is a growing field which needs regulation. Guards are employed in ever increasing numbers, in private business and at all levels of government as well. Some are specialized and others provide general protective services. Their responsibilities range from drug detection, a specialty, to preventing unlawful activities, a general duty. In short, the security industry is providing a level of service that traditional law enforcement agencies cannot supply. It was estimated that the security force in New York State is in excess of 100,000 members. They serve a large number of employers and clients. The State has a compelling interest in protecting those employers, clients and the public from ill intending or other misfits who pose as guards and from guard companies who hire the so called "warm bodies."

In realizing its duty to protect the residents of New York State, the legislature has decided that security guards who are employed to detect, deter, observe and report should be trained, registered and undergo a criminal history check. To accomplish these ends, the State has set standards of employment, mandated specific training, established a registration process, required liability insurance for guards and created an enforcement unit within the government.

1-3   EIGHT-HOUR PRE-ASSIGNMENT TRAINING COURSE, WHAT WILL BE LEARNED

The eight-hour pre-assignment course has been developed in accordance with the law. The course has seven topics, including this introduction (¼ Hr). The remaining topics are: Role of a Security Guard (1¼ Hrs), Legal Powers and Limitations (2 Hrs), Emergency Situations (1 Hr), Communications and Public Relations (1 Hr), Access Control (½ Hr) and Ethics (1 Hr). Finally, each student will review the material and take an examination (1 Hr). When the students successfully complete the course each one will receive a State issued certificate.

The introduction to this course provides an overview of the Security Guard Act of 1992 and discusses the objectives of the pre-employment course.

The roles security officers play are many. The industry is diverse. Some security officers will be generalists, jacks of the trade, others may decide to specialize, become experts in one area. This block of instruction offers an overview of the industry and outlines the general responsibilities, functions and duties relevant to security professionals.

The legal powers of security officers are no different than the powers given to New York State residents. Can a guard make an arrest and use force on some person are questions that will be answered in this topic. Security officers will realize that their powers in this area are less than the powers that police and peace officers have.

Any seasoned guard has experienced some sort of an emergency situation. Professional security officers realize that coolness and readiness are assets in coping with emergencies. Good plans result in good outcomes. This area of instruction provides an overview of potential emergencies and explains how guards should react to them.

Communication and public relations are very important parts of the job. Poor communication can result in aggressive behavior on the part of the person who is receiving the communication. It is for certain that a rude guard will leave a bad impression not only about him or her but about the company as well. Positive communication gains positive results for all involved. Knowing the process and the accompanying perceptions will help security officers be effective communicators.

Access control is a major part of the security function. Who and what are allowed into a premises and how this control is exercised are important aspects of security officer training and function. The elements of access control range from simple signs that read "keep out" to computerized key cards. Control is maintained through security personnel, physical security and environmental design.

Not many people would argue against the idea that people in the security industry should adhere to and abide by an ethical code. For one thing, by following that code a security professional will truly become that, a professional. All accepted professions have a code of ethics. The code defines behavior and conduct. It is a standard of measurement, a path to follow. Those who choose an alternate course should be weeded out because they bring the occupation down and are the cause of public disrespect.

The examination, a moment of dread for some, contains twenty- five multiple choice and true-false questions. The questions are based on the objectives of the topics. If there are misunderstandings regarding the questions or wording, they should be discussed with the instructor. Cheating is a violation of the code of ethics and will not be tolerated. If caught, those who choose to cheat will fail. Notification of this behavior will be made to the State via the class roster.

The certificate is a record of an accomplishment. It is a right of passage into the security field. The original certificate is to be kept by the student, hopefully in a secure place. A copy of that document is to be given to the employer as a validation that the student passed the required training. Remember give the employer a copy, not the original.

1-4   MISCELLANEOUS INFORMATION

The information that follows is useful for the student to know, but is not required in the pre-assignment training. This includes: further training, fingerprinting and photographing, criminal history and application for a registration card.

The Security Guard Act mandates further training. Once a guard is employed, he or she must complete a sixteen-hour, On-the-Job course. He or she must do this within ninety days of starting work. Every calendar year thereafter, the guard must complete an eight-hour, in-service course. Both courses should relate to the functions that that particular guard performs. These courses must be taken at a certified security guard training school. Armed security guards must attend a forty-seven-hour firearms training session. Each calendar year after the initial firearms training, the armed guard must return for an eight hour firearms in-service class.

Once employed, the guard must provide his employer with two sets of fingerprints and two photographs. These can be taken at the security guard training school or by the employer. Sometimes police department personnel will take fingerprints for the guard. Often there is a fee for these services. The fingerprint cards and photographs are sent to the New York State Department of State with the guard's registration card application and a background check. Be advised, that the submitted fingerprint cards will be used to compare the individual's rolled impressions with those fingerprints maintained on file in the Division of Criminal Justice Services.

An employer is obligated by law to run a background check on each new employee. This check is to determine if the new worker has been truthful on his or her application for a registration card. This includes a criminal history. If the perspective guard has been convicted of certain crimes, he or she may not be eligible to become a security officer. For a detailed list of those crimes and conditions consult section 89-f, subdivision 13 of the G.B.L. (most public libraries have New York State law books). Remember, they will compare fingerprint cards to determine if an individual has been convicted of a crime.

Once a guard is employed, he or she must file an application for a New York State security guard registration card. There are two varieties, armed security guard registration card and security guard registration card. The Department of State will process the application and run a criminal history check through the New York State Division of Criminal Justice Services. If the criminal history and application are acceptable, the department will issue the guard a registration card with one of the guard's pictures embossed on it. The cards are valid for two years. The State imposes a fee for issuing the registration card and for conducting a criminal history.

1-5 CONCLUSION

New York State has determined that there is a public need to regulate the security industry. To meet that end security officers must register with the state and meet certain standards. The standards include training and an acceptable background.

The State provides the minimum curriculum for this training in the form of mandated topics. Those topics range from the role of a guard to adhering to a code of ethics.

A professional security officer will enter or remain in the field only if he or she has been deemed to have an acceptable background, is of good moral character and is free from certain criminal convictions.

NOTES

CHAPTER 2

THE ROLE OF A SECURITY GUARD

2-1 INTRODUCTION

The functions of security officers are as varied as the types of employers or clients. One officer could be the personal body guard of a beautiful Hollywood star, another a watch person at an automobile dealership. Their specific functions and duties would be radically different. However, in a broader sense, all security officers have similar responsibilities, the protection of life and property on the terms of the employer.

Whether a guard protects a star or an automobile, each has the directives of detecting, deterring and reporting. Many types of situations must be detected. At times, detection can aid in deterring potential problems. In any event, these incidents must be reported, either orally or in writing or both.

Each guard must realize that he or she is a professional in a highly competitive service industry. To meet this end, being professional, each guard should have full knowledge of his or her duties, functions and responsibilities.

2-2 FUNCTIONS OF A SECURITY GUARD

The main function of a security guard is to provide his or her employer or client with professional protective services. Professional means being alert, honest, courteous, attentive, responsive, neat and clean. A lax guard is a negligent guard. He or she will miss much information, detect or deter little and give the appearance of not caring about the job. A discourteous security officer is very offensive. The average person has dignity and does not like being disrespected. A rude guard does not promote the reputation of the security industry and may, in the end, be the victim of harsh treatment, including violence.

Public Relations

Public relations is increasingly becoming an important aspect of a security guard's functions. This, in part, may be attributed to the public's growing awareness of the security field and the guards who perform security duties.

Public relations requires paying attention. An attentive guard is one who listens and responds positively to people. The appearance of not listening is a turnoff to people seeking or giving information. The communication process will stop and the other person will leave frustrated and possibly annoyed. Naturally, in negative contact situations, respect and cooperation is greatly weakened. To overcome this problem, a security officer should be responsive. Responsive means to show a positive interest in what is being communicated or a positive interest in a person's particular problem. It could mean being sympathetic or enthusiastic, depending upon the situation. In enforcement situations the response should always be firm and fair. When responding to people, words and phrases such as: "sir", "ma'am", "may I help you", and "thank you" should be used frequently. Words such as: "pal", "buddy", "boy", "girl" and vulgar or demeaning words should be left in the locker room. A security officer must be concerned with public relations between him or herself and co-workers, the employer, the public and agencies such as police and fire departments. Qualities such as character, attitude, appearance and knowledge of the job enhance a positive public image of the security professional.

Character

Character is a quality that consists of honesty, discipline and loyalty. Obviously, these are qualities essential in the protective service field. A person of character is respected and will prevent loss or damage, not accept unauthorized gratuities or bribes. He or she will not tolerate violations of company policy or unlawful activity. He or she will realize that moral courage is required to fulfill duties which may rub others the wrong way such as reporting violations and enforcing the various rules, be they laws or company rules. A guard with character will realize that much of the job can be routine and that he or she should not let the routine lull him or her into a lax attitude regarding the mission of protecting the employer, co-workers, the public and property.

Attitude

The concept of attitude has and will continue to be a sub-theme of this chapter. Here attitude will specifically be addressed as a function and responsibility of a security officer. The guard is often the first person a visitor or a co-worker encounters when dealing with a specific organization. A first impression, whether positive or negative is a lasting one indeed. A positive impression will enhance the image of the organization and may facilitate the future needs of the organization, such as increased business. A negative impression will have the opposite effect. Therefore, it is essential to good public relations that the guard be courteous, considerate, alert and responsive.

In part, the proper attitude consists of consideration for others. By demonstrating consideration, the guard will reduce friction and gain cooperation. Consideration takes into account that other people may, for example, make foolish inquiries of the guard or seem not to understand simple explanations. In these cases patience is required, not curt or discourteous responses. Consideration does not mean that someone should allow another to abuse him or her. It means being firm without being belligerent or being firm without demonstrating a threatening attitude. One should also avoid the threatened use or use of force in situations unless that threat or use of force is absolutely necessary.

Security officers should be fair and impartial when dealing with others. This does not imply that they must present a cold as steel attitude or demonstrate a lack of interest. A friendly approach to situations is appropriate unless circumstances make another approach is more suitable.

Finally, a security officer should be interested in doing his or her job. A lack of interest is conveyed to others verbally and through body language as having a poor attitude. Interest's rewards are job satisfaction and a feeling of accomplishment. When one feels good about one's self the expressions of self-satisfaction and accomplishment are conveyed to others as a positive attitude.

Appearance and Security Programming

Currently there are two types programming. They are the "hard approach" and the "soft approach." The hard approach utilizes the police type uniform and training is along paramilitary lines. The soft approach is less rigid. Clothing may consist of a sports jacket with a small identification plate or insignia, slacks, shirt and tie.

The hard approach is utilized when a command presence is needed such as during traffic or crowd control situations and in the deterrence mode. The police type uniform usually has the psychological power of implied authority. Since we were children, we were taught that the uniformed police officer is the person who controls people and situations. After repeated exposure to this thinking, we automatically associate a uniform with authority. Most of us are willing to submit to that authority without too much hesitation. This is particularly true if the person wearing it acts in a professional manner.

A soft approach is best used when an organization wants the public and coworkers to know that security is present, but does not want the often uncomfortable authoritative presence. In certain situations, this type of programming fosters cooperation and professionalism. Imagine, for a minute, walking into the lobby of a fine hotel, only to find a tall, burley security guard in a police type uniform, wearing a utility belt full of menacing gadgets. The first thought is, "This place has big problems." On the other hand, if one enters the lobby and notices a security officer dressed in a jacket and tie, that person begins to have a sense of security. The person would know who to go to for assistance and not feel uncomfortable about the establishment.

All security officers should present a neat and clean appearance. The clothing should be clean and worn properly. Ties, for example, should be worn from the collar, not from an open button hole. Hats, if worn, should be placed squarely on the head, not worn casually back on the crown. Personal hygiene is very important. One should not go on shift dirty, unshaven or reeking of body odor. If a security officer reasonably behaves as a professional, he or she will command respect and have fewer problems when dealing with people.

An attentive guard is one who listens to people. The appearance of not listening is a turnoff to people seeking or giving information. The communication process will stop and the other person will leave frustrated and possibly annoyed. Responsive means to show an interest in what is being communicated or an interest in a person's particular problem. It could mean being sympathetic or enthusiastic, depending upon the situation. In enforcement situations the response should always be firm and fair. When responding to people, words and phrases such as: sir, ma'am, may I help you, and thank you should be used frequently. Words such as: pal, buddy, boy, girl and vulgar or demeaning words should be left in the locker room. As a communicator the security officer must be concerned with public relations between him or herself and coworkers, the employer, the public and agencies such as the police and fire departments.

Knowledge of Job

Knowledge of the job is another important theme for the professional to consider. Learning is continuous because of change, addition or subtraction. In the security officer's work place rules are subject to modification. Employees are hired as some are fired, retired or moved up in the organization. Organizations are fluid, people are constantly moving about within the facilities (who belongs where). Cargo may continually come and go, thus conditions in a warehouse are changing. Laws change to meet the changing demands of society. Many of those laws affect how organizations operate. Changes in technology affect security operations. To meet this objective, security officers should be familiar with State and local laws, company rules and regulations, fire, safety and other emergency plans. Security officers should be familiar with first aid guidelines as well. The reasons for staying current with change is obvious. If one falls behind in this knowledge, security is compromised.

The security officer should also be familiar with the organizational structure, who does what and who is answerable to whom. This knowledge will aid in the public relations effort of properly directing visitors and employees seeking information.

2-3 PRIMARY DIRECTIVES

Security officers accomplish their responsibilities through three primary directives. They are detect, deter and report.

Detect

Detect means to actively go out and find something or someone. One could be looking for a potential accident or seeking a criminal. Detection requires patrol, observation and perception. To be successful in detecting, one must make an active effort to move about the post. For observation sake, there is no speed in patrol, the slower the better. While on patrol, security officers should note the conditions of safety equipment such as fire extinguishers and become familiar with their operations. The more he or she learns while on patrol the better prepared he or she will be to deal with an emergency.

Observation, as was noted earlier requires focus and attention. While on patrol one looks for that which is normal. If one does not know what is normal, one cannot tell what is abnormal or unusual. A broken window in an abandoned or unused building may very well be normal. A broken window in a retail store probably is not normal.

Perception is a combination of: observation, sight, hearing, smelling, touching, circumstance, past knowledge, experience and investigation. Perception is what one concludes after analyzing what the above combination reveals. For instance, a guard is on duty in a jewelry store and he or she observes a shiny yellow metallic bar secured in a locked glass case. He or she concludes that the bar is gold. This conclusion is based on the following facts: The guard is in a jewelry store. Gold is found in jewelry stores. Gold is a shiny yellow metal. Precious metals are usually secured in areas where the public has access. His or her conclusion may be enhanced if he or she picked up the bar, felt the metal and the weight. On the other hand, if the guard is in a novelty store and he or she observes what appears to be several shiny yellow metal bars on top of a display counter the conclusion would be very different.

Deter

Deterrence means prevention. The security guard should make every possible effort to prevent crimes, fires, accidents and other unacceptable incidents from taking place. This is accomplished through high visibility, uniformed appearance and random patrol.

A guard must maintain a command presence. He or she must be visible and alert while in a deterrence mode. A visible guard who is non-attentive to the surroundings and happenings will not deter the criminal who seeks an opportunity to commit crimes or an employee who violates company policy. He or she will not see the potential accident.

A uniformed appearance is a key to deterrence. That is one reason why the police wear uniforms and drive highly identifiable marked cars. A wrinkled, dirty uniform gives the appearance of disinterest. This can lead the would be criminal to believe that the guard does not care about deterring. Obviously, a neat, clean appearance is an important psychological aspect in deterring criminal behavior.

As was mentioned earlier, criminals seek opportunity to commit crimes. With the exception of crimes committed in anger, criminal activity is highest when the opportunity is present. Therefore, random patrol is an important aspect of deterrence. Random patrol takes effort because human beings are creatures of habit. We like routines. If our routines are disrupted we feel unsettled. In varying patrol, the criminal looses opportunity because he or she does not know where the guard will turn up next. A routine patrol, such as a watch clock system can be timed and the criminal knows exactly how long each round will take. He or she has an opportunity set by time. Guards should double-back, take different routes, speed up and slow down and move in different patterns.

Report

It has been said that, "The job is not done until the paperwork is in." In other words a report must be filed. Reports, either orally or in writing should describe unusual incidents. It is not necessary to report the usual. As was noted earlier, reports serve several different purposes. They show and record activity, define the job and can be used in legal actions (one security officer's report in New York City helped convict a man of murder).

Reports must contain details which record the following information: who, what, when, where why and how. No report is complete unless it describes every one of those essentials. Who is the most complex because there may be many of them. For instance, who reported the situation, who was involved, who witnessed it, who committed it and so on. When, where and how are the simplest to figure and record. Why involves a motive and may never be known, particularly when a crime is committed and the criminal is never caught. For more information regarding the six elements of a report see chapter 7.

2-4   DUTIES OF A SECURITY GUARD

Society has increased the responsibilities of public law enforcement through specialization and a focus on community policing. These increased responsibilities have created a void, in that the police no longer provide the routinely expected protective services of the past. This void must be filled and security officers are the logical choice. Additionally, in the past, private security has traditionally been the protective arm of industry. The era of the watchman is gone. Rapidly advancing technology with its ever changing needs, legal requirements and sophisticated company policies require trained and versatile security officers.

Today's security officers must possess knowledge of the organizations which they protect. This includes policies, post assignments, building layout, the hours of operation and the security operation. Guards must be aware of the demographics (population) of the area. Poorer neighborhoods present greater protective problems. In addition to the penal and criminal procedure laws, they must be familiar with laws that pertain to the facility's operation, such as safety (OSHA) and fire regulations. They must be cognizant of alarm and fire fighting procedures. They must know when and how to contact emergency first responders such as police, fire and emergency medical teams.

The duties of a security guard are broken down into two categories, they are general duties and site specific duties. General duties are the duties that the average guard may be assigned during any given work shift. They include: escort service, alarm response, crime prevention constant localized patrol, crowd control, traffic control, customer or client service, investigation and any other tasks that the employer deems to be necessary. Site specific duties are, in a way, specialist functions. For example, Guards assigned to retail outlets may only be concerned with arresting shoplifters. They would be taught the investigative techniques and suspicious actions associated with that particular incident. Some of the site specific tasks include the prevention, detection and deterrence of the following: theft, drug abuse, employee theft and white collar crime.

General Tasks

Escort Service

Escorting valuable property and people is a common occurrence in the industry. Security officers may be called upon to escort money from the organization to the bank. Others may escort visitors to destinations within the facility. Depending upon the employer, there are many situations that call for escorts. During these times the guard should be alert to his or her surroundings, happenings and suspicious people. It is wise to proceed directly from point A to point B. Any delay can be costly.

Alarm Response

Countless alarms are activated every day. Some are tripped by criminals or fires, others accidentally go off. With the increased public demand on the police and the limited tax dollars available to hire more, security officers are increasingly called upon to handle these situations. Alarms should not be handled routinely. Each call has the potential for danger. It is very easy to fall into the bad pattern of being careless, especially when one has handled a particular alarm many time in the past. Initially the guard should respond and survey the exterior of the building, looking for breaks in the glass, open doors and smoke. The security officer should also be alert for suspicious vehicles and people in the area of the alarm. If the survey reveals a problem, the dispatcher should be advised of it and a back-up requested. The back-up might very well be the police. They are trained in this area and have other resources, such as dogs, that will aid them in securing the building. If the building appears secure check the doors and windows to see if they open. Also feel the door for heat. If one opens or is very hot notify the dispatcher and call for the back-up. If nothing seems wrong, a professional will realize that the roof may have been broken through or someone may have remained in the building until after closing. The building should be carefully checked and the alarm reset. It is a wise idea for each guard to become familiar with the building's lay-out before an alarm response situation. This will aid during a later building search. If this is not possible, the guard should become familiar with the lay-out during a search.

Crime Prevention

Crime prevention is a responsibility of most security officers. This is accomplished through detection, deterrence, awareness, patrol and a professional demeanor or attitude. The most frequently committed crimes of concern to security officers are: larceny (stealing), criminal mischief including graffiti (vandalism), burglary, criminal trespass and robbery.

Constant Localized Patrol

Constant localized patrol is required to reach two of the three mandated directives, detection and deterrence. If a guard is not at a fixed post, he or she will most likely be patrolling in a motor vehicle, on a foot post or monitoring a closed circuit television. Remember patrol should be random, not routine.

Crowd Control

Among other situations, crowd control may be necessary at rock concerts, grand openings of shopping centers and public disturbances. It is important for security officers to maintain a uniformed, command presence and remain calm, especially in tense situations. During these times, guards may be called to direct the movement of the crowd. A firm clear voice is required.

Traffic Control

Traffic control can also occur where crowd control is necessary. It may also be required in other situations, such as the emptying of a parking lot after a major event. In controlling traffic the security officer should realize that verbal communication is hampered by closed windows, radios and the noise of car engines. In these situations the guard will rely on hand signals. They should be clear, obvious and crisp. When asking a motorist to stop, the guard should raise one stiff arm slightly above his or her head, with the palm of the hand facing the motorist. He or she may point the index finger of the other hand at the car he or she wishes to stop. The guard should not allow other vehicles to move until after the one he or she has signaled to stop has stopped. In moving traffic the guard should point with one hand and vigorously move the other arm in a circular, sweeping movement. During traffic control, the guard should dress in bright colored vests with reflective tape. At night reflective vests and flashlights are essential.

Customer-Client Service

Customer-client service is a general task that encompasses assisting visitors or co-workers who seek information such as those seeking directions to a specific location. This is a public relations aspect of the job. Attitude, appearance and character are important elements of it.

Basic Investigations

Basic investigation constitutes information gathering. All events that come to the guard's attention must be investigated. This means that sufficient information about the incident must be gathered to allow for the completion of an accurate report.

Other Tasks Assigned

Depending on the needs of the employer, security officers may be assigned to other duties that are not listed here. In each case those guards should be fully aware of what is expected of them. If there is a doubt as to this, then ask questions.

Specific Tasks

Theft

The detection of theft could be a specific task if that is the main duty of a security officer. This is the case when a guard is assigned to arrest shoplifters in a retail outlet. These guards are usually undercover, therefore they are not interested in deterrence or prevention. A person who knows that the store is protected by undercover agents may be deterred, but the main job is to arrest thieves. Another area of concern is pilferage by visitors, vendors, sales people and co-workers. A security officer can prevent pilferage by being aware of delivery times, access levels and visitor policy.

Substance Abuse

To say that drug abuse is a problem in this country is an understatement. Company owners realizes that drug abuse creates massive problems in business and industry. Substance abuse causes poor quality work, absenteeism, aggressive behavior, theft and a host of other problems that cost millions of dollars. This is a growing area for the security specialist.

Employee Theft

Employee theft is a major problem today. The victims range from the corner grocery store to the United States Government. Anything a thief deems valuable is subject to theft. This includes candy from a market to secret government documents on nuclear weapons. In addition to regular theft and theft of paid work time, espionage is a concern in this area. The secret formula for a popular perfume may be very valuable to another perfume manufacturer. A career in the area of detecting, preventing or deterring employee theft may be a very rewarding experience.

White Collar Crime

White collar crime is the crime of greedy businessmen and women. It could involve employee theft, often at the management level, but it may also consist of arranging stock market prices, defrauding investors, stealing from escrow accounts, kickbacks, bribes, sabotage, coercion, computer fraud and certain forms of corruption. Security officers in this specialty are highly trained professionals.

2-5 EMERGENCY SITUATIONS

The fact is unavoidable, sooner or later career security officers will face emergency situations. The keys to successfully dealing with them are calmness, preparation, training and practice. Calmness is important, if the guard panics so will others. Calmness comes with self-confidence. Self-confidence is gained through preparation, training and practice.

Security officers may encounter eleven emergencies. They are: fire, explosions, bomb threats, riots, civil disturbances, strikes and picketers, hazardous material accidents, natural disasters, medical emergencies, evacuations and crimes in progress. These will be covered in chapter four so they need not be addressed at length here.

At this point a security officer should realize that he or she must be prepared to handle these situations and still provide other services as they are called for by the employer or client. The guard must also realize that he or she is employed for specific tasks which are designated by the employer or client.

Security officers are limited in the scope of their duties and responsibilities to their respective companies' policies. Security officers do not have general police authority nor are they duty bound to act on behalf of the public, unless specified by law. They are not police or peace officers.

2-6   RESPONSIBILITIES OF THE SECURITY OFFICER

Security officers have seven responsibilities. If they approach these responsibilities with the demeanor described earlier they will be more successful in fulfilling their duties. These responsibilities include: enforcing company policy, maintaining order and security on the post, protecting people and property from harm, preventing crimes, fires and accidents, observing and reporting, access control and communicating with others.

Enforcing Company Policy

Enforcing company policy is a major aspect of the security officer's responsibility. He or she is often hired for this particular purpose. Company policies vary with the needs of each organization. These policies might include: enforcing regulations, such as "no smoking," logging-in specific visitor information, monitoring cargo flow, to name a few. All security officers should become knowledgeable in what portion of the rules and regulations he or she is responsible for enforcing.

The security officer should be aware that he or she must act in accordance with the company policy. There may be rules regarding arrests and the use of force, for example. Company policy will determine whether security officers are authorized to make arrests, use physical force against another person, use restraining devices such as handcuffs and carry weapons. They should be aware that company policy may prevent them from enforcing New York State or local laws. Company policy will determine what is reportable and how it is reported, when police involvement in company affairs is required, when to evacuate, how to patrol and so forth. Security officers are responsible to know what rules and regulations apply to their conduct and what limits are placed on them. In short, they should know their job descriptions.

Maintain Order and Security

All security guards should maintain order and security on their posts. They should have the area under control. This is accomplished by being aware of the surroundings and happenings on the post and by taking the appropriate action when necessary. To meet these objectives, the guard must be aware of the post orders and any changes or amendments to those orders. He or she should be briefed on the events of the previous tour by the guard he or she is relieving. A guard should brief the oncoming tour about any events that happened on his or her completed tour of duty.

Protecting from Harm

The foundation of the security industry rests with the concept of protecting people and property from harm. This is accomplished, in part, through prevention. Protection does not just mean safeguarding people and property from the dangers posed by a criminal. It includes the ability to perceive any potential problem and to take action before a harmful incident can occur. It means the ability to see that an unattended wet floor or an extension cord carelessly placed has the potential to cause an injury. This responsibility is very closely related to the fourth one, the mandate to prevent crimes, fires and accidents. Crimes, fires and accidents are harmful to the employer, coworkers and the visiting public. Protection via prevention is accomplished by following the directives of detect, deter and report.

Observing and Reporting

Observing and reporting are essential aspects of a guard's duties. Observation is a skill which is developed. On a daily basis people see a lot of things, but they do not observe them. For example, we see hundreds of license plates daily, not many of us observe them. Observe means to focus, to concentrate on a particular item or situation. If, through observation, a guard realizes a problem or a potential problem exists, he or she should take the proper action. Reporting is required as a means to explain what has occurred and what action was taken or should be taken. To this end, reporting also serves as a preventative measure. For example, a guard notices a frayed electrical wire. There is no action that the guard can take other than report the incident so an electrician can fix the problem. One aspect of reporting is self-protection. By reporting unusual incidents, criminal activity, dangerous or unsafe environmental conditions, the guard cannot be accused of negligence.

Access Control

A tremendous amount of time is dedicated to access control. Access control is controlling the movement of people and property into, within and out of a facility. This can be accomplished through escorts, passes and control logs. Those people whose access is controlled include: visitors, vendors, contractors or coworkers. It is safe to concluded that most areas not open to the public rely on some form of access control. Access control can range from a simple sign reading "employees only" to a complex arrangement employing guards, key cards and employee badges. More time will be dedicated to this subject.

Communication

Communication is a basic responsibility in the security industry. Security officers must communicate company policy to coworkers and the visiting public alike. Through communication guards direct and control situations, enforce rules and laws and assist people in their daily affairs. To effectively communicate, guards must know what company rules they are responsible for enforcing and what federal, state, and local laws affect the work place, such as fire codes that prohibit the locking of certain doors.

2-7   TYPES OF POSTS

Security officers are assigned to three types of posts, mobile patrol, foot patrol and fixed posts with or without closed circuit television (CCTV).

Many security officers are assigned to mobile patrol. They may be assigned to operate motor vehicles, scooters, motorcycles, bicycles, all terrain vehicles and horses. After reporting for duty and being briefed by the outgoing guard, security officers should check the vehicle. This is generally done by following a vehicle check list. If no check list is required, security officers should check the vehicle to determine if it can be operated safely and properly. They should check the lights, tires, oil, coolant, emergency and other equipment and, if the vehicle contains one, a radio control log. They should also check for new damage. Once this has been completed a note stating the results of the inspection should be recorded in a daily activity log.

Mobile patrol is adaptable for the outer defense of the employer's property. Mobile patrol enables guards to patrol and respond to calls faster than a foot patrol. Radio or cellular phone equipped vehicles allow for instant communication with the base and other patrol vehicles. A conspicuously marked patrol vehicle is a deterrent against crime provided that it is used in random patrol. The vehicle offers protection against the elements and from assaults as well.

Because of the radio and the mobility, these security officers may be the first responders to calls for service, including emergency calls. They are responsible for the safe and legal operation of the vehicles. They must obey the vehicle and traffic laws and company policy while operating the vehicles. They must also remember that they do not have the special privileges afforded to emergency vehicle operators. If they violate the law, they are subject to arrest.

Safe operation of the vehicle is essential. A security officer who becomes involved in a motor vehicle accident can no longer provide his or her employer with the protective service or respond to the assigned call. In addition to facing an arrest for reckless driving, the unsafe driving security officer may face civil litigation. His or her employer may be liable as well.

Foot patrol can be used in both the outer and inner defense. A security officer on foot patrol will have more contact with people than one engaged in mobile patrol. During these encounters, the security officer should be mindful that public relations or good will is an important factor in maintaining a positive image for both the guard and the employer. As with mobile patrol, the guard should be highly visible. Foot patrol should be a random undertaking. The security officer assigned to this patrol should be alert for potential hazards, accidents and rule violators. Because conditions on a post change, the alert guard will note those changes and be aware of how they affect safety on the post.

Whether the guard is assigned a foot post or mobile patrol, he or she is responsible for knowing the zones, sectors or post areas. This includes knowledge of the boundaries of those areas and the businesses within those boundaries. He or she should be familiar with the employees, proprietors and emergency phone numbers of each business. A security guard should realize that a supervisor may oversee the security operation of several zones. He or she should know which supervisor he or she is working for and what that supervisor expects of him or her in the way of job performance.

There are four types of fixed posts: base stations, access control posts, information post and stationary posts. The duties at a fixed post base station could include telephone and radio communications, routine administrative tasks such as completing logs, activity sheets and other reports. Base stations also serve as monitoring points for the variety of alarms in use today. Officers assigned to access control gates, guardhouses and the like have the responsibilities of keeping unauthorized people from entering the facility and keeping unauthorized property from leaving. They must not become indifferent when examining entry authorization documents. Informational posts are generally located where there is public access, in corporate lobbies for example. These guards should be aware of the building's layout. They should also know how to direct people to areas within the building or the area they are responsible for knowing. If these guards cannot provide a satisfactory answer to an inquiring person, they should not dismiss the person with an "I don't know," but rather make every effort to assist that person. This can be accomplished through phone calls, radio communication or consultation with maps, directories and other sources of information. Stationary posts are usually temporary assignments. Guards assigned to them may be required to control traffic, both vehicular and pedestrian or access. An example of this type of post could be at a temporary assignment at a rock concert where guards control traffic and access to the musicians.

Security officers assigned to fixed posts may be responsible for scrutinizing closed circuit television monitors (CCTV). CCTV is an extension of the fixed post's eyes and ears. They should be placed to focus on entry and exit points, corridors where access is limited, strategic access points within the building, where valuable property is stored or where ever management deems them necessary. The guards should be alert for unusual activity at those points. Tapes should be changed periodically to keep the quality of the images clear and crisp. Security officers should be aware that these tapes can be used as evidence in court provided that they are processed properly as evidence. When taping for evidence, the taping device should contain a clock. The clock should continuously record the date, day and time on the tape. This shows that the tape was not edited. Once taken for evidence the tape should be marked as such and stored where it will not be tampered with or contaminated, see Chapter Two in *New York State Criminal Law For Security Professionals*. To maximize the use of CCTV, each guard should be familiar with the operation and functions of the unit employed.

Every trade has its tools and the security business is no exception. Before assuming responsibility for the shift, each guard should make certain that the tools and equipment required to provide the protective service are available or operational. They include forms, reports, memo books, pens, radios, CCTVs and so forth. He or she must have an operating flashlight on all tours. Many locations lack electricity or sunlight. If restraining devices are authorized by company policy, each guard should possess a quality pair of handcuffs. Occasionally, they lock and cannot be operated until unlocked. The locks should be checked daily. Security officers should be aware of the weather conditions and make certain that their clothing is appropriate. Quality rain wear and boots can help keep security officers comfortable during inclement weather.

2-8   HISTORY AND CURRENT STATE OF AFFAIRS

Security has been with mankind since the beginning. One reason ancient people banded together was for the protection of both the individual and the group. The development of private security is a response to the public's needs and pressure. As cities grew and the communities became impersonal, communal protection was placed in the hands of the night watchman and private interests. Many of the night watchmen had no legal authority or training. Business concerns hired private individuals to protect businesses' interests. In rural areas reactive sheriffs responded to complaints then investigated them. Citizen groups known as vigilantes were formed to apprehend criminals.

In 1829 Sir Robert Peel of England introduced a law that would replace the loose protective effort with London's Metropolitan Police. Within thirty years major cities in the United States followed Peel's example and organized the forerunner of today's modern police agencies. In the beginning these agencies were not charged with law enforcement. They were peace keeping organizations. Unfortunately, they were politically corrupt and the hired officers were often the thugs and strong arm men of the controlling political party. Businesses that suffered losses had to rely on private citizens for theft investigation and loss recovery.

At the same time, in the mid-eighteen hundreds several security agencies were formed to meet the various new needs of an growing country. Pinkerton formed an agency to provide security for the railroads. He also investigated train robberies and other crimes committed against the westwardly expanding railroad industry. Brinks started a delivery service and expanded that operation into payroll protection. Henry Wells and William Fargo formed a freight transportation company and provided guards to protect the freight from theft. Holmes offered burglar alarms and developed a security business from this 1858 endeavor. By the latter half of the eighteen hundreds private security was solely responsible for industrial security.

Today, security is a growing and diverse field. This has resulted from an increase in crime, fear of terrorist attacks, budgeting problems in government that affect the police, and the expanding role of the police as social agents. Currently, the security industry supplies two and one-half times more guards than the police supply police officers. The amount of police officers today is about the same as it was in 1965. Our nation spends eighty billion dollars more for private security than the governments spend on police forces. The businesses and residents on whole New York City blocks, for example, have banded together to pay security officers to patrol those areas. They have done this in spite of the fact that there are hundreds of New York City Police Officers on patrol at any given time. As a cost cutting factor, one New Jersey municipality fired the entire police force and replaced them with security officers. Government is replacing the police with code enforcement security officers and assigning guards to posts at government buildings.

Today, the security industry is not only concerned with preventing crime and apprehending criminals, it is concerned with safety, waste, fire, new technology, environmental issues and in meeting the standards set by the Occupational Safety and Health Act (OSHA). To meet these demands, career minded security officers must become professional and formal training is important in reaching that goal.

2-9 SUPERVISION

Some security officers may decide that they would like to become supervisors and eventually managers in the business. Supervision requires leadership. To a certain degree, leadership can be gained through a college education. Depending upon the company, a college education may or may not be required for the position, but the education certainly can help. Several of the more reputable companies advertise for employment candidates with some college background. Also, the experience gained through military service or a law enforcement organization can be an asset for the potential leader. Leadership is learned. Anyone who desires to become a supervisor can learn leadership traits and become an effective supervisor. The keys are leading by example, knowing the job and understanding human nature.

The role of a supervisor is to make sure that the job gets done. In doing so he or she may use one or a combination of three approaches. They are the autocratic, democratic or free reign approach. The autocratic supervisor is the constant overseer. He or she demands that the objectives be gained in a specific manner. He or she is the "You do exactly what I say, when I say it." type of boss. The employee is not free to choose another method of reaching the objective. This type of supervision works well in emergencies and with new employees who lack confidence and do not know the alternative methods of reaching the goals. With experienced employees this style builds resentment and frustration because they are not allowed any latitude in reaching the goals.

The democratic supervisor lets the subordinate working group help decide what course of action will be used to reach an objective. He or she will take an active role in the discussions and may make the final determination, but the group has input in the process. This leadership style allows for employee growth and job satisfaction. The workers feel that they are part of the operation and that they are contributing to the organization. This style is effective with experienced employees who understand their roles and can contribute to the solution. It also helps new employees gain confidence and understand alternative methods of reaching the goals.

The free reign supervisor does not take an active role in helping his or her employees reach the organizational goals. Each employee is on his or her own and can reach the objective any way each chooses. In essence, this supervisor does not interfere with a chosen course, even if it is incorrect. This style works well with seasoned, trusted security officers who thoroughly know their jobs. It does not work with new employees who need guidance or experienced workers who require some support. New employees become confused as to how to proceed under this style and do not learn. Experienced workers become frustrated with the lack of support and can loose confidence. The group under a free reign leader is without direction.

Depending upon the situation, an effective supervisor will use all three methods. New or lax employees require strong direction. The autocratic approach is useful under those circumstances and in emergency situations that call for immediate action. Under normal conditions democracy will bring a cohesive work group into the field. With seasoned veterans a free reign approach will allow the supervisor time to attend to other responsibilities.

2-10 CONCLUSION

Security is one of the fastest growing occupations of the 1990s. All indications are that this trend will continue into the future. The field is expanding in part to fill a void left by law enforcement agencies. In filling this void, security officers will have expanded contact with the public and others. A professional attitude and demeanor will gain and reinforce a positive image of both the security officers and the industry.

To some degree the void has increased the duties and responsibilities of the security service. No longer are security personnel assigned strictly to the so called boring "warm body jobs." Jobs where very little intelligence, creativity or education is needed. Today, security officers are required to be flexible, often completing a variety of tasks on one given shift. Unlike their watchmen predecessors, guards are assigned to high profile, public relations positions in all types of settings, including but not limited to: public and private educational facilities, airports, hospitals, retail outlets, government buildings, municipal patrol, warehouses, manufacturing facilities, office lobbies, hotels and whole city blocks. They are employed to protect both public and private interests.

Regardless of the setting or the function, security officers should always realize that they are private citizens acting in accordance with employers' or clients' policies. They are not police or peace officers.

CHAPTER 3
LEGAL POWERS AND LIMITATIONS

3-1 INTRODUCTION

When the public order is disturbed, steps must be taken to restore it. In New York State criminal conduct is considered a public injury, in part because the public order has been disturbed. This idea applies even if the victim is a private person in his or her own home. Because public order must be restored as quickly as is possible, the law has allowed private people to make arrests and, at times, use force in doing so. These arrests and the use of necessary force must occur either during the commission of the offense or immediately thereafter. They cannot take place a day or a week later.

Security guards are private people. Private people are people who do not have police or peace officer status. One of the status differences lies in arrest powers. There is a difference in the arrest powers between private people and police or peace officers. Furthermore, police and peace officers are duty bound by law to take the necessary action in situations where arrests may be involved. Security officers are not duty bound to act, they can merely observe and report if that is what the employer requires. They must, however, take whatever action the employer mandates or possibly face a negligence action.

Anyone who chooses a career in security will eventually face a potential arrest situation. In every case the guard will be guided by his or her employer's policy. Some officers will be ordered to gather information and turn it over to the employer or the police, others will have the power to arrest.

In addition to knowing employer policy, every security officer should know what his or her legal obligations are in the area of arrest, detention and the use of force. If guards do not know this information, they can bring trouble to themselves and to their employers too. This is a gray, troublesome area. If a guard abuses this area or acts without knowledge or authority, at the very least he or she can be reprimanded. In some instances, they can be terminated. Others could face criminal charges ranging from harassment to murder. Finally, the guard and the employer could be named in a civil action for a variety of damages.

A complicating factor in these issues is public perception. People often mistake security officers for police officers and expect them to act accordingly. The public may expect security officers to arrest people who have committed crimes such as assaults and robberies when they occur in public. The guard can only be guided by company policy and the law of arrest, not by the excitement of the situation or the demands of the public. They must remember that their authority is different from police officers or peace officers in that police or peace officers can make an arrest based on probable cause. Security officers do not have this legal benefit. Security officers can only take the action that an ordinary person could take under those circumstances. They had better be right.

3-2 ORIGINS FOR ARREST AUTHORITY AND LIABILITY

Our law, whether it is federal or state, criminal or civil is based on English Common Law. English Common Law is based on precedent or the doctrine of *Stare Decisis*. This means that a court's decision today will be based on a court decision that was made in the past on a case involving similar circumstances. For example, if, today, a person owns an apple tree and an apple falls onto a neighbor's property, the apple belongs to the neighbor. This decision will be reached because long ago a court ruled that the apple belonged to the person whose property it fell onto. In addition to court decision, common law is based on daily practices and customs. Common law became the law of the land in the eleventh century when a king declared it to be the Law of England. It gained further support in 1613 when Sir Edward Coke, Chief Justice of England, declared that legislated law which contradicted Common Law was illegal. Common law is the foundation of the Bill of Rights, known as the Ten Amendments to the United States Constitution. The Amendments include protection against unreasonable search and seizure and self-incrimination.

New York State Law and Common Law provide arrest authority to police officers, peace officers and citizens, including security guards. Under this authority and conditioned upon certain restrictions police or peace officers have latitude in making arrests. They have the protective blanket of probable cause. This means that they can be wrong and are still protected against civil liability. A security officer cannot be wrong and is not protected if he or she is wrong. Loosely, probable cause is a conclusion that a person of average intelligence, judgement and experience would reach after reviewing the facts and circumstances of a situation. A police officer can arrest another person without a warrant when a person has committed:

a. any offense when he has reasonable cause to believe (probable cause) that such person has committed such offense in his presence.

b. a crime when he has reasonable cause to believe (probable cause) that such person has committed such crime, whether in his presence or not.

Later in this chapter the discussion will focus on the security officer's arrest authority. The attentive guard will note the phrases "in fact committed" and "in his presence." In security guard arrest situations the phrase "in fact committed" is substituted for "reasonable cause to believe" (probable cause). "In his presence" is a general arrest requirement for guards, however, it is not a necessary requirement for a felony. Police officers only need to witness minor offenses before they can make arrests. They do not have to witness crimes to make arrests for them.

Again, security officers must be aware of the company policy, company rules and regulations regarding arrests, custody and the use of force in meeting security goals. If there are any doubts about the policy, the guard should discuss them with a supervisor or company official. He or she should know exactly what is expected of him or her in those situations.

Offensive behavior, the resulting arrest and crime or offense classification are complex issues. Police officers receive extensive training in these areas and then, for practical reasons, are given a margin of error. Because of these complexities and many more, a security officer should seek the direction and assistance of a supervisor when handling arrest situations. A well-trained supervisor should be able to assist in determining: facts such as what offense has been committed, is being committed or is about to be committed. The supervisor should be able to help establish the identity of the perpetrators, complainants or witnesses. He or she can also help establish the time sequence of an offense. The supervisor should also be able to help in determining the amount or force required to subdue or restrain an individual.

Security officers should be aware that proving illegal conduct can be difficult. For example, the guard may realize that a theft was committed, however, if the guard cannot produce an owner who can state that he did not give the thief permission to take an item, the guard cannot prove that a theft occurred. When in doubt, if company policy allows, summon the police to investigate the situation. At the very least one should summon a supervisor. In the meantime, collect all of the available information and take notes.

The importance of knowing the laws of arrest, the laws governing the use of force, the prohibited conduct statutes and company policy is clear when one understands the problems a guard or guard company can encounter if a guard acts improperly. The guard and possibly the employer can be defendants in civil lawsuits. The guard can suffer in other ways as well. As was noted in the introduction, a guard could be reprimanded or terminated. Improper custody, excessive use of force or other unlawful conduct could also lead to a guard's arrest and prosecution.

A civil lawsuit is a claim of injury made by one person against another person, a corporation or the government. The injury can be an intentional one such as physically injuring another person on purpose. The injury can also be a negligent injury, not done on purpose, but rather done recklessly such as leaving a puddle of water in a hallway where a person slips and breaks an arm. If a person wins the case in a civil lawsuit, money is awarded to the person who made the claim. The award takes one of two forms, or both. One award is compensatory. The claimant is given money to compensate for an injury. The other award is punitive. In this case, the defendant is being punished for causing the injury. In some cases the claimant can receive money for both compensatory and punitive damages. A security guard can be sued for compensatory damage when he acts improperly or fails to take an appropriate action. He or she can be sued for punitive damages in the following circumstances: fraud, malice, oppression or wanton conduct to name a few instances.

Under the doctrine of *respondeat superior* the company employing a security officer can also be sued if the guard engages in misconduct while acting within the scope of his or her authority. In this situation the guard and the employer may both become defendants in a civil action.

3-3 FACTORS THAT SUPPORT ARRESTS

All incidents that result in arrests should be investigated as thoroughly as is possible before, during and after the arrest. The results of the investigations should lead juries to guilty verdicts. The following considerations should be included in the investigations: physical evidence, confessions, fingerprints and photographs, identification of the defendant, observations of the guard, information from the police and other sources.

Physical Evidence

Physical evidence can be important in proving guilt. Physical evidence is something tangible. It can be seen, heard, felt and possibly smelled. Physical evidence can be as small as a sperm filled with DNA or as large as the Twin Towers in New York City. Physical evidence plays two roles, one, it can show that a crime was committed, and, two, physical evidence can show who committed a crime. In the first case, for example, if an item is stolen, the stolen item shows the result or objective of the theft. In the second case, a fingerprint found at the scene of a crime can identify the criminal. In some cases the evidence can show that a crime was committed and that a particular person committed it. A sperm can show that a woman was raped and through DNA testing it can show who raped her.

Physical evidence must be handled in a certain way before the courts will accept it as evidence. This is known as the chain of custody. Once property is seized or recovered it must be listed and accounted for until it is either turned over to the police or brought to court. Evidence should be marked for identification and stored in a secure place. Additionally, an evidence log should be maintained. The log should note who took custody of the property, where it is stored, when it was placed there and who, if anybody, removed the evidence from storage and why. Naturally dates and times should be a part of the log. For further details regarding evidence consult with *New York State Criminal Law for Security Professionals* or legal sources.

Confessions and Miranda Warnings

Confessions are admissions of guilt. This is very strong evidence against accused individuals. Confessions can be given both orally and in writing. For a confession to be valid it must be freely and voluntarily given. In other words the person cannot be forced into giving it.

In 1966 the United State Supreme Court rendered the Miranda decision. In short, the court ruled that defendants are protected by the Constitution against making self-incriminating statements to the police. The court ruled that the police have to issue Miranda Warnings before taking confessions. Miranda Warnings are the "rights warnings" and start with the sentence, "You have the right to remain silent." A security officer does not have to give the Miranda Warnings unless he or she is acting at the request of a police officer. It is also recommended that the following security officers issue the Miranda Warnings, police officers moonlighting as security officers and security officers who are directly employed by any governmental agency, including those assigned to public schools.

Fingerprints and Photographs

Fingerprints and photographs are valuable as physical evidence. These are not the fingerprints and photographs taken from a defendant after processing. These are fingerprint impressions left at the crime scene and photographs taken during the commission of a crime or other offense. Fingerprints require technical processing, therefore, if discovered consideration should be given to protecting them from destruction and requesting the police to collect and process them. Photographs are routinely taken in instances where fraud may occur such as during transactions at automatic teller machines. Closed Circuit televisions are employed in many areas of the security field to detect and deter. Fingerprints and photographs can help show that a crime was committed and they can help show the identity of the perpetrator.

Identification of Defendant

Identification of the defendant is absolutely necessary if a conviction is to be obtained. Generally, the security officer must be able to state in court that the defendant is the same person who committed the offense. If this connection cannot be made, the defendant can be found not guilty. It is important that a guard remember the defendant. Detailed notes may help in bringing this recollection about. Any person who can identify the perpetrator should remain at the site until the information can be processed or until the police have completed that aspect of the investigation.

Observations of Guard

What the guard saw and heard during an illegal incident is very important. Most arrests involving guards and private people will result from what they saw. In many cases the law does not allow guards to make arrests unless they observed the offense during its commission. What a guard heard can also be important. If the security officer heard the accused tell another that he or she committed a crime, that information can be used against the accused.

Information from Police and Other Sources

Information from police and other sources can be useful in starting an investigation. For reasons that will become clear later, this information should not be used as the basis for an arrest. If the information comes from sources other than the police, the security officer must be prepared to prove two points. The first point is the reliability of the source. Several questions must be answered before reliability is determined. Some of them are: How reliable has this informant been in the past? Has he or she given the guard previous information that turned out to be true? If so, how many times in the past? The second point focuses on how the informant came by the information. Some questions in this area are: Is the information first-hand, based on the personal knowledge of the informant? Is the offense continuous in nature? How old is the information? There are no pat answers to these and other questions because each case is judged on its own merits, on a case by case basis.

3-4 DEFINITIONS OF FELONY, MISDEMEANOR AND VIOLATIONS AND OFFENSE

For arrest purposes the law is broken down into three categories: felony, other offenses and age. Basically, one must understand two concepts. One, the law that controls an arrest for a felony is different than the law that controls arrests for other offenses. Two, in certain circumstances a person under the age of sixteen cannot be arrested for violating laws that are not crimes. To understand this more clearly one must understand the following penal law definitions: offense, felony, misdemeanor, violation and crime. One must also understand the "defense of infancy."

"Offense" roughly means any illegal conduct which can result in jail time or a fine. Felonies, misdemeanors and violations are offenses punishable by jail time or fines (10.00-1, PL). If a person commits an offense he or she can be arrested and punished by the state. Some conduct is illegal but arrests are not authorized. The penalty in these cases is an award for damages. The victim receives the award, not the State of New York. In these cases the illegal activity is a violation of civil law. Civil law violations do not result in jail time, nor is a fine levied.

According to Black's Law Dictionary a felony is "a crime of a graver or more atrocious nature than those designated as misdemeanors." According to the penal law a felony is **"...an offense for which a sentence to a term of imprisonment in excess of one year may be imposed" (10.00-5, PL).** This means that if a person is sentenced for committing an offense and the term is one year and one day in jail, he has been sentenced for a felony. In the United States the most severe punishment for a felony is death.

According to Black's Law Dictionary misdemeanors are "offenses lower than felonies and generally those punishable by fine or imprisonment otherwise than in a penitentiary." "Misdemeanor" literally means misbehavior. Its penal law definition is **"...an offense, other than a "traffic infraction," for which a term of imprisonment in excess of fifteen days may be imposed, but for which a sentence to a term of imprisonment in excess of one year cannot be imposed (10.00-4 PL).** This means that if convicted of a misdemeanor the defendant can receive a sentence of between sixteen days and one full year jail.

A "violation" is **"...an offense, other than a traffic infraction, for which a sentence to a term of imprisonment in excess of fifteen days cannot be imposed (10.00-3, PL).** If a person is sentenced to between one and fifteen days in jail, he has been convicted of a violation. Notice, as the offenses get more serious, the punishment gets tougher.

"Crime" is defined by Article 10.00-6 of the penal law as either a misdemeanor or a felony. The only offenses of concern here are those that are punishable by between sixteen days in jail and, as of September, 1995, possibly death.

New York State Law provides a "Defense of Infancy." Basically, this means that people under the age of sixteen are immune from criminal prosecution. There are exceptions in serious felony cases. The police and the court systems handle these cases very differently than they handle cases involving people who are over sixteen years old. People under sixteen can be arrested if they commit "crimes" but, they cannot be arrested if they commit violations. Certain penal law offenses are violations. Harassment, disorderly conduct and trespass are among the violations. People under the age of sixteen cannot be arrested for those offenses. For example, if a security officer is slapped in the face by a fifteen year old, he cannot arrest that person. If a sixteen year old did the same thing, he or she could be arrested. Anyone over the age of seven can be arrested if he or she commits a "crime" which is either a misdemeanor or felony.

3-5 ARRESTS BY A SECURITY OFFICER OR A PRIVATE PERSON

When and Where

The New York State Criminal Procedure Law (CPL) authorizes arrests by private people. That law states:

1 **Subject to the provisions of subdivision two, any person may arrest another person (a) for a felony when the latter has in fact committed such felony, and (b) for any offense when the latter has in fact committed such offense in his presence.**

2 **Such an arrest, if for a felony, may be made anywhere in the state. If the arrest is for an offenses other than a felony, it may be made only in the county in which such offense was committed (140.30).**

This seems simple enough, yet subdivision one is the basis of much civil litigation. The law suits develop because people do not fully understand this law and how the courts have interpreted it. Subdivision one requires an analysis.

Firstly, an arrest is the taking of a person into custody so that he may be held to answer for the commission of an offense. The person is being deprived of his or her liberty or freedom of movement. If, one detains another person against that person's will for suspicion of committing an offense, the latter's detention is an arrest. Arrests take place in any number of ways. If a person is cornered by three of four security officers and that person is not allowed to leave, he has been arrested. A person is arrested if he or she is not allowed to leave the building. A person is arrested if he or she is detained by fear, threat, intimidation or physical force. Remember, an offense is any conduct that is punishable by jail time or a fine.

Standard of Proof

Subdivision one has two areas of concern. One area involves only felonies which are very serious crimes. The other area covers all offenses ranging from traffic infractions to felonies. The law states that one can arrest a person who has in fact committed a felony. This means two things. One, the felony has in fact been committed. Two, that the person being arrested has in fact committed that particular felony. Because of the phrase "in fact" there cannot be a mistake on either issue. If the arrested person is found not guilty or it has been determined that, for some reason, the felony was not committed, the security guard's arrest may be held to be invalid. He or she can be sued for false arrest.

Notice that there is no "presence" requirement in the felony area. The arresting person does not have to witness the felony. The arrest can be based on the facts of the situation as long as the guard is right. The problem with this aspect is if a guard arrests another for a felony which he or she did not witness and the offense in reality is a misdemeanor, the arrest will be deemed to be invalid because of the "presence" requirement needed for offenses other than felonies.

The second area of this law states that a person can arrest another person for any offense when the latter has in fact committed the offense in the arresting person's presence. Again the phrase "in fact" is present, subsequently the arrested individual must have committed the offense in question. The added requirement of "in the arresting person's presence" means that a guard must actually eye witness the offense's commission. Arrests in non-felony cases cannot be based on the facts of the situation, no matter how much those facts point towards guilt, unless the security officer sees the offense being committed.

Arrests for felonies can be made anywhere in the state. Arrests for offenses other than felonies can only be made in the county of occurrence. One might think that a guard can make an arrest in Buffalo a week after a felony was committed in New York City. That is not correct. Private people can only arrest during the commission of an offense or immediately thereafter. This means that one could pursue a felon to Buffalo and arrest him there. In non-felony cases, one could pursue the offender throughout the county of occurrence. If the non-felony offender makes it over the county line, the chase must end.

Procedure for Taking People into Custody

Section 140.35 of the CPL describes when and how arrests are to be made. Arrests can be made "**at any hour of any day or night**." Clearly, there is no time constraint. Once a person is arrested, subdivision two states that the arresting security officer "**must inform the person whom he is arresting of the reason for such arrest unless he encounters physical resistance, flight or other factors rendering such procedure impractical**." Obviously if a person is resisting the arrest or is running away the concentration is focused on stopping either the resisting or running. To make this notification is an ineffective waste of energy. Another situation that would render the notification impractical is arresting a person while he or she is committing the offense. Subdivision three authorizes the use of physical force in making an arrest. Force can only be used in accordance with the laws of justification, a topic that will be discussed shortly.

Section 140.30 CPL explains what is done with an arrested person after the arrest. Subdivision one states that the guard "**must without unnecessary delay deliver or attempt to deliver the person arrested to the custody of an appropriate police officer...he may solicit the aid of any police officer and the latter...must assist in delivering the arrested person to the appropriate police officer.**"

An unnecessary delay is an unreasonable delay. The courts understand and accept the idea that there can be reasonable delays. A reasonable delay will not hurt the security officer's case. Reasonable delays include time to process the prisoner, time to record confessions and finish the immediate investigation. The key to a reasonable delay is a justifiable explanation of how the time was spent. What is reasonable is a conclusion that a person of average intelligence, judgement and experience would reach after reviewing all of the facts.

The appropriate police officer is one who has the authority to enforce laws at the location of the arrest. An arresting security officer need not bring the arrestee to a police station to satisfy the delivery requirement. Calling the police and turning the arrestee over to them at the arrest location is acceptable. Subdivision 3-4 of this law states that the police are not obligated to receive custody of the arrestee if they believe that the arrest is invalid or unauthorized.

After the defendant is turned over to the appropriate police officer, the security guard must make any and all required court appearances resulting from that arrest. Failure to do so could result in a dismissal of the charge against the defendant. This situation could result in a civil lawsuit against the guard and the employer.

3-6 USE OF FORCE IN EFFECTING AN ARREST OR PREVENTING AN ESCAPE

Every arrest situation poses hazards for the arresting agent. They include resistance and possible injury. When effecting an arrest, the guard should have a plan. He or she should consider safety first. The guard should pick the time and place of arrest, when he or she has the advantage. Care should be taken to avoid involving innocent bystanders who could suffer injuries if the arrest turns into a resistive confrontation. The area should be devoid of potential offensive weapons. Two officers should be deployed to arrest. Once an arrest is made the security officer is responsible for the safety of the arrestee. The arrestee should be constantly supervised to avoid potential problems such as escape or weapons access.

Security officers should be mindful that people, even criminals, do not want to be disrespected. If one approaches the arrest situation with this in mind, the possibility of resistance is greatly reduced. If one approaches the intended arrestee with a hostile or belligerent attitude the potential for resistance increases. It is much easier to escalate than to defuse a situation. When a security guard approaches a situation in a firm, business-like manner, most arrestees will be more inclined to submit to an arrest. If it is needed, one can, by degree, become more forceful. By approaching the situation forcefully, one cannot, by degree, become business like. An offended person will remain hostile. Public relations has its place even in arrest situations.

If resistance is met or escape from custody is occurring, Article 35 of the New York State Penal Law (PL) authorizes the use of force in making an arrest or preventing the escape. Under specified circumstances the law authorizes the use of two types of force, "physical force" and "deadly physical force." Security officers may use force under two conditions. The first is at the direction of a police or peace officer. The second circumstance occurs when they are acting on their own account. In the first case it is unlawful to refuse to aid the police or peace officer unless the guard knows that the police or peace officer is wrong or unauthorized (35.30-3, PL).' In the second case the law reads as follows:

4. **A private person acting on his own account may use physical force, other than deadly physical force, upon another person when and to the extent that he reasonably believes such to be necessary to effect an arrest or to prevent the escape from custody of a person whom he reasonably believes to have committed an offense and who in fact has committed such offense; and he may use deadly physical force for such purpose when he reasonably believes such to be necessary to:**
    (a) **defend himself or a third person from what he reasonably believes to be the use or imminent use of deadly physical force; or**

(b) Effect the arrest of a person who has committed murder, manslaughter in the first degree, robbery, forcible rape or forcible criminal sexual act and who is in immediate flight therefrom (35.30-4, PL).

For a security officer to fully understand this law he or she must know and understand the following: Certain Article 10 definitions, what "reasonably believes" and "necessary" mean and the statutes regarding murder, manslaughter, robbery, rape and criminal sexual act. Once these notions are understood, this law is more easily understood.

Laws and legal terms are often defined by law and judicial interpretation, not by the dictionary. The phrase "physical force" has no current legal definition. Its meaning is confined to a certain category of force because the phrase "deadly physical force" has a penal law definition. Therefore "physical force" is any force that is not "deadly physical force." Deadly physical force" is: "**...physical force which, under the circumstances in which it is used, is readily capable of causing death or other serious physical injury**" (10.00-11, PL). Notice the phrase "readily capable." One does not have to actually injure another to use deadly physical force. Assuming a combat crouch, pointing a cocked and loaded gun at someone's head is using deadly physical force. This is true because the weapon in this position is readily capable of causing death or other serious physical injury. One must also remember that the use of deadly physical force can be intentional or accidental.

To more fully understand what "deadly physical force" is all about the guard must know what constitutes "serious physical injury." "Serious physical injury" also has a penal law definition which is "**...physical injury which creates a substantial risk of death, or which causes death or serious and protracted [lengthy] disfigurement, protracted [lengthy] impairment of health or protracted [lengthy] loss or impairment of the function of any bodily organ**" (10.00-10, PL).

Reasonably believes is a rational belief that a certain course of action is required. The actor draws this conclusion based on the attending facts of a situation. In many cases physical contact occurs during an arrest. Contact is a means of exercising control over the arrestee. Control is essential during the arrest process. The contact may be as little as taking hold of the arrestee's arm or as serious as killing him. The key to this contact is reasonableness. There are two standards of reasonableness. One is the subjective standard, the other is the objective standard. The subjective standard is what the actor thought was necessary under the circumstances. The objective standard is a conclusion that a person of average intelligence, experience and judgement would reach after reviewing the facts of a situation. Most people would agree with the amount of force used if an actor advised a person the he was under arrest, took hold of his arm and escorted him to a processing room. However, the average person would disagree with the actor if, after taking hold of the arm, he punched the arrestee three times in the face to ensure compliance to the actor's demands.

Necessary means that the actor believed that there was no other alternative but to use force. Necessary also means that the amount of force used was just enough to accomplish the objective. In the case noted above, grabbing the person's arm may have been necessary, but without further resistance, punching the arrestee three times in the face was unnecessary.

The crimes outlined in the immediate flight section of this law are very serious crimes. The security professional should become familiar with them by consulting *New York State Criminal Law For Security Professionals* or the *New York State Penal Law.*

The use of deadly physical force is the last resort. The criminal justice system will closely analyze every situation where that force is used. The courts strictly interpret these laws in those cases. The United States Supreme Court has already ruled that the police cannot employ deadly physical force when attempting to arrest non-dangerous, unarmed felons. If the police are prohibited from the use of deadly force in those cases, certainly, security officers should not use it either. If there is a doubt, or the conduct could be seen as reckless conduct, do not use this force.

The security officer should also remember that the use of deadly force can be done by accident. If in the heat of an arrest situation a security officer goes from poking someone with a flashlight to hitting the person on the head with it, he may well have gone from using physical force to using deadly physical force. Smashing someone's head with a heavy flashlight can cause a skull fracture and, by definition, that could be a serious physical injury. Under the wrong circumstances, a choke-hold could be seen in the same light.

3-7 ARTICLE 10, DEFINITIONS

A person's knowledge of the Penal Law must include Article 10. The phrases defined there will appear throughout the law. At this point, all of the relevant definitions will be reviewed. Some of the definitions have been excluded.

§10.00 Definitions of terms of general use in this chapter (law).

Except where different meanings are expressly specified in subsequent provisions of this chapter, the following terms have the following meanings:

1. **"Offense"** means conduct for which a sentence to a term of imprisonment or to a fine is provided by any law of this state or by any law, local law or ordinance of a political subdivision of this state, or by any order, rule or regulation of any governmental instrumentality authorized by law to adopt the same.

2. **"Traffic infraction"** means any offense defined as "traffic infraction" by section one hundred fifty-five of the vehicle and traffic law.

3. **"Violation"** means an offense, other than a "traffic infraction," for which a sentence to a term of imprisonment in excess of fifteen days cannot be imposed.

4. **"Misdemeanor"** means an offense, other than a "traffic infraction," for which a sentence to a term of imprisonment in excess of fifteen days may be imposed, but for which a sentence to a term of imprisonment in excess of one year cannot be imposed.

5. **"Felony"** means an offense for which a sentence to a term of imprisonment in excess of one year may be imposed.

6. **"Crime"** means a misdemeanor or a felony.

7. **"Person"** means a human being, and where appropriate, a public or private corporation, an unincorporated association, a partnership, a government or a governmental instrumentality.

8. **"Possess"** means to have physical possession or otherwise to exercise dominion or control over tangible property.

9. **"Physical injury"** means impairment of physical condition or substantial pain.

10. **"Serious physical injury"** means physical injury which creates a substantial risk of death, or which causes death or serious and protracted disfigurement, protracted impairment of health or protracted loss or impairment of the function of any bodily organ.

11. **"Deadly physical force"** means physical force which, under the circumstances in which it is used, is readily capable of causing death or other serious physical injury.

12. **"Deadly weapon"** means any loaded weapon from which a shot, readily capable of producing death or other serious physical injury, may be discharged, or a switchblade knife, gravity knife, pilum ballistic knife, metal knuckle knife, dagger, billy, blackjack or metal knuckles.

13. **"Dangerous instrument"** means any instrument, article or substance, including a "vehicle" as that term is defined in this section, which, under the circumstances in which it is used, attempted to be used or threatened to be used, is readily capable of causing death or other serious physical injury.

14. **"Vehicle"** means a "motor vehicle", "trailer" or "semi-trailer," as defined in the vehicle and traffic law, any snowmobile as defined in the parks and recreation law, any aircraft or any vessel equipped for propulsion by mechanical means or by sail.

15. **"Public servant"** means (a) any public officer or employee of the state or of any political subdivision thereof or of any governmental instrumentality within the state, or

    (b) any person exercising the functions of any such public officer or employee. The term public servant includes a person who has been elected or designated to become a public servant.

17. **"Benefit"** means any gain or advantage to the beneficiary and includes any gain or advantage to a third person pursuant to the desire or consent of the beneficiary.

Article 10 is relatively straightforward. However, there are a several points which should be considered. Four of the definitions of this article have been addressed earlier. They include, deadly physical force, serious physical injury, felony and offense. At this time there is no need for further discussion regarding them.

3-8 CULPABILITY

Culpable roughly means criminal responsibility. Culpability is a state of mind. In New York there are four mind-sets that affect criminal conduct. They are: "intentionally," "knowingly," "recklessly" and "with criminal negligence." Generally, a person cannot commit a penal law offense if he does not have "...the accompanying mental state which constitutes each offense" (1.05-3, P.L.). Unless the law clearly indicates otherwise, culpability should be considered to be an element of every penal law offense. The security professional should understand that a defendant will not be convicted if the element of culpability cannot be proved beyond a reasonable doubt.

The few offenses that do not require culpability are offenses of "strict liability." Strict liability means that a person can be found guilty of an offense merely because he engaged in the offensive conduct, regardless of his mind-set. Generally, "strict liability" applies to penal law offenses which involve the ages of children. Statutory rape is an example. Under proscribed circumstances, it is unlawful for a person over the age of twenty-one to have sexual intercourse with a person under the age of seventeen. Legally, it does not matter what the twenty-one year old thought the age of the other person was. The twenty-one year old cannot claim that he is not guilty because he thought that the other person was seventeen or older. Likewise, it is illegal for a bartender to serve an alcoholic beverage to a person under twenty-one, even if the bartender thought that the patron's age was over twenty-one.

The laws prohibiting conduct usually express a culpable state. The wording could appear in a statutory definition, as is the case with larceny, (155.05-1, P.L.) or in the area that explains the prohibited behavior, such as assault, (120.00, P.L.). However, if a certain conduct obviously requires a mental state the law may not specifically mention culpability. The mind-set is assumed to exist. For example, if a tattoo artist plies his trade on a person under the age of eighteen, he can be found guilty of unlawfully dealing with a child (260.20-3, P.L.). That law does not define a culpable state. However, the artist cannot tattoo a figure into another person's skin unless he does so intentionally and knowingly.

For a complete understanding of culpability a review of the pertinent statutes are in order:

§15.00   Culpability; definitions of terms.

The following definitions are applicable to this chapter:

1. **"Act"** means a bodily movement.

2. **"Voluntary act"** means a bodily movement performed consciously as a result of effort or determination, and includes the possession of property if the actor was aware of his physical possession or control thereof for a sufficient period to have been able to terminate it.

3. **"Omission"** means a failure to perform an act as to which a duty of performance is imposed by law.

4. **"Conduct"** means an act or omission and its accompanying mental state.

5. **"To act"** means either to perform an act or to omit to perform an act.

6. **"Culpable mental state"** means "intentionally" or "knowingly" or "recklessly" or with "criminal negligence," as these terms are defined in section 15.05.

§15.05   Culpability; definitions of culpable mental states.

The following definitions ar applicable to this chapter:

1. **"Intentionally."** A person acts intentionally with respect to a result or to conduct described by a statute defining an offense when his conscious objective is to cause such result or to engage in such conduct.

2. **"Knowingly."** A person acts knowingly with respect to conduct or to a circumstance described by a statute defining an offense when he is aware that his conduct is of such nature or that such circumstances exists.

3. **"Recklessly."** A person acts recklessly with respect to a result or to a circumstance described by a statute defining an offense when

he is aware of and consciously disregards a substantial and unjustifiable risk that such result will occur or that such circumstance exists. The risk must be of such nature and degree that disregard thereof constitutes a gross deviation from the standard of conduct that a reasonable person would observe in the situation. A person who creates such a risk but is unaware thereof solely by reason of voluntary intoxication also acts recklessly with respect thereto.

4. **"Criminal negligence."** A person acts with criminal negligence with respect to a result or to a circumstance described by a statute defining an offense when he fails to perceive a substantial and unjustifiable risk that such result will occur or that such circumstance exists. The risk must be of such nature and degree that the failure to perceive it constitutes a gross deviation from the standard of care that a reasonable person would observe in the situation.

The following aspects of culpability are overviews of the sections. For an advanced understanding a security officer should refer to the penal law.

§15.10 Requirements for criminal liability...

This section explains that the minimum requirement for the commission of an offense is an act or omission. The section also distinguishes the difference between offenses involving strict liability and mental culpability.

§15.15 Construction of statutes with respect to culpability.

Phrases such as "with the intent to defraud" and "knowing it to be false" can be substituted for two of the four mental states described above. If one such term appears in a statute it applies to every element of the whole section. Sometimes the culpable mental states do not appear in the law, but by the very nature of the conduct culpability is present (the tattoo artist noted above). Generally an offense is a culpable offense unless the legislature clearly indicates that the offense is one of strict liability. This subdivision applies to the penal law and other laws also.

§15.20   Effect of ignorance or mistake.

Generally, neither is an excuse for unlawful conduct. A security officer should be aware that there are exceptions. This section describes strict liability regarding the ages of children discussed earlier.

§15.25   Effect of intoxication upon liability.

Intoxication is not a permissible defense unless it negates an element of an offense.

All of the statutory law that follows will require culpability. Because of this fact, a security officer should be more than familiar with the concepts embodied in the four mental states of mind.

Intentionally means that the offender has thought about what he wants to accomplish. Intentionally is the decision to engage in a conduct. This does not mean that a lengthy plan has to be formulated. It could mean that, but intentionally would also include the idea that a thought flashed across a person's mind before he acted. Intentionally can effectively be described as committing an offense "on purpose."

Knowingly should be understood to mean that a person is aware of what he is doing. If a person decides to steal something, he has intent. When he actually moves to take the article, he is aware of his actions and knows that he is stealing.

Recklessly can be interpreted to mean that a person is aware that his conduct can cause an injury to another person or property but he "consciously disregards" that awareness and engages in the conduct anyway. If the result or circumstance are proscribed by law, the person acted with this culpable mental state. The risk he took must be substantial and unjustifiable. Furthermore, the risk must be a gross deviation from what a person, of average intelligence, judgement and experience would consider doing. In issues involving recklessness the objective standard is, what is reasonable and what is beyond reasonable. For example, a person attending a large gathering of people hurls a fist-sized rock into the crowd, not intending it to hit anybody. He is aware that the stone can hurt someone, but does not care. The rock strikes another on the side of the head causing substantial pain. In this case, it is obvious that the act was a gross deviation from normal conduct. The risk was substantial and unjustifiable. The rock hurler acted recklessly.

Criminal negligence parallels reckless culpability. The difference in criminal negligence is that a person does not perceive the substantial and unjustifiable risk. He does not see that his actions are a gross deviation from the norm. He does not comprehend that a proscribed result or circumstance will be the outcome of his actions. The example used in reckless culpability would apply in this section if the person did not understand that the rock could cause an injury to another person.

The answer to the scenario regarding the stolen radio is that Steve Adore would probably not be found guilty of criminal possession of stolen property. True, he did possess a stolen radio by exercising dominion and control over it, but Steve did not have the culpable state of mind for the crime. That statute clearly states that a person is guilty of the crime when he "knowingly" possess the stolen property. Knowingly is a culpable mental state which means that he is aware that the property was stolen. Steve was not aware of the status of the radio.

3-9 COMMON PENAL LAW VIOLATIONS

The following are the most frequently committed offenses. Remember one must consider Article Ten definitions, statutory definitions and culpable mental states when interpreting these laws. Not all of the statutes are included. For a fuller understanding consult *New York State Criminal Law for Security Professionals* or the *Penal Law*.

Assault in the Third Degree

The assault sections of the penal law are located in Article 120. They begin with assault in the third degree which is:

§120.00 Assault in the third degree.

A person is guilty of assault in the third degree when:

1. With intent to cause physical injury to another person, he causes such injury to such person or a third person;
   or
2. He recklessly causes physical injury to another person;
   or

3. With criminal negligence, he causes physical injury to another person by means of a deadly weapon or a dangerous instrument.

Assault in the third degree is a class A misdemeanor.

The Article 10 definitions found in the statutes are: **person, physical injury, deadly weapon, dangerous instrument and misdemeanor**. These were addressed in chapter four. A wise security professional would review them.

The culpable mental states described in the laws are: **intentionally, recklessly and with criminal negligence**. These are elements of the crime and must be proved in court beyond a reasonable doubt.

Arrest situation: A guard may arrest for this offense if it was in fact committed, in his observable presence. This prohibited conduct is an offense other than a felony. A guard may arrest an adult. He may also arrest an infant, a person older than seven, because a misdemeanor is an Article 10 defined crime. The arrest can only occur in the county of occurrence.

In reviewing the scenario to determine if any of the assault in the third degree statutes were violated, a guard must remember that our system of justice is an adversarial system. This means that one situation can be seen from different angles and in court people argue their points of view based on the angle from which they see the issue. The two adversaries are the prosecutor and the defense attorney. The former argues for conviction, the latter offers a defense against the conviction. In the scenario one can take a differing position than the side that will be presented. Holding a differing position is fine because it stimulates thought and an open mind can help one appreciate another's perspective. If argued successfully the differing position will prevail.

The argument that will be presented here is not guilty. Intentional assault is not the right charge. True, Lou Easeanna did punch Carl E. Flour, but he did it out of anger and for no particular reason. The circumstances of the scenario cannot prove the culpable mental state of intentionally. Remember, culpability is an element. The prosecutor must prove every element of an offense beyond a reasonable doubt before a conviction can be secured. If Lou had repeatedly punched Carl, intent to injure might have been proved, but he only hit him once.

A more appropriate charge, one that could support a guilty verdict, is subdivision two, recklessly causes physical injury to another. To reach this conclusion two elements must be reviewed. One, the culpable state of recklessly and two, did the voluntary act cause a result, namely a physical injury.

Reckless includes an awareness and a disregard of a substantial and unjustifiable risk. The risk itself is a gross deviation from normal conduct. The fact that Lou has taken boxing lessons can show that he was aware of the risk and disregarded it. There is a substantial risk of injury to the nose when one punches another in the face with all of his might. Anger is hardly a justifiable reason to physically abuse another person. Additionally, a reasonable person would not punch another because of a promotion. Lou's action was a gross deviation from normal behavior.

A physical injury is defined as substantial pain or the impairment of a bodily function. The facts will demonstrate that Carl suffered substantial pain. He received hospital treatment for the injury. For a three day period he suffered pain sufficient enough to require prescribed medication. As a result of the pain, Carl lost three days of work. In this case substantial pain is evident.

Subdivision three does not apply. Lou did not use a deadly weapon or a dangerous instrument. The fact that he took a few boxing lessons hardly supports the idea that his hands could be dangerous instruments.

These sections of law are misdemeanors. If Lou Easeanna was convicted of this offense, he could receive a term of imprisonment. The sentence could be as little as sixteen days, or as much as one year.

Assault in the Second Degree

Assault in the second degree is a higher level crime than assault, third degree. This is a felony. If a person is convicted of this charge he could receive a prison sentence of up to seven years. Added elements known as aggravating factors can cause the punishment to be increased. One of the aggravating factors is serious physical injury. For example, in the assault third statute, subdivision one, the law requires two elements, intentional culpability and a physical injury to another. In the assault second section the law requires two elements also, an intentional act and a serious physical injury to another. Another aggravating factor is the use of a deadly weapon or a dangerous instrument to inflict either type of injury.

The sections of assault in the second degree which a security officer may encounter are:

§120.05 Assault in the second degree.

A person is guilty of assault in the second degree when:

1. With intent to cause serious physical injury to another person, he causes such injury to such person or to a third person; or

2. With intent to cause physical injury to another person, he causes such injury to such person or to a third person by means of a deadly weapon or a dangerous instrument; or

4. He recklessly causes serious physical injury to another person by means of a deadly weapon or a dangerous instrument; or

6. In the course of and in furtherance of the commission or attempted commission of a felony, other than a felony defined in article one hundred thirty which requires corroboration for conviction, or of immediate flight therefrom, he, or another participant if there be any, causes physical injury to a person other than one of the participants; or....

(Article 130 describes sex offenses, felonies involving mentally defective or mentally incapacitated victims are excluded from this assault section.)

Assault in the second degree is a class D felony.

The Article 10 definitions found here are: **person, physical injury, serious physical injury, deadly weapon, dangerous instrument and felony.**

The culpable states required for the commission of assault, second degree are, **intentionally and recklessly**.

Arrest situations: An officer may arrest for these offenses when they have in fact occurred. Because they are felonies the guard need not witness them. The arrest can be based on probable cause, providing that the arrested person did in fact commit the felony. Infants over the age of seven and adults, age sixteen and older, can be charged with these crimes. The arrest can occur anywhere within New York State.

§140.00 Criminal trespass and burglary; definitions of terms.

The following definitions are applicable to this article:

1. **"Premises"** includes the term "building" as defined herein, and any real property.

2. **"Building,"** in addition to its ordinary meaning, includes any structure, vehicle or watercraft used for overnight lodging of persons, or used by persons for carrying on business therein, or used as an elementary or secondary school, or an inclosed motor truck, or an inclosed motor truck trailer. Where a building consists of two or more units separately secured or occupied, each unit shall be deemed both a separate building in itself and a part of the main building.

3. **"Dwelling"** means a building which is usually occupied by a person lodging therein at night.

4. **"Night"** means the period between thirty minutes after sunset and thirty minutes before sunrise.

5. **"Enter or remain unlawfully."** A person "enters or remains unlawfully" in or upon premises when he is not licensed or privileged to do so. A person who, regardless of his intent, enters or remains in or upon premises which are at the time open to the public does so with license and privilege unless he defies a lawful order not to enter or remain, personally communicated to him by the owner of such premises or other authorized person. A license or privilege to enter or remain in a building which is only partly open to the public is not a license or privilege to enter or remain in that part of the building which is not open to the public. A person who enters or remains upon unimproved and apparently unused land, which is neither fenced nor otherwise enclosed in a manner designed to exclude intruders, does so with license and privilege unless notice against trespass is personally communicated to him by the owner of such land or other authorized person, or unless such notice is given by posting in a conspicuous manner. A person who enters or remains in or about a school building without written permission from someone authorized to issue such permission or without a legitimate reason which includes a relationship involving custody of or responsibility for a pupil or student enrolled in the school or without legitimate business or a purpose relating to the operation of the school does so without license and privilege.

The word **"premises"** as defined here is a catch-all word. Its definition includes buildings and real property, that is land. Dwellings are buildings that are usually used for overnight lodging of people. They are still buildings and, though not specifically mentioned, are included in the definition of "premises." A house, for example, is a dwelling if people sleep there at night. It is a building if it is used for business or if it is vacant.

"Building" has the usual meaning which includes dwellings. This definition has been expanded to include any structure used for overnight sleeping purposes or for conducting business from within. This includes boats and vehicles if they are used for those purposes. A tent could be considered to be a building if someone lived in it or conducted business from within of it. Schools are obviously buildings. In an effort to make crimes involving enclosed trucks and enclosed trailers more serious, the law includes them in the definition of building. If a person was stealing lumber from the back of a flatbed truck, the crime would be larceny. If he was stealing lumber from within a box truck or box trailer the crimes would be burglary and larceny because they are considered to be buildings. In hotels each living unit is considered to be a building within the main building. Each living unit is a dwelling while the hotel itself is just an ordinary building. This also applies to apartment buildings or multiple dwellings. Certain areas, such as hallways or lobbies may be open to the public.

"Dwelling" is a building which is used for overnight lodging. The word dwelling is often associated with homes or apartments. However, the definition of "building" expands the meaning of dwelling to include any structure which people usually sleep in. A tractor-trailer can be a dwelling if the truck driver usually sleeps within the sleeping compartment of the tractor cab. If the tractor is pulling a box trailer, the trailer is an ordinary building.

"Enter or remain unlawfully" is broken down into several areas. The general rule is that a person enters or remains unlawfully in or on a premises when he does so without the owner's permission. Owner includes: the actual owner, an agent of the owner, or someone who rents from the actual owner or an agent of the renter. If a person rents a premises then the actual owner may not have license and privilege to enter or remain there. An agent is a representative of the owner, and includes: security officers, store employees or any other people who the owner delegates to be the agent.

The second idea involves buildings that are open to the public. All people are allowed into those buildings, regardless of their intent once inside. Posting signs prohibiting certain types or classes of people from entering the building does not legally stop those people from entering. However, an owner or agent can keep people out of a building by revoking their license and privilege to be there. This can only be done through a personal communication. A personal communication can be verbal or in writing (as long as the person can read). It should be both. Once issued, the communication bans a specific person or a specific group of people from entering or remaining. If it is possible, the guard should ask for personal identification and record that information, including name, date of birth, address, height, weight, eye and hair color, along with the date and time of the communication. Keep the record in a daily log book or official report. These documents are business records and can be used later in court. An excellent idea is to have the banned people sign forms stating that they know that their license and privilege to be in the building is revoked. An owner or agent cannot bar a person for unlawful reasons. Unlawful reasons include banishment because of age (unless provided for by law), sex, color, creed, religion or national origin. This part of the "enter or remain unlawfully" definition also covers public buildings with private areas. People do not have license and privilege to enter those private sections. Doorways with signs that state "employees only," for example, lead to areas that are off limits to the public.

Unimproved and apparently unused land is the next aspect of the definition. Anyone can travel onto unimproved and apparently unused land without the owner's permission. Of course, if the owner or his agent personally communicates that entry onto the land is forbidden, then the person is trespassing. Properly posting the property with signs is also a sufficient means of communicating that entry is forbidden. Those signs must warn a viewer against trespassing and, or other activity such as hunting, fishing or trapping. They must include the owner's name and address. Signs that merely state, "no trespassing" are insufficient for this purpose. The signs must be posted around the entire property at spaces close enough to give trespassers fair warning. The signs should be on a flat surface not wrapped around trees or poles. Note, it is illegal to place posted property signs on utility poles (145.30, P.L.). Likewise, entry is denied if the land is fenced or otherwise enclosed to keep people out. A six foot chain-link fence with a barbed wire topping is a fence designed to exclude intrusion. A five foot wall is an enclosure that is designed to keep trespassers out. Shrubbery such as a thick privet hedge may have been grown to prevent access.

The final area of the definition involves school buildings. Any building can be a school if it is so designated by the proper authority. School does not always have to be held in a traditional school house. Shopping center stores can be school buildings. One cannot enter or remain there without a legitimate reason or without consent from a person who is authorized to give permission for such entry or continued presence.

Trespass and criminal trespass are comprised of four sections of law. Trespass is a violation, a non-crime. Therefore, no person under the age of sixteen can be arrested for that offense. An arrest can only be effected in the county of occurrence. Criminal trespass starts in the misdemeanor category and, through aggravating factors, reaches the felony level. Notice that the aggravating factors include "dwelling," "physical injury" and possession of explosives or other weapons. Anyone over the age of seven can be arrested for criminal trespass. If the crime is a misdemeanor the person can only be arrested in the county of occurrence. If the crime is a felony, the arrest may take place anywhere within New York State. With the exception of the felony, all arrests must be based on personal observation. The culpable mental state involved in these statutes is "knowingly," which means that "he is aware" of his actions.

§140.05 Trespass.

A person is guilty of trespass when he knowingly enters or remains unlawfully in or upon a premises.

Trespass is a violation.

§140.10 Criminal trespass in the third degree.

A person is guilty of criminal trespass in the third degree when he knowingly enters or remains unlawfully in a building or upon real property
(a) which is fenced or otherwise enclosed in a manner designed to exclude intruders; or
(b) where the building is utilized as an elementary or secondary school or a children's overnight camp as defined in section one thousand three hundred ninety-two of the public health law or a summer day camp as defined in section one thousand three hundred ninety-two of the public health law in violation of conspicuously posted rules or regulations governing entry and use thereof; or
(c) located within a city with a population in excess of one million and where the building or real property is utilized as an elementary or secondary school in violation of a personally communicated request to leave the premises from a principal, custodian, or other person in charge thereof; or

(d) located outside of a city with a population in excess of one million and where the building or real property is utilized as an elementary or secondary school in violation of a personally communicated request to leave the premises from a principal, custodian, school board member or trustee or other person in charge thereof; or

(e) where the building is used as a public housing project in violation of conspicuously posted rules or regulations governing entry and use thereof; or

(f) where the building is used as a public housing project in violation of a personally communicated request to leave the premises from a housing police officer or other person in charge thereof; or

(g) where the property consists of a right-of-way or yard of a railroad or rapid transit railroad which has been designated and conspicuously posted as a no-trespass railroad zone, pursuant to section eighty-three-b of the railroad law, by the city or county in which such property is located.

Criminal trespass in the third degree is a class B misdemeanor.

§140.15 Criminal trespass in the second degree.

A person is guilty of criminal trespass in the second degree when he knowingly enters or remains unlawfully in a dwelling.

Criminal trespass in the second degree is a class A misdemeanor.

§140.17 Criminal trespass in the first degree.

A person is guilty of criminal trespass in the first degree when he knowingly enters or remains unlawfully in a building, an when, in the course of committing such crime, he:

1. Possesses, or knows that another participant in the crime possesses, an explosive or a deadly weapon; or

2. Possesses a firearm, rifle or shotgun, as those terms are defined in section 265.00, and also possesses or has readily accessible a quantity of ammunition which is capable of being discharged from such firearm, rifle or shotgun; or

3. Knows that another participant in the crime possesses a firearm, rifle or shotgun under circumstances described in subdivision two.

Criminal trespass in the first degree is a class D felony.

Now that the definitions and laws regarding trespass have been reviewed, the answers to the questions pondered in the scenario should be apparent. The sign reading "shoplifters are prohibited from entering this store" is not a personal communication. Therefore, the thief entered and remained legally. The guard could not have arrested him for trespassing. The thief did not commit burglary either. As will be seen shortly, the phrase, "knowingly enters or remains unlawfully" is also a necessary element of burglary. In the scenario the thief entered the store legally, therefore a burglary charge is invalid. However, if the owner or his agent had previously warned the thief that his license and privilege to enter the store was revoked, then a burglary charge may be a valid one. Once a person is told that he is not allowed in a building his license and privilege to be there is taken away. If he enters again, criminal trespass in the third degree or burglary, when applicable, are acceptable charges.

Burglary

All burglaries are felonies. They are serious crimes. The elements needed to prove burglary are:

§140.20   Burglary in the third degree.

A person is guilty of burglary in the third degree when he knowingly enters or remains unlawfully in a building with intent to commit a crime therein.

Burglary in the third degree is a class D felony.

At this point the phrase "enters or remains unlawfully" deserves further discussion. A person can enter a building in a variety of ways. He can open the door and walk in, break a window and climb in, or break a window and put his hand in. A person has unlawfully entered a building and is committing burglary if he breaks a window and pokes a fishing pole through the opening to aid in the commission of a crime. "Remains" means that a person legally enters the building and he remains hidden there until after closing. The concept of "remains" does not include situations such as breaking into a building to keep warm then as an after-thought, stealing property while remaining there. Unlawfully means without the owner's permission.

In any burglary circumstance a person must knowingly either enter or remain in the building with the intent to commit a crime within. In the burglary sections two culpable mental states are applicable. They are "knowingly" and "intentionally." "Knowingly" was discussed earlier, and means that "he is aware" of his conduct. Intentionally means that his "conscious objective" is a certain course of action. Knowingly and intentionally are elements of these crimes and must be proved. Additionally, Article 10, defines crimes as either misdemeanors or felonies. Subsequently, a person commits burglary when, "he is aware" that he is unlawfully entering or remaining within a building and that his "conscious objective" is to commit a misdemeanor or felony inside.

Article 35 authorizes the use of deadly physical force to prevent or terminate burglaries of occupied buildings. This force is authorized only when a person reasonably believes its use is necessary to prevent the crime from occurring or to stop a burglary in progress. This force should not be used against unarmed, non-dangerous criminals. Because of the Article 35 authorization, the following burglary statutes have been included:

§140.25 Burglary in the second degree.

A person is guilty of burglary in the second degree when he knowingly enters or remains unlawfully in a building with intent to commit a crime therein, and when:

1. In effecting entry or while in the building or in immediate flight therefrom, he or another participant in the crime:
   (a) Is armed with explosives or a deadly weapon; or
   (b) Causes physical injury to any person who is not a participant in the crime; or
   (c) Uses or threatens the immediate use of a dangerous instrument; or
   (d) Displays what appears to be a pistol, revolver, rifle, shotgun, machine gun or other firearm; or

2. The building is a dwelling.

Burglary in the second degree is a class C felony.

Burglary in the first degree is essentially the same as burglary in the second degree, subdivision one, except that the building is a dwelling. The aggravating factor of entering a person's home while armed or by causing a physical injury to a non-participant raises the crime to a class B felony. An affirmative defense attaches to burglary in the first degree, but it is of minor importance to security guards. For a fuller understanding of this section consult the penal law.

Criminal Mischief

When a person commits criminal mischief, he is committing a crime. Criminal mischief in the first, second and third degrees are felonies. Criminal mischief in the fourth degree is a misdemeanor. Anyone over seven years of age can be arrested for these crimes. There are no statutory definitions applicable to criminal mischief. The culpable mental states include "intentionally" and "recklessly." Criminal mischief in the fourth degree is set forth as follows:

§145.00 Criminal Mischief in the fourth degree.

A person is guilty of criminal mischief in the fourth degree when, having no right to do so nor any reasonable ground to believe that he has such right, he:

1. Intentionally damages property of another person; or

2. Intentionally participates in the destruction of an abandoned building as defined in section one thousand nine hundred seventy one-a of the real property actions and proceedings law; or

3. Recklessly damages property of another person in an amount exceeding two hundred fifty dollars.

Criminal mischief in the fourth degree is a class A misdemeanor.

Subdivision two discusses abandoned buildings as they are described in 1971-a of the real property actions and proceedings law (R.P.A.P.L.). Briefly, in a city with a population of one million or more people, an agency may exist which is responsible for the enforcement of the multiple dwelling law (M.D.L). Under certain circumstances that agency can declare that a multiple dwelling is abandoned. Once the building has been certified as abandoned:

"Destruction of an abandoned dwelling" occurs when a person having no right to do so or permission of the [above noted] agency or the owner to take, remove or otherwise damage the fixtures or structures of the building, nor any reasonable ground to believe that he has such right or permission, intentionally removes or damages any fixture or part of the structure of a building... (1971-a, R.P.A.P.L.).

Once the agency, known as the department, certifies that a multiple dwelling is abandoned, the agency must:

> ...immediately affix to the dwelling in a prominent and conspicuous location, a notice that the building has been found to be an abandoned building and that it is a crime to take, remove or otherwise damage any fixture or part of the building structure (1971-2, R.P.A.P.L.).

After the agency has affixed the notice to the building, the criminal mischief law can be enforced. The notice warns would-be vandals that by damaging or removing the fixtures and structures their conduct is criminal. In terms of criminal mischief, this concept conflicts with the general rule regarding abandoned property. Abandoned property is considered to be ownerless, therefore, it is not the property of another. To prove criminal mischief one must, in part, prove that another person owned the property and he did not give anyone permission to damage it *People v. Kittel* (1971). For the purposes of this law, after the city has affixed the sign, it has assumed control of the building. The warning notice demonstrates that fact. If the warning notice is not affixed to the building or it has been removed a problem arises. Theoretically, a person could enter the abandoned building, believing that he had that right under the general rule, noted above, and vandalize it. Before enforcing this subdivision, security officers should make certain that the required warning is posted on the building in a noticeable place.

Subdivision three requires reckless conduct and a resulting damage in excess of two hundred and fifty dollars. Remember, "recklessly" entails an awareness and a conscious disregard of a substantial and unjustifiable risk that a result will occur. Recklessly is not accidental nor is it necessarily careless conduct. One acts recklessly when his conduct is unjustifiable as viewed through the eyes of an ordinary person of ordinary intelligence, judgement and experience. For example, a security officer is on post in front of an eight-hundred dollar plate glass window. A person throws a large rock at the security guard. The rock misses the guard, but shatters the window. The rock thrower is guilty of criminal mischief under this subdivision because he acted recklessly and caused damage in excess of two-hundred and fifty dollars.

Criminal mischief in the third and second degrees involve the intentional damaging of another's property. The aggravating factors in each instance is money. The third degree felony requires that the property be damaged in excess of two hundred and fifty dollars. The second degree crime requires intentional damage in excess of fifteen hundred dollars.

§145.05 Criminal mischief in the third degree.

A person is guilty of criminal mischief in the third degree when, with intent to damage property of another person, and having no right to do so nor any reasonable ground to believe that he has such right, he or she damages the property of another person in an amount exceeding two hundred fifty dollars.

Criminal mischief in the third degree is a class E felony.

Graffiti

Because "making graffiti" is unsightly and very common, in 1992, the legislature enacted a specific law prohibiting it. The legislature also outlawed the related conduct of "possession of graffiti instruments." Both statutes clearly depict intent as an element of the crimes. They are misdemeanors. Anyone over the age of seven years, who commits these crimes, can be arrested. The guard must observe the criminal conduct before an arrest is valid.

§145.60 Making graffiti.

1. For the purposes of this section, the term "graffiti" shall mean the etching, painting, covering, drawing upon or otherwise placing of a mark upon public or private property with intent to damage such property.

2. No person shall make graffiti of any type on any building, public or private, or any other property real or personal owned by any person, firm or corporation or any public agency or instrumentality, without the express permission of the owner or operator of said property.

Making graffiti is a class A misdemeanor.

Graffiti is often found in an expressive form, written or drawn on buildings, bridges, water towers, in public bathrooms and on other suitable objects. Most graffiti artists are young people, teenagers. Some of them may be juveniles, people under the age of sixteen. Some may be adults, people over the age of sixteen. Older people also engage in this conduct, particularly in public bathrooms. A person is not guilty of this crime if he expresses himself by marking his own property. The crime is committed if, with the proper intent, he marks another's property without permission.

§145.65 Possession of graffiti instruments.

A person is guilty of possession of graffiti instruments when he possesses any tool, instrument, article, substance, solution or other compound designed or commonly used to etch, paint, cover, draw upon or otherwise place a mark upon a piece of property which that person has no permission or authority to etch, paint, cover, draw upon or otherwise mark, under circumstances evincing an intent to use same in order to damage such property.

Possession of graffiti instruments is a class B misdemeanor.

The phrase, "circumstances evincing an intent" means that under the circumstances, it is quite clear that a person was using or is about to use graffiti instruments. This could encompass a variety of situations. For example, after business hours, a guard discovers one single person behind the building he is protecting. Green, wet paint is running down the building's wall. The person the guard discovered is holding a can of green spray paint. The cap is off of the can and the nozzle is wet. Under these circumstances, possession of graffiti instruments is an appropriate charge.

Experience indicates that most graffiti is made with paint, markers, pens and pencils. Cutting or gouging instruments such as knives are used as well. With the exception of paint, these items are often carried by people every day. The mere possession of them, including paint, does not warrant an arrest for this crime. A valid arrest is based on proof of two points. One, that the person does not have permission to mark the object. Two, he intended to damage property by making graffiti with the instruments.

Larceny

1. A person steals property and commits larceny when, with intent to deprive another of property or to appropriate the same to himself or a third person, he wrongfully takes, obtains or withholds such property from an owner thereof.

This definition incorporates other definitions found in section 155.00. Those definitions are: property, deprive, appropriate, obtains and owner. Property is anything of value. Deprive means to withhold permanently. Appropriate means to permanently exercise control over property or dispose of it. Obtains means to transfer property or legal interest. Owner is the person who has more of a right to possess the property than the person who stole it.

According to this definition a person can steal in four ways: take the property, permanently withhold it, exercise control over the property, dispose of it, or transfer the property to his or another's name. The usual means of theft is taking the property.

The definition identifies the culpable mental state required for larceny. The mind-set for larceny is "intentionally." The thief's "conscious objective" is to steal. This is the only time in the larceny sections that the culpable mental state is mentioned. However, intentionally is an element of every section in this article. The prosecutor must prove beyond a reasonable doubt that the defendant intended to steal the property.

Subdivision two of this section describes several different ways which larceny can be committed. Many of them are of little importance to the security officer (subdivisions: c, d and e). The relevant definitions are as follows:

2.   Larceny includes a wrongful taking, obtaining or withholding of another's property, with the intent prescribed in subdivision one of this section, committed in any of the following ways:
      (a) By conduct heretofore defined as common law larceny by trespassory taking, common law larceny by trick, embezzlement, or obtaining property by false pretenses;
      (b) By acquiring lost property. A person acquires lost property when he exercises control over property of another which he knows to have been lost or mislaid, or to have been delivered under a mistake as to the identity of the recipient or the nature or amount of the property, without taking reasonable measures to return such property to the owner...

Common law is the law the United States inherited from England through the colonization of this continent. It is the familiar old law, the law that everyone basically understands. For instance, it is generally understood that another person's property belongs to him and that if someone takes it, he steals it. Our society does not need to review a law book for an explanation of this. Therefore, when the statute refers to common law larceny by trespassory taking or by trick no further explanation is required. Trespassory taking, the act of walking into a store, for example, and stealing something is understood to be illegal. Trespassory entry can be legal or illegal. A person who enters a retail establishment, enters legally, a burglar enters illegally. Regardless of the manner of entry, it is understood that the property within belongs to someone else.

Lost property includes packages that are delivered in error. This includes accepting delivery under another's name or taking it because of its nature or value. Lost property may be acquired if a reasonable effort is made to locate the true owner. Often the property is given to the police. If, after some time, the owner does not come forward to demand the property, the finder may claim it. Security officers may on occasion receive lost property. They should make every effort to identify the owner and return the property.

Petit Larceny

The relevant sections of petit larceny and criminal possession of stolen property are as follows:

§155.25 Petit Larceny.

A person is guilty of petit larceny when he steals property.

Petit Larceny is a class A misdemeanor.

Petit larceny is a frequently occurring event. The value of the stolen property cannot exceed $1000.00. An amount in excess of $1000.00 is an aggravating factor and the crime is raised to felony level. Most shoplifting falls into the petit larceny category. Security officers are often involved in arrest situations involving petit larceny. The possibility of civil litigation in these situations is often present. Guards and their employers can be defendants in actions arising from false arrest or false imprisonment. Some of the litigation results because the security officer does not witness the crime in progress.

There is one alternative to a charge of petit larceny when the guard does not actually witness the theft. A more appropriate charge might be "criminal possession of stolen property" (165.40, P.L.). This law states:

§165.40 Criminal possession of stolen property in the fifth degree.

A person is guilty of criminal possession of stolen property in the fifth degree when he knowingly possesses stolen property, with intent to benefit himself or a person other than an owner thereof or to impede the recovery by an owner thereof.

Criminal possession of stolen property in the fifth degree is a class A misdemeanor.

This is particularly useful in mercantile establishments (retail trade) because of section 218 of the general business law. This law offers a defense to the retailer or his agent against "false arrest, false imprisonment, unlawful detention, defamation of character, assault, trespass or invasion of civil rights." Basically, section 218 allows the merchant or agent to detain a person whom he has reasonable grounds to believe (probable cause) "unlawfully possessed an anti-security item as defined in section 170.40, P.L. or was committing or attempting to commit larceny on such premises of such merchandise." The law requires that the detention be done in a reasonable manner and for a reasonable amount of time. The detention can occur in the establishment or in the vicinity of the establishment. A "reasonable time" includes the time to allow the detained person "to make a statement or refuse to make a statement...to examine employees and records...relative to the ownership of the merchandise or possession of such an [anti-security] item."

Reasonable grounds to believe is the same as probable cause. Remember, it is a conclusion, based on the facts of a situation, that a person of average intelligence, judgement and experience would reach. According to section 70.10-2 of the criminal procedure law, the definition regarding the commission of an offense is:

"Reasonable cause to believe that a person has committed an offense" exists when evidence or information which appears reliable discloses facts or circumstances which are collectively of such weight and persuasiveness as to convince a person of ordinary intelligence, judgement and experience that it is reasonably likely that such offense was committed and that such person committed it...

Section 218 states that " **'reasonable grounds' shall include, but not be limited to, knowledge that a person has concealed possession of unpurchased merchandise of the retail mercantile establishment or has possession of an [anti-security] item..."** The fact that the wording does not limit "reasonable grounds" strictly to the knowledge of possession requirement, warrants the inclusion of the criminal procedure law definition. The C.P.L. definition is the acceptable standard for probable cause. It offers the security officer more latitude in these situations.

An example of how the alternative course of action might work can be found in the case of *People v. Williams* (1968). Minnie Williams was being followed by a store detective who suspected her of shoplifting. At one point Ms Williams entered the dressing area with five items of clothing and returned with three items. The detective checked the dressing area and the two missing items were not there. Williams left the store and the detective arrested her for petit larceny. The case was dismissed because the judge ruled that the detective did not witness that particular crime. According to 218 of the G.B.L., if the detective had reasonable grounds to believe that Ms Williams was shoplifting, the detective had a right to detain and question her. The total circumstances in this case indicate that the detective had probable cause, though the judge referred to it as surmise and suspicion. If upon detaining Williams, the detective learned that she possessed the stolen property, and she did, then today criminal possession of stolen property would have been the right charge. The circumstances surrounding the possession could prove that Williams knowingly possessed the stolen property with the intent to benefit a person other than the owner. At that point in time the detective actually witnesses the criminal possession, therefore, the crime was committed in her observable presence.

Two other sections of law further support the criminal possession charge. Section 165.55 offers presumptions, facts that are assumed.

> 1. A person who knowingly possesses stolen property is presumed to possess it with intent to benefit himself or a person other than an owner thereof or to impede the recovery by an owner thereof (165.55, P.L.).

Section 165.60 blocks the defense that a thief cannot be convicted of criminal possession of stolen property because he was involved in the theft.

> In any prosecution for criminal possession of stolen property, it is no defense that:

> 2. The defendant stole or participated in the larceny of the property; or (165.60, P.L.)...

In Misdemeanor larcenies, the security professional should consider the alternative charge of criminal possession of stolen property as opposed to a charge of petit larceny. Remember "possess" has an Article 10 definition and means, "to have physical possession or otherwise to exercise dominion and control over tangible property." In shoplifting cases, the thief will possess the stolen property whether it is on his person or in the trunk of his car.

Grand Larceny

Grand larceny has four degrees. In grand larceny, fourth degree the property varies. Some of the property may have little monetary value. The property is placed in the more serious crime category because of the nature of the property. Another element of grand larceny is the raised value of the property. Grand larceny can be committed if a person steals property worth more than $1000.00. Not all of the grand larceny sections or statutes will be addressed here. Enough will be presented to give security officers a working knowledge of the law. Grand larceny is as follows:

§155.30 Grand Larceny in the fourth degree.

A person is guilty of grand larceny in the fourth degree when he steals property and when:

1. The value of the property exceeds one thousand dollars; or...

3. The property consists of secret scientific material: or

4. The property consists of a credit card or debit card; or

5. The property, regardless of its nature and value, is taken from the person of another; or...

7. The property consists of one or more firearms, rifles or shotguns, as such terms are defined in section 265.00 of this chapter; or...

Grand Larceny in the fourth degree is a class E felony.

Robbery

Robbery has one definition with two subdivisions. That definition is:

§160.00 Robbery; defined.

Robbery is forcible stealing. A person forcibly steals property and commits robbery when, in the course of committing a larceny, he uses or threatens the immediate use of physical force upon another person for the purpose of:

1. Preventing or overcoming resistance to the taking of the property or to the retention thereof immediately after the taking; or

2. Compelling the owner of such property or another person to deliver up the property or to engage in other conduct which aids in the commission of the larceny.

This definition states that robbery is a form of larceny. Therefore, some of the definitions of larceny apply to this article. Those definitions are "larceny" and "property." They were paraphrased in the chapter 11. The use of force in this definition is the "immediate" use of force. Immediate means all of the action will occur at the time of the event. "Give me the wallet now or I will kill you now" is immediate. If the threat involves future use of force for the delivery of property at the time of the encounter, robbery has not been committed. For instance, if Mike Rophone threatens Phil A. Buster with bodily harm tomorrow if Phil does not give Mike his watch today, there is no robbery. That is another crime known larceny by extortion (155. 40-2, P.L.).

Robbery can be seen as an aggravating factor of larceny. It requires the use of, or threatened use of, physical force to steal. The use of force, or the threat, can accomplish three results: prevent resistance of the larceny, overcome the resistance or compel a person to give the robber the property. The first two results are self-explanatory. The third result requires some discussion. Compelling another to deliver property or to engage in conduct which aids in the commission of a larceny can take several forms. The most obvious means of compulsion is the pointing of a gun at a bank teller and demanding the bank's money. One could also compel the teller's aid in the larceny by having him empty out all of the other tellers' draws.

Robberies take many forms. They range from pushing an elderly person down and stealing her pocketbook to sophisticated well planned armored car heists. Robberies are always crimes against people. One cannot rob a building, per se. One can burglarize a dwelling with the intent to rob the people inside of it. Robberies are:

§160.05 Robbery in the third degree.

A person is guilty of robbery in the third degree when he forcibly steals property.

Robbery in the third degree is a class D felony.

§160.10 Robbery in the second degree.

A person is guilty of robbery in the second degree when he forcibly steals property and when:

1. He is aided by another person actually present; or

2. In the course of the commission of the crime or in the immediate flight therefrom, he or another participant in the crime:

(a) Causes physical injury to any person who is not a participant in the crime; or

(b) Displays what appears to be a pistol, revolver, rifle, shotgun, machine gun or other firearm; or

3. The property consists of a motor vehicle, as defined in section one hundred twenty-five of the vehicle and traffic law.

Robbery in the second degree is a class C felony.

Robbery in the first degree is paraphrased here. The crime contains aggravating factors that elevate it from robbery in the second degree. Those factors are: cause serious physical injury to anyone not involved, the displaying of a loaded firearm, use or threatened immediate use of a dangerous instrument or the robber is armed with a deadly weapon. Robbery in the first degree is a class B felony. For a fuller understanding of robbery, first degree, consult the penal law.

In addition to the statutory definitions, the robbery sections rely on Article 10 definitions to clarify the meaning of the laws. They include: physical injury, serious physical injury, deadly weapon and dangerous instrument.

The prohibited conduct defined in the robbery sections is self-explanatory. Some comments regarding the injury aspects and the displaying of firearms is called for. An element of robbery, second degree, is a physical injury to anyone who is not a participant. The injured person could be the robber's victim or someone blocks away who was struck, in the robber's immediate flight, by the get-a-way car. If the injury is a serious one, then robbery, first degree was committed. In robbery, second degree, the firearm displayed does not have to be loaded or even real for the crime to be committed. In robbery, first degree, the weapon must be real and loaded.

Harassment

Harassment laws can serve to protect security officers from belligerent people and visa versa. They prohibit the intentional harassing, annoying or alarming of individuals. Logically, harassment laws can be seen as prevention statutes. They offer a legal remedy to people who might otherwise respond violently. A violent response further disrupts the public order. This breach could result in higher criminal charges being brought against the person who was initially harassed. By enforcing these laws, the more serious break of public order can be avoided. No volume regarding security officers and the law would be complete without noting these sections. They are:

§240.25 Harassment in the first degree.

A person is guilty of harassment in the first degree when he or she intentionally and repeatedly harasses another person by following such person in or about a public place or places or by engaging in a course of conduct or by repeatedly committing acts which places such person in reasonable fear of physical injury. This section shall not apply to activities regulated by the national labor relations act, as amended, the railways labor act, as amended, or the federal employment labor management act, as amended.

Harassment in the first degree is a class B misdemeanor.

§240.26 Harassment in the second degree.

A person is guilty of harassment in the second degree when, with intent to harass, annoy or alarm another person:

1. He or she strikes, shoves kicks or otherwise subjects such other person to physical contact, or attempts or threatens to do the same; or

2. He or she follows a person in or about a public place or places; or

3. He or she engages in a course of conduct or repeatedly commits acts which alarm or seriously annoy such other person and which serve no legitimate purpose.

Subdivisions two and three of this section shall not apply to activities regulated by the national labor relations act, as amended, the railways labor act, as amended, or the federal employment labor management act, as amended.

Harassment is a violation.

The security officer should not be lulled into a false sense of protection regarding these laws. Harassment requires the culpable mental state of "intentionally." A person's "conscious objective" must be to harass, annoy or alarm someone. If someone is annoyed and is yelling and screaming at a person, he is not harassing that other person. He is merely venting his frustration. Likewise, if someone accidentally bumps into another person, he is not committing harassment. If a security officer is following a suspected shoplifter around a store, he is not harassing that person. His intent is legitimate. He is protecting his employer's property. He is not following the suspect to annoy or alarm him.

Harassment in the first degree and subdivisions two and three of the second degree offense do not apply at strike scenes. Picketing workers often harass fellow employees or managers who cross the picket lines. Those striking workers are specifically exempt, probably because arrests under this section would constitute strike breaking.

Harassment in the first degree requires that a person reasonably fear physical injury. "Reasonable fear" has a two prong test, one, the subjective test, two, the objective test. The subjective prong is the victim's view of the situation. The victim must be able to state how the facts surrounding the encounter made him afraid of being physically injured. The objective prong is the conclusion that a reasonable person would reach after examining the facts. A reasonable person is a person of average intelligence, judgement and experience.

A person under the age of sixteen years old cannot be arrested for harassment in the second degree because this offense is not a crime. Any person over the age of seven can be arrested for harassment, first degree. The arrest in either case must take place in the county of occurrence.

3-10 CONCLUSION

Security officers should be aware of both their legal powers and limitations and their employers' policy regarding arrests and the use of force. They should know that they are not "duty bound" to enforce laws, make arrests or use physical force against other people. They are required to act in good faith and to discharge the duties that are establish by the employer. If they have the authority to make arrests, arrests should be accomplished with safety in mind. If there is any doubt as to the legal requirements for the arrest or if the situation could obviously create a serious danger to others, a professional security guard would stay back, observe and notify the employer or the police of the situation. There is absolutely no reason for a security officer to unnecessarily risk his or her life to protect property from the results of criminal conduct.

CHAPTER 4

EMERGENCY SITUATIONS

4-1 INTRODUCTION

During the course of a career in the field of security it is likely that the average guard will encounter emergencies. Due to the nature of the work, he or she may be the first to discover or arrive at the emergency.

One method of meeting the responsibility of protecting people and property from harm is patrol. While on patrol the guard should be mindful of the several types of emergencies that he or she may encounter. He or she should be able to recognize and seek out circumstances that can create emergencies. Upon discovering those circumstances, the guard should correct the situation before there is a problem. To meet that end, a professional should consider conducting safety checks. When, if on patrol, a guard discovers an emergency he or she should be familiar with the proper response. The first rule in handling an emergency is to assess the problem in terms of threat potential to life and property, then report it. The second rule is to document all emergencies.

Every guard should know the employer's policy regarding his or her role in emergency response. If there is an emergency response plan, the guard should know and follow it.

4-2 POTENTIAL EMERGENCIES

Security officers may encounter several types of emergencies. Their potential exposure to these will depend upon the business activities of their employers and the volume of public contact. A security officer assigned to duty at a shopping mall will encounter more crimes in progress than one employed in a chemical storage facility. However, the potential for a hazardous material accident or an explosion is probably higher in the storage facility.

Emergencies can occur as the result of intentional acts, accidents and naturally occurring events such as hurricanes. Intentional acts can be motivated by personal, political or social interests and can result in sabotage, espionage or criminal behavior. Accidents do happen, however, many can be eliminated through prevention and training. Naturally occurring events happen with or without warning. The best response results from preparation and planning.

The emergencies a guard should expect to encounter are: fires, explosions, bomb threats, riots, civil disturbances, strikes and picket actions, hazardous material accidents, natural disasters, medical emergencies, evacuations and crimes in progress.

Fires

Fires are extremely dangerous. Security officers should be aware that smoke inhalation kills more people than the actual fires kill. Entering a smoke filled room is dangerous, deadly and ill advised. Smoke may contain lethal gases released through combustion and entering that condition can produce swift unconsciousness and death. Another reason for staying out, is that disorientation occurs shortly after entering. A person who enters a smoke filled room cannot see. He or she will lose his or her bearings, become lost and my not be able to find the entrance again. If a room is that full of smoke it is not likely that any survivors exist there. Another point to remember, if smoke is coming from under a door, do not open it. Feel the door first, if it is hot, then opening it will feed air to the fire. This will probably cause an explosion. Anyone standing in the doorway will receive serious burns and is likely to inhale deadly hot air. The best possible course of action is to assess the situation and report it. If the fire is manageable extinguish it, if not evacuation may be necessary. Security officers should be prepared to escort emergency responders to the fire location and stand ready to assist the responders if required. The incident should then be documented.

In evacuating the building, the security officer should be mindful that smoke rises. It accumulates at the ceiling first then is forced lower as it builds-up. The available breathing air may be between the floor and a height of one to two feet. It may be necessary to crawl under the smoke to escape. If it is possible attempt to cover the mouth and nose with wet cloth. This can function as a temporary smoke filter.

There are four classifications of fires: "A," "B," "C" and "D." The security officer should be aware of these classifications because each type of fire has a fire extinguisher that is designed to put it out. All fires require heat, oxygen and fuel to exist. If any one of the three is removed the fire must die out. Each extinguisher removes at least one of the three sustaining elements.

Class "A" fires consist of ordinary combustibles such as wood, paper, cloth and plastic. A class "A" fire extinguisher will have a label displaying either an "A" or the symbol of a triangle somewhere near the top of the extinguisher. Some display both, others have the display and a picture of the material the extinguisher is capable of putting out. Class "A" extinguishers cannot be used to put out any other types of fire.

Class "B" extinguishers are used to extinguish fires caused by flammable and, or combustible liquids, gases and greases. These extinguishers display a "B," the symbol of a box, or both. A picture may or may not be present.

Class "C" fires consist of fires in energized electrical equipment. These range from fires in faulty wiring to those in electrical panels. The extinguishers display the letter "C" or the symbol of a circle. Again a picture may or may not appear on the extinguisher.

Class "D" fires are fires from combustible materials such as magnesium and titanium. These are super hot fires and are difficult to extinguish. The letter "D" appears on the extinguisher. The symbol for this type of extinguisher is a five pointed star.

Many fire extinguishers are capable of putting out a variety of fires. They have multiple letters and symbols. One typical extinguisher is able to control "A," "B," and "C" class fires. This extinguisher can be used on fires consisting of ordinary combustibles, flammable and combustible liquids, gases and greases and on electrical fires as well.

While on patrol, a professional will note several points regarding fire extinguishers. A diligent guard will know the location of every fire extinguisher and what type of fire or fires each one is capable of putting out. He or she should learn how to operate each one. The procedure is simple: pull the pin, aim the hose, squeeze the lever and sweep the base of the fire. Fire extinguishers become stale. To prevent this they are periodically inspected. A tag indicating the date of inspection and who inspected it is usually attached to the extinguisher. A guard should check the tag to ensure that it has been inspected according to the inspection schedule. Some extinguishers have gauges that indicate the state of readiness, they should be checked regularly. Because people play with fire extinguishers, they should be examined for discharged contents. They should be picked-up and the weight judged. An empty fire extinguisher mounted on the wall is of little use in an emergency. Problems with fire extinguishers should be reported immediately.

One of the purposes of patrol is prevention. Fires can be prevented if the security patrol officer is looking for potential fire hazards. Potential fires can be caused by any of the following conditions: Dirt or rubbish build up, improperly stored rags particularly those containing solvent, grease or other petroleum based additives, smoking in unauthorized areas, open flame or unattended heaters, improperly stored hazardous materials, defective electrical equipment including unattended coffee pots left on and combustibles stored near heating or electrical devices. These conditions should be reported immediately and corrected as soon as is possible. The guard should also report unlit or unmarked emergency exits.

For the purposes of effectively handling fire and other emergencies, a dedicated security officer should know the assignment address, be totally familiar with the building layout and co-worker activity. Many of us travel from point "A" to point "B" without knowing the names of the streets we travel. We often use landmarks and exit numbers to guide us. This may be particularly true if a security officer reports to different locations during the course of a tour of duty or has varying weekly assignments. The guard should record the address of the assignment and nearest cross street. This information is helpful when dialing 911 or other emergency numbers. The person who answers the 911 phone call could be miles away and not be familiar with the incident location.

Knowledge of building layout is important. It is necessary to know which doors are exit doors and which doors lead to dead ends. Exit doors have lighted exit signs and open outward. A guard should make certain that the lights and the emergency exit hardware are functioning properly. While on patrol, the guard should be aware of the fact that exits become unintentionally blocked by pallets of goods, machinery and other movable equipment. In an active area some doors may be blocked, then available as exits several times during a shift. The guard should look for doors that may be barred closed. These conditions should be reported and remedied. An alert security officer should note which windows are available for emergency exit. He or she should be aware of the existence of fire alarms and posted evacuation routes. The guard should know if any telephones are internal phones only. They have lines which cannot make connections outside of the building. The guard should know what areas of the building are occupied, during what time periods and by how many people.

When encountering a fire situation, the first step is to assess and decide upon a course of action. The main concern is the safety of the guard. A down or endangered guard is of little value because the safety of others is jeopardized. Once the guard's safety is confirmed, he or she must report the fire. This can be done by pulling an alarm, radio communication or telephone. Should the guard elect to fight the fire he or she must seek and use a fire extinguisher of the proper classification. Security officers must remember that they are not professional fire fighters and if the fire becomes unmanageable they must consider the safety of every person in the area. Under these circumstances, the best course of action is to clear the area and wait for and direct the fire department.

Explosions

Explosions have many causes. Some are accidental, such as: gas main or transformer explosions, chemical spills or mixes, or other industrial accidents. A security officer should be aware that if there is one accidental explosion others may follow. Some explosions are intentional. Intentional explosions can be the result of terrorism caused by social, political, domestic or personal motives. Sabotage can also be accomplished via explosives. Suspects could include employees, former employees or vandals. Regardless of the motive, bombs can be planted randomly, placed as the result of a plan or placed to protest an aspect of an organization's operation.

Explosions due to terrorism are of recent and rising concern. Security officers should pay attention to suspicious vehicles left unattended in parking areas or parked in unusual or illegal places. They should also be on the alert for suspicious packages, particularly if the packages seems out of place. Suspicious vehicles and packages should not be tampered with, but rather reported. Should an explosion occur, the first concern is for human safety. Notification of the explosion should be made and people should be evacuated from the area. The area then should be searched for victims.

Should an explosion occur, the security officer has several responsibilities. They include: dealing with the injured, suppressing panic, the safety of all in the area and security breaches. Injured parties could include employees, visitors and the public. Their medical needs and safety are major concerns. The security officer must attempt to prevent panic by being calm, maintaining order and minimizing confusion. The security officer is responsible for keeping people at a safe distance from the explosion site due to the fact that a secondary explosion may occur. An explosion will create a security breach. Once the safety of all concerned parties has been established, the guard should turn his or her attention to access control and general security. The affected area should be sealed off to prevent further loss or injury.

Bomb Threats

Many businesses will receive some sort of a bomb threat during the course of operation. Bomb Threats can warn of a real danger, or as is usual, they may be nothing more than harassment. On occasion a bomber will make several false calls in order to catch the intended victim off guard when the real device is detonated. Each threat should be treated as a genuine threat until it is determined otherwise. Security officers should be aware of and follow his or her employer's procedures and guidelines regarding bomb threats. Safety of people and assets should be foremost on the security officer's mind.

If the threat is by phone, one of the objectives is to keep the caller on the phone for as long as is possible. Some agencies have a bomb threat check-list sheet which requires security officers to fill out certain information. If one is not available, the security officer should try and determine the following information: name and address of caller, who placed the bomb and what was the motive, type of bomb, its location, appearance, time of detonation, background noise, gender and approximate age of the caller, speech patterns, dialect or accent and the exact wording. When receiving these calls it is important to remain calm and to write down all of the information. The incident should be reported to the police, a supervisor or company official immediately. The phone in which the threat came in on should not be used until after the investigation has been concluded. There is a possibility that the call can be traced through the telephone company.

If the threat is in writing, Once the realization sets in that the letter is a bomb threat, try not to handle the letter or envelope. They become physical evidence. Set them aside in a place where they will not be disturbed because they may contain unseen, latent fingerprint impressions. Additionally, the writing or typing can be analyzed and possibly compared to a future suspect's writing, typewriter or printer.

Bombs can enter a building in a variety of ways. Security guards should be aware of this fact. An alert guard will realize that bombs can enter via: the mail, courier, parcel post, messenger, a disgruntled or former worker, an emotionally disturbed individual, any one of the host of protest groups and by car or truck.

To be effective, a bomb does not have to be placed inside of the building. They can be placed outside of it as well. Hiding areas could include: dumpsters and trash cans, mailboxes and vehicles to name a few. Security guards should know their surroundings and understand what is a normal condition and what is not normal.

After the threat is received a search for the bomb should be initiated. The best method of searching is to summon the police and ask them to search. Many police departments have trained personnel in this area who employ the use of robots and dogs. If the search is conducted without the police, all searchers should be aware that their mission is to observe and report. They are to look for suspicious packages and vehicles. Common hiding spots include: public areas, such as lobbies, electrical and janitor closets, bathrooms, stairwells and parking lots. If they discover something out of the ordinary they are not to touch it. The searchers should be mindful that bombs can be detonated in a variety of ways. They include: radio transmission, heat, barometric pressure, time devices and any other manner in which an electrical current can be switched on. It follows then that radios and cellular phones should not be used during the search phase.

If an evacuation is required, choose a route that has been thoroughly searched first. If a bomber's intent is to terrorize by injuring people, he or she will have the greatest success by destroying the evacuation route during evacuation. At this point the concentration of people will be the greatest.

At the very least a bomb threat, whether by phone or by mail, constitutes the crime of Aggravated Harassment In The Second Degree, section 240.30 of the penal law. This crime is a misdemeanor, an offense other than a felony.

Hazardous Materials

A hazardous material (HAZMAT) accident can be dangerous to health, cause substantial disruption of work and damage property. If a hazardous material accident occurs during a guard's tour of duty, he or she is obligated to protect people from harm. The security officer must be concerned with his or her safety and the safety of coworkers and the public. To accomplish this end, the professional will know what hazardous materials are on the site, where they are located and what procedure he or she should follow to decontaminate and remedy.

Many employers are involved in hazardous material awareness training (HazCom). Whenever possible security officers should seek this training. Furthermore, security officers should be aware that each employer must maintain Material Safety Data Sheets (MSDS) on every hazardous material involved in the operation of his or her enterprise. These sheets describe the material, exposure symptoms, decontamination procedure and the remedy, which may be a medical follow-up. The sheets are open to review by all employees. A well trained guard should know where these sheets are kept, what materials are listed on them and how to proceed in an accident. The security officer should be mindful that the *National Fire Protection Association (NFPA) has developed a placarding system designed to alert people to the dangers of certain materials. Other hazardous materials are marked with a single diamond placard. The placard contains a number. When the number is checked with the *Emergency Response Guide (ERG), the officer can determine what the material is and what classification the hazardous matter is in. Shipping labels may also contain information regarding hazardous material.

In the event of a hazardous material accident the guard should proceed to the area via the safest and quickest route, assess and notify. He or she should adhere to the following general rules: make notification by phone, a radio could cause an explosion, keep people out of the area, do not touch or smell the material, do not try to mop up any liquids and remember that only trained and equipped personnel should clean the area. If a person has been contaminated, that person should be isolated from those who have not been exposed. When appropriate, the victim should be decontaminated or if necessary treated as a medical emergency. If the contaminated person is still in the accident area, the guard should not attempt a rescue unless it can be done in complete safety to the guard. Remember, if the accident occurred out of doors keep the unexposed people upwind from the accident. Keep all exposed people downwind from the unexposed.

The key to solving the problems presented with hazardous material accidents rests with knowledge. A guard should make every effort to know the level of danger and harm each material presents. He or she should know the limitations placed on his or her role by that level of danger and harm. A spill of household ammonia, for example, is easily relieved by washing with water, exposure to a high concentration of radioactive material is not easily remedied.

Hazardous materials are grouped into nine categories. Of those, the State of New York requires security officers to be aware of six categories, they are: toxic agents, corrosive chemicals, flammable material, explosives, radioactive material and spontaneous heaters.

Toxic means poison. The effects of toxic material vary between skin irritation to lethal poisoning. These materials have the capability of damaging

*See Chapter 10 for details.

any bodily organ. Poison can enter the body through physical contact, breathing contaminated air or ingestion via food or drink. Security officers should note that toxic fumes will result when certain chemicals, such as ammonia and chlorine, are mixed together.

Corrosive chemicals are those that contain either acids or bases (alkalis). Sulfuric acid is an example of a corrosive substance that has an acid quality. Common household baking soda (sodium bicarbonate) is an example of a base. Strong acids or bases are capable of destroying skin by contact and mucous membranes by inhalation of the fumes.

Flammable materials are found in three forms, liquids, gases and solids. Flammable vapors can emanate from liquids, such as gasoline or propane. They can exist naturally as a gas, such as hydrogen or helium. Other flammable materials are found in solid form such as rocket fuel. Ignition can be caused by flame, sparks from electrical switches, friction, and high temperatures. When ignited, rapid, spontaneous combustion results. Security officers should be aware that the result of combining certain chemicals is spontaneous combustion.

Explosives come in a variety of forms ranging from dynamite (sawdust and nitroglycerin) to plastic explosives. As with other flammable material, some explosives are unstable, like nitroglycerin. Concussion may cause detonation. Some explosives, like the plastic variety, are very stable. They require detonation by a blasting cap.

Radioactive materials consist of elements that shoot out tiny particles. Plutonium and uranium are examples of elements that emit radiation. These elements are used to create nuclear weapons. The particles they release pass through the body and can damage cells. Security officers should be aware that radioactive material is used in a variety of ways, ranging from medicine to smoke detectors to bombs.

Spontaneous combustion results from oxidation or bacterial decay. Oxidation is a chemical reaction that causes heat. Many chemicals react with other substances to create combustion. Some react with air or water. Some materials, such as oxygen, may not burn, but increase the rapidness of combustion. The more oxygen that is added to a fire, for example, the faster that fire will burn. Bacterial decay occurs when bacteria digest organic matter. That process also causes heat. When the heat builds up to the combustion point, ignition occurs. A pile of oily rags, for example, has the potential to oxidize and burn.

Natural Disasters

Natural disasters take many forms. They include: hurricanes and high wind weather situations such as tornados and gales, thunder storms, blizzards, floods, tidal waves, and earthquakes. Through advanced technology, we may be warned of an impending natural disaster, particularly if it involves the weather. In those cases the security officer should take steps to ensure that the disruption of normal service and property loss is minimal. The guard should also be concerned with the protection of life. He or she should secure loose objects, equipment, opened doors and windows. It is important to make sure that emergency exits are not blocked or locked. In the event of high winds, large windows should be crisscrossed with masking tape. This adds strength to the glass and helps prevent them from being blown in. In general anything that can be harmed as a result of the disaster should be moved to a safer location. For example, if the area is expecting a flood, property on the floor should be elevated.

Natural disasters often cause utility services to fail. This disrupts normal service. The guard should make sure that emergency lighting is functional. This includes the lighted exit signs. He or she should determine if the smoke and fire detectors are functional. If the building is equipped with an electrical generator, the guard should determine if it is functioning. He or she should make sure that all flashlights and radios, commercial and two way, have a fresh supply of battery power. Commercial radio stations should be tuned to the Emergency Alert System. This system will provide updated information regarding the disaster. Two way radios are essential for internal communication. If the building has an elevator system the guard should be mindful that it may fail if the electrical service fails. He or she should caution people not to use the elevators during the disaster. He or she should also know the procedures involved in elevator evacuation. If there is a refrigerator system, the guard should consider recommending other methods of cooling the perishables, such as dry ice.

During the disaster, people on the premises should be congregated in the safest place possible, away from external windows. The security officer should continue to patrol and be alert for potentially harmful developments and possible victims. If damage has occurred non-essential people should be evacuated from the area. The guard should be aware that situations change as the disaster progresses. For example, during a hurricane winds will change direction as the storm passes by. The threat then comes from a different direction. To follow the progress of a disaster, a guard should monitor the Emergency Alert System described above.

Once the disaster has run its course, the guard should conduct a patrol. Depending upon the disaster, the guard should consider checking for fire, damage, leaks, flooding, falling ice, icy sidewalks, icy parking lots and dangerous conditions, including downed electrical lines and weakened building structures. If any of these conditions exist, the guard should secure the area, keep people away and make the proper notifications.

Again, the security officer should be familiar with and follow any emergency plan established by the employer.

Crimes in Progress

All crimes have a progress stage, the time during which the crime is being committed. It is highly likely that a career security officer will eventually encounter a crime in progress. His or her response, as in all emergency situations, will be determined by the employer's policies. That policy may be observe and report, stop the crime or arrest on sight.

Two of a security guard's objectives in these situations is to minimize the impact of the crime on the employer and reduce the risk of injury to potential victims. To meet these objectives security officers should respond with at least one other officer if possible. They should listen to and communicate with the dispatcher and monitor the radio activity of other responding guards. By paying attention to the radio, they can receive and relay updated information. They should consider calling for the police, fire or ambulance service. They must be aware of the law that is being violated and consider the options open to them regarding the use of force. They should identify and isolate possible witnesses. Once at the scene, they should identify the crime scene and protect it from contamination or disturbance. They should maintain control over the scene until the police arrive.

Security officers who receive a call of a crime in progress should attempt to gain as much information as is possible about the situation. This information should include: the incident location, the nature of the incident, the number and description of the perpetrators, whether any weapons are involved, a description of any motor vehicles used in the crime. all of this information will be helpful to the responding guards and can help reduce the unknown factor for them.

In any case the first steps in dealing with these situations is to respond in a safe manner and evaluate it. Considerations in the evaluation should include: safety of the guard and other people, the type of crime being committed and the means available to the guard to intercede effectively. Once the evaluation has been made the second consideration is to immediately report the incident to a supervisor, base station or the police. The observing guard should remain in constant contact with other guards or the base station giving up-dates.

Criminal conduct varies from non-violent graffiti writing to violent crimes such as robbery, assault and homicide. Obviously, some crimes are committed with weapons, ranging from rocks to bombs. A guard should be aware that at times an unarmed criminal may arm him or herself upon being detected. If action is required on the guard's part, the means to act effectively is an important consideration. An unarmed guard does not have the means to act effectively in a situation where the criminal is armed with a weapon. In these cases the guard should remain a safe distance from the criminal and attempt to keep cover between him or her and the criminal.

Generally, when crimes in progress are discovered the police will be notified. The police may serve several functions when dealing with a crime in progress. They will respond and arrest the perpetrator, take custody of someone who was arrested by the guard and process physical evidence. In most cases a police report will be completed. To aid the police, the guard should report the location of the incident. This should include the nearest cross street. The guard should describe: what type of offense is being committed, how many criminals are involved and their descriptions, if weapons are involved and if applicable the type of vehicle involved. The guard should also furnish a description of him or herself, where he or she will be and if applicable what type of vehicle he or she is in. If an arrest has been made, the reporting guard should advise the police contact as to how many people have been arrested. If a base station operator or a supervisor is making the report, he or she should advise the police who to contact at the scene and furnish the scene guard's description.

Evidence may be found at the scene that will aid the criminal justice system in prosecuting the case. Remember, physical evidence can help identify the criminal and show that a crime was committed. If evidence is at the scene, the guard's function is to protect it from contamination, tampering or destruction. The evidence must be secured or sealed off. To meet this end, the guard should not touch it, keep other people away from it and only let authorized people approach it. Witness evidence, some thing someone, other than the guard, saw or heard, can be used later in court. The professional would be wise to record any witness's name, address and phone number and furnish this information to the police. For a more thorough understanding of evidence handling consult *New York State Criminal Law For Security Professionals.*

When the police arrive they will assume control of the scene and the investigation. For the purposes of the security officer's report, he or she should note the name and shield number of the police officer who assumes control. The security officer should brief the police regarding the facts of the incident and advise them of the location of any evidence. The police will decide how to proceed from this point. They will determine who has relevant information regarding case preparation and what evidence will be collected.

Interviewing is a developed skill. An interview has a specific objective. A security officer should not attempt to interview witnesses, perpetrators and victims unless he has the authority to conduct an investigation, arrest perpetrators and has been trained in interviewing techniques.

Riots

Riots often occur because of political or social unrest. Political causes for riots stem from dissatisfaction with the government's handling of issues ranging from police brutality to involvement in wars. Social conditions that spark riots vary from race, ethnic and religious relations to poverty and other undesirable social conditions. Riots may occur as the result of civil disturbances or they can erupt when any group feels politically, socially or economically deprived and a controversial issue sparks them to act. A riot can occur anywhere where groups of people congregate, ranging from athletic stadiums to city streets to abortion clinics. The results are uncontrolled violence, property destruction and looting. Because of the likelihood of injury and damage, rioting is a crime under the penal law.

Riots are extremely dangerous and difficult situations to handle because many include large numbers of angry, violent people. The security officer's primary concern is the protection of life, including his or her own. He or she must be aware that because of a uniformed appearance, he or she may become the target of the mob. The guard must also consider the fact the he or she will be outnumbered. For these reasons a guard should never confront or agitate rioting people. The protection of property is a secondary consideration. In most rioting situations the police will be needed to disperse the crowd. Obviously notifying them should be a first consideration.

Civil Disturbances

Civil disturbances may result from protests of dissatisfaction. Many of the protests occur because of controversial political issues. Some result because of social discontent. When engaged in protesting, the protestors want to draw attention to their side of the issue. The protesting people feel very strongly about the various causes in which they are engaged. Generally, when a person or a group of people takes issue with a policy or circumstance the potential for a civil disturbance should be a matter of concern.

Civil disobedience is the willful breaking of laws to draw public attention to a cause. The protestors violate the law in plain view of the police and security. The violations usually include, trespassing, obstructing traffic and other non-violent illegal conduct. The protestors are aware that they will be arrested and passively resist arrest by not cooperating. Many of them must be carried to waiting custody vehicles.

A security officer assigned to crowd control should realize that the best way to deal with riots or civil disturbances is to prevent them from occurring in the first place. Professional appearance and attitude are the starting points. The appearance should be neat and clean, maintaining a command presence. The attitude should be one of neutrality. This attitude is important, particularly if a guard's stand on an issue is the opposite of the protestors. A security officer should never engage a protestor in debate or provoke an argument. If possible avoid confrontation. Security officers should not touch any of the protestors either. If an agitator is starting to stir the crowd towards anger, it is recommended that he or she be removed from the scene. The cardinal rule in handling potential crowd control problems is, "never commit a force to small to do the job." If the potential for civil disturbance or riot seems to be increasing call for back-up, consider notifying the police and protect the employer, coworkers, customers, patients and property from harm.

In either the case of riot or civil disturbance, utility service may be effected. Telephone, electric and gas service may be temporarily discontinued. To be prepared for this contingency security officers should make certain that radios and emergency lighting are in operating order. They should also make sure that emergency exits are not blocked.

Strikes and Picket Actions

Strikes and picket actions can be seen as methods of expressing dissatisfaction. A strike usually involves a work stoppage by employees because of dissatisfaction with an employer. A picket action is a means of drawing attention to any dissatisfaction, including a strike. Picket lines are not limited to striking workers. They can be formed to draw attention to any particular issue. The security officer should handle these situations similarly to the way in which he or she would handle any other crowd control situation. In situations involving picket lines, there is usually advanced notice. It would be wise for the security officer assigned to these cases to police the area before the day's action starts. Pick up any item that could be used as an offensive weapon, such as rocks, sticks, bottles and the like and remove them from the scene. Picketing protestors are not allowed to block the entrances to the facility in which they are protesting against. They cannot stop workers, clients, patients and others who have business within the facility from entering or leaving the place. They do not have the right to picket near the property of the facility. They do have a right to picket peacefully and to express themselves in accordance with the free speech amendment of our constitutions. The New York State General Business Law makes certain actions by security officers assigned to strike-picket duty illegal. Consult that law or *New York State Criminal Law For Security Professionals* for an overview.

Medical Emergencies

Medical emergencies are not unusual occurrences in the work place. They range from industrial accidents to heart attacks. Some medical emergencies can be remedied with a band-aid, others require an emergency medical technician team and an ambulance. The security officer should understand that he or she should not administer any first aid procedures which he or she is not certified to administer. If the guard is not properly certified, there is little that he or she can do in terms of first-aid. The main role of a guard in this situation is to make sure that the proper emergency response team was notified and is responding. To meet this objective, the guard should assess the situation and make the proper notification. He or she should be prepared to: describe the emergency, name, age and sex of the victim, make the victim feel as comfortable as is possible and guide emergency responders to the location. Serious injury is accompanied by traumatic shock. The victim feels cold. By placing a blanket over the victim, the cold feeling may be reduced. The guard should keep spectators away from the area. Spectators make the victim feel uncomfortable and can increase psychological shock by commenting on the seriousness of the injury or illness. Spectators can also impede the response and work of the emergency medical technician team. The guard should be available to assist the emergency responder if necessary.

Security officers should refrain from certain actions at a medical emergency. They should never move the victim unless the victim's position is endangering his or her life. For example, if a victim is in a vehicle, leave him or her there unless the vehicle catches on fire and the victim's life is in jeopardy. The reason for this is simple, any movement can increase an injury. A broken spine, if moved, could severe the spinal cord causing paralysis. Security guards should never remove items that are imbedded into the body. By removing those items the injury could be increased. One of the results of a serious injury is thirst. Even though the victim may ask for water, it is ill advised to give it. Likewise do not feed an injured person. Security officers should not administer any medication.

After the medical emergency, accident or public health concern has passed, the guard should inspect the area. He or she should look for blood, slippery floors broken glass and debris left by the emergency responders such as gloves, bloodied gauze pads, syringes, et cetera. The area should be secured and people kept out until the location can be properly cleaned. The guard should be mindful that body fluids such as blood can transmit diseases. Acquired immune deficiency syndrome (AIDS) and Hepatitis B are examples of blood borne diseases. Whether security officers are involved in handling medical emergencies, accidents or other public health concerns, he or she should follow the universal precautions. Where appropriate, the guard should wear a face mask, gloves and medical gowns. If fluid spills onto the guard, he or she should wash the area immediately and apply an antiseptic such as betadine. Other surfaces can be disinfected with household bleach.

Security officers should be mindful of the Good Samaritan Law. This law exempts qualified people from civil litigation when they administer first-aid within their certified area. The law is voided if they exceed their qualifications. A wise security officer will not exceed his or her qualifications. Another point of law states that the person administering the aid cannot receive compensation for the service. If they do, the law is voided. This means that a security guard should not accept a gift from a grateful, recuperated victim. That gift is considered to be compensation. The civil litigation area becomes accessible to the victim.

Accidents

Accidents are treated similarly to medical emergencies. The responding security officer must assess and report. The security officer has one additional duty in those cases. He or she must safeguard the victim from further injury and the curious.

Evacuations

Evacuation is a procedure designed to bring people from harm's way to safety. Evacuation may be a consideration in any emergency situation. The idea should be given careful consideration. Evacuations can range from removing one person from a burning automobile to withdrawing hundreds of people from a skyscraper. During times of evacuation, security officers should consider the panic factor. To avoid the dangerous conditions panic creates, the security officer should maintain a command presence. He or she should be firm and authoritative. In these instances they must direct people to safety, not lead them to it. They must be calm and self-assured. Self assurance is gained through knowledge. The security officer should know all of the posted evacuation routes and what his or her responsibilities are according to an emergency response plan.

Elevators and Escalators

Occasionally security officers will encounter emergencies involving elevators or escalators. In emergencies involving theses conveyances the initial step is to evaluate the situation. If the event involves an elevator, any boarded passengers should be calmed and reassured that help is on the way. To subdue panic, someone should maintain constant contact with the passengers. The building's engineering department or the elevator company should be informed of the problem. Occasionally people become entangled in escalators. To avoid further damage or injury, power to the escalator should be turned off. Once this has been accomplished, those who are not entangled should be escorted off and the entangled person should be calmed and assured. Engineering or the escalator company should be notified and respond to extract the entangled person. In either case, if a greater emergency exists, such as an injury, an emergency responder should be notified.

During other emergencies, such as fires, the elevator bank should be brought down to the lobby of the building. Elevators that do not drop to the lobby should be dropped to their lowest floor. This prevents passengers from being trapped between floors during the emergency and makes them available to the emergency responder.

4-3 EMERGENCY PREPAREDNESS PLAN

A written emergency preparedness plan should aid in reducing the effects of an emergency. The plan saves time, effort and coordinates the response. The plan should explain what course of action should be followed by whom to successfully handle the situation. A good plan will make the most efficient use of all resources, including personnel.

A good plan describes the procedures that are to be followed in a crisis. During an emergency each person involved in the response will have certain duties and responsibilities. Each responder should know exactly what is expected of him or her. For this reason, each of them should review and be familiar with the plan's details.

The details should include a chain of command. The chain is a structure which shows who is accountable to whom in the organization. The chain shows the lines of authority and responsibility from the top manager of the organization down to the working level. Accountability should be limited to one group of responders reporting to and taking orders from one other person only. Through this reporting and directing method, the chain of command minimizes confusion and fixes accountability. For example, if a security officer is told by a supervisor to evacuate an injured person and another supervisor tells him or her not to evacuate, confusion will be created. Confusion will occur because the guard will not know whether to evacuate or not to evacuate. In that case, the guard cannot be held accountable for the action or lack of action because he has been given conflicting orders from two supervisors. Time and effort will have been wasted and perhaps a life lost because the chain of command was not followed properly. That guard should answer to, and be directed by one supervisor only.

The plan should detail that in major emergencies, responses should be coordinated by a manager with undisputed authority and total responsibility. This person should set-up a command post near the emergency. All communication regarding the crisis should be funneled into the command post for evaluation. After evaluating the information, the manager should coordinate and direct the course of the operation through the chain of command. He or she should seek feedback to determine whether the effort is going according to plan. Coordination eliminates duplication of work and maintains optimum effort. In the event that the emergency response is turned over to a civil authority, such as the police or fire department, that agency will assume the duties of coordinating the response.

Training is an important element of an emergency response plan. Every person involved should be trained in both the classroom and through drills. Classroom discussion is focused on understanding the plan and its implementation. Drills cause conditioned, automatic responses. Training leads to self-confidence and can reduce panicked responses. Through training, the security department learns what is expected of it, and each guard knows what is expected of him or her. Each guard learns to be familiar with the overall plan, including the responses of other departments and outside agencies. Training will dictate the plan's procedure regarding who is to be notified in each type of emergency.

Plans should consider responses to every potential emergency. They should include procedure for notification and evacuation. Notification plans should include information regarding who makes what notification inside and outside of the chain of command. The plan should describe the circumstances when a civil authority should be notified. Evacuation routes should be established in the plan and evacuations signs posted. The plan should consider what organizational assets are available for handling fire and medical emergencies. Assets include equipment and trained personnel. These assets may include utilizing an employee's outside interest. During emergencies, the plan may call for enlisting the aid of an employee who, while off duty, is an emergency medical technician or a fire fighter. The plan should establish procedures for property protection and life saving steps.

4-4   MISCELLANEOUS INFORMATION

Response to Emergencies: General Procedures

In many emergencies some of the response steps taken are the same. The initial step is assessment. Basically this is asking and answering the questions, "What is going on here and how do I correct the situation?" Once these answers have been determined, the second step, depending upon the severity of the emergency, may be to notify the proper authority. The proper authority does not have to be a public responder, such as a fire department. The proper authority can be a supervisor, a base station or a person designated by an employer. The third step is to remedy the situation. The remedy may be found in an employer's policy or it may be a response described in a first-aid manual, a Material Safety

Data Sheet, a Fire Safety Officer's Training Course or any other emergency response manual. If the employer has an emergency plan, it is very important for the guard to know it and to know what is expected of the guard. All security officers should know and practice their specific roles in emergency situations. The remedy should also include steps to secure or isolate the emergency area. People should be kept a safe distance from the location. The fourth step is to resume normal security as quickly as is possible. Once the emergency has been stabilized, the security officer should not linger at the scene unless he or she is needed there. He or she should realize that criminal conduct is based mostly on opportunity. If the guard is unnecessarily lingering, he or she is distracted and an opportunity is open for the criminal.

The security officer should realize that after the incident a report may be required. The guard should make mental notes as well as field notes. He or she should note the name, date of birth, home address and home phone number of any victims in the emergency. He should also record any other information that will help complete the report's requirements.

Security officers should maintain and update the phone numbers of emergency responders. The list should be kept in an available location.

Security officers should know their limitations. Limitations can be imposed by policy, law or physical tasks. A security officer who works within his or her limitations will be more effective and less vulnerable to injury or legal problems.

The more effective security officers are those who know the facility within which they are employed. They should be familiar with every nook and cranny. Those guards know which doors are exit doors, where the extinguishers, alarm stations and emergency showers are located. This knowledge greatly enhances the guard's ability to respond in emergencies.

Alert security guards know that in emergency situations people will be looking to them for guidance and direction. The people are aware that guards' knowledge of procedures, building lay out and the proper responses to the variety of emergencies will aid in protecting them and property in the event of an emergency.

If there is a doubt about an emergency response or the role one plays in the emergency, the guard should not hesitate to ask what is expected of him or her.

Security officers may elect to consider RAIN, discussed in Chapter 10, as an appropriate response in certain emergency situations.

Security Guard Safety

Safety is the first rule. When handling emergency situations the safety of people always takes precedent to the safety of property. Security officers should not unnecessarily risk their lives or the lives of others. They should be mindful that reckless conduct, such as entering a smoke filled room without protection, can be dangerous. In protecting people, security officers should respond in accordance with company policy, training and common sense.

To prevent unnecessary injury, a security officer should assess the situation to determine what aspects can cause injury or be too dangerous to act upon. Upon assessing the circumstances, he or she may decide to approach the situation and take action. In that case it is important to notify a supervisor or base station of the situation and the intended action. Calling for a back-up officer may be required. However, if the situation reaches a critical point, the guard should consider evacuating and notifying the appropriate civil authority such as the police or fire department. Once this has occurred, the guard should stand ready to assist the emergency responder. If the security officer is the base station operator, he should periodically check with the officer at the emergency scene to make sure that the officer handling the situation is safe. A supervising officer should respond to the scene to make sure that the proper procedure is being followed.

Security officers should be mindful that, at times, failure to act could bring undesirable consequences such as termination or negligence litigation. The key phrase in deciding whether to act or not to act is "do what is reasonable under the circumstances."

To reduce the risk of injury, the security officer should be firm and fair when dealing with people. He or she should avoid demeaning other people by talking down to them or by using racial or ethnic slurs. The guard should avoid arguing with people. Arguing tends to escalate a problem because people become irritated as the argument progresses. When dealing with irate people the professional will remain calm and try to sooth the angry person. He or she should casually remove available offensive weapons within reach of the irritated individual.

In handling emergencies such as fire, explosion, bomb threats hazardous wastes and disasters, the guard should realize that trained professionals are available to help. If the situation calls for professional first responders, seek their assistance.

A calm, guard in a uniform represents authority, people will react more calmly to that self assured authority and follow directions more easily. Calmness tends to suppress panic, thereby avoiding injury.

Available Equipment

While on patrol, the professional will assess the post for available emergency equipment. He or she will note what fire fighting apparatuses are available and their state of readiness. A guard should make sure that emergency lighting is operable. He or she will know where the decontaminates are stored and how to use them.

Security officers should possess certain items which can aid in avoiding injury. A working flashlight should be on hand day or night. There are many areas that are not exposed to light during the day. Entering these areas can be dangerous, particularly if the guard does not know what the area contains. If company policy allows, the guard should consider owning a quality pair of handcuffs or tie raps. These can be used to restrain and control people in custody. A restrained person is less likely to injure than one who is not restrained. Two way radios are essential for communication during an emergency. They can serve as personal protection through a deterrent factor. A person with harmful intent may realize that help is a radio call away and be discouraged from further action. Radios can also serve to bring help to an injured person in the field.

Security officers should not consider possessing billy-clubs including a police nightstick while on or off duty. Those items are illegal.

4-5 CONCLUSION

Security officers must be prepared to deal with a variety of emergency situations. The more familiar they are with the procedures, the better they will be able to cope with the emergency. To meet this end, a professional will seek certification in handling the various emergencies. They will strive to know the company policy regarding emergencies and when to seek the help of emergency responders, such as the police, fire department or ambulance crew.

The best way to deal with an emergency is to prevent it from occurring in the first place. This is done by diligent patrol, good observation skills and reporting potential problems for correction.

CHAPTER 5

COMMUNICATION AND PUBLIC RELATIONS

5-1 INTRODUCTION

The ability to communicate is probably the most important skill a person can possess. Without the capability to communicate, a person could not function as a human being. We learn to communicate early in life. Cultural upbringing and our value systems play important roles in interpreting communication. This country consists of a multi-cultural population. Therefore communication can be a difficult process. In communicating with people from other cultures, we must understand that they may have different customs than our mainstream culture. We need not know a culture's particular traditions. What we need to do is to have patience and understanding when communicating with a person of another culture. However, having a basic knowledge of another's customs is very helpful in the process of passing or receiving information.

Public relations is part of the communication process. Public relations can make or break a security officer and the organization which he or she represents. Good public relations consists of being helpful, friendly, polite, neat, clean and professional.

To meet the objectives, the security officer will be introduced to the following topics: the components of communication, the three methods of communication, obstacles to communication and the components necessary to be an effective communicator.

5-2 COMPONENTS OF THE COMMUNICATION PROCESS

The communication process has three components. They are sender, receiver and feedback. In the classroom setting the instructor is sending the information. When a security officer has to direct people or enforce company policy, he or she is the sender. In the classroom the student is the receiver in the communication process. In the field, the person the security officer is directing is the receiver. Feedback is seeking to know if the receiver understands the message. This is accomplished by questioning or testing. In the classroom the instructor questions students to determine if they understand the message. On the job, the security officer should question the person he or she is directing to determine if that person truly understands the message sent. If the message is not received properly, the communication should be repeated or rephrased until it is understood.

5-3   USES OF COMMUNICATION

There are five uses of communication in the security field. Public relations is the most common use. The other four are: compliance or order maintenance, describing events (needed for good reports), emergencies (for the protection of people and property) and interviewing (as an investigative tool).

There is no doubt that effective communication is important. It plays an important role in public relations. This is particularly true in combating prejudice, for prejudice is, as will later be discussed, an effective communications terminator. Tact is important, without it the security officer's approach to a situation could be grating and irritating. In the courtroom setting communications can sway a jury in either direction. If the guard is a poor communicator, he or she will not be received well and the testimony will be less credible. The Public Relations aspect of communication is necessary in gaining cooperation from other agencies. Finally, the effective communicator knows how to document information for reports and possible future court testimony.

The security guard supervisor is responsible to make sure that the company policy is followed, thereby maintaining order and compliance to company policy. Because they cannot be at every situation, management issues orders, regulations, rules and policy in the written form. When reading written orders one usually does not have the opportunity to question their meanings. Because of this problem, the writer must make certain that the written communication is understandable. It has been said that one who can communicate well in this medium has an important skill.

When the public observes a security officer, they see a communication process. Appearance is the first aspect of communication. Secondly, they will observe the demeanor or attitude. This can also communicate positively or negatively. Finally, when the public speaks with a guard, his or her spoken responses and accompanying body language will be observed. All of these observations reflect the public relations effort of that particular security officer and the organization he or she represents.

For an employer, whether contractual or proprietary, the ability to communicate well in emergency situations is important. The rapid and accurate deliverer and the understanding receiver of information can reduce injury and loss during an emergency event.

The security guard is charged with conducting investigations into situations that fall within his or her scope of responsibility. This requires two abilities. One, the ability to communicate what information is needed to complete the investigation and two, the ability to gain information from those who are involved in the situation. Additionally, he or she should be skillful at recording observations and facts.

5-4 THREE METHODS OF COMMUNICATION

There are three methods of communication, verbal, non-verbal and written. Two of the three, verbal and written, obviously require the use of words. The third, non-verbal communication, is achieved through, signs, symbols, gestures, posture, movements, attitude, and physiological responses. In verbal communication, non-verbal communication is present. Also present are tone, pitch, emphasis and intensity. Non-verbal communication and the other aspects such as tone help define the meaning of the verbal communication. Written communication stands alone. The other forms of communication are not present to support the meaning of the written document.

Verbal Communication

Verbal communication consists of spoken words and the hearing of those words. Aspects of verbal communication include tone: friendly, neutral or offensive, volume: loud, soft or mid-range and message content. Hearing, in this case, means listening and understanding. If one does not understand, one should seek clarification until one does understand. During verbal communication one should consider enhancing it through the conscious use of body language.

Oral communication is used in public relations, seeking compliance to orders, rules or regulations, verbal reports, radio conversations and emergency communications. Regardless of which communication one is engaged in, the communication must be clear and understandable, particularly in emergency situations.

The verbal communication process is not without problems. People are prejudice and this hampers the process. Sometimes the receiver has difficulty hearing and the message does not get across. Insensitivity and offensive language do not enhance communication, neither does a poor attitude. Poor speaking skills tend to reduce the listening aspect of verbal communication. Lack of knowledge of the topic negatively impacts on the process also.

A significant problem with verbal communication is the word selection. Words have different meanings to different people. Each of us defines a word based on our own cultural heritage, social and economic class and value system. To a person who was raised in poverty the word "work" may mean long, hard hours at a low paying job. To a wealthy person the word "work" may mean art or music. To overcome this problem the sender must choose words which he or she knows the receiver will understand. In addition the sender may want to select adverbs or adjectives to make the meaning of the communication clearer. For example, if one states, "Give me a four letter word for intercourse." The usual response is "fuck." However, the response to that question could also be "talk." According to the dictionary, intercourse deals with communication or sexual activity. To clarify the question, one only needs to add a word which limits the focus of the question. For example, if the statement is, "Give me a four letter word for verbal intercourse." The answer can only focus on a communication word such as "talk." The word "verbal" clarifies the question and confines the answer.

Overcoming Problems

One can overcome verbal communication problems by practicing the skills necessary to be an effective communicator. These skills include learning to be a better listener, learning to speak with tact, that is, using non-offensive language, paying attention to the accompanying body language, maintaining a positive attitude, remembering that security work is a service industry and knowledge of the job, the responsibilities and duties.

Non-verbal Communication

Non-verbal communication takes many forms. The components include: gestures, symbols, posture, appearance, demeanor, contact, distance, confidence and eye contact. A wave of the hand is a sign which may indicate a greeting. A wedding ring is a symbol of a commitment. A closed posture may mean that a person is on the defense or does not want to communicate. On the other hand, an open posture indicates that the person is receptive to the communication process. Aggression is often accompanied by body language, particularly if a person moves from an open stance to the side stance and raises the hands to chest level. Depending upon the culture, lack of eye contact can indicate lying or lack of interest. Physiological or bodily changes such as increased pulse rate or faster breathing, sweating, dryness of the mouth may indicate that a person is not truthful. An observant guard will learn to read and interpret body language and other forms of non-verbal communication.

Non-verbal communication has other important aspects. From a public relations point of view, non-verbal communication can be the basis of the first impression. As was stated earlier in the volume, a first impression can be a lasting impression. Therefore it is in the interest of the guard and his or her company to create a positive first impression. Non-verbal communication can also: prepare a guard for an aggressive act about to be committed against him or her, aid in knowing that someone understands a verbal communication and helps to determine if someone is listening.

Lack of eye contact, closed posture and physiological changes often accompany lying. The reason is stress. Generally, people do not like to lie. When they do lie, they become stressed. Stress shows itself in a variety of ways. Looking away from the questioner's face when giving an untruthful answer is a common way of dealing with that stress. The security officer should note that people also look away from the questioner's face when they are asked to remember something. To determine the difference between memory glances and lying glances, the guard should ask a person innocent questions such as "What did you have for dinner last Sunday?" Questions such as that one will show the guard which way a person glances when asked to recall something. When lying, the glance will usually go in a different direction. Closed posture occurs when people cross their arms in front of themselves and hunch up. This is a defensive posture and can occur when people do not want to communicate. Often people do not want to communicate a lie so they close-up. When people are willing to communicate and tell the truth the posture will open-up gradually. As any polygraph technician can explain, stress causes physical reactions that the person under stress cannot usually control. On the lie detector these reactions are measured on graph paper. An alert guard can observe some of these reactions. Someone wiping his or her hands on his or her clothing may be a sign of sweating, a stress reaction. Because adrenalin is released into the blood stream during times of stress, heart rate and breathing become increased. A lying person's neck may pulsate or the breathing becomes more rapid.

Before determining that any these conditions are the result of false statements, the guard should assess the situation. People have different stress levels. Some people get stressed-out at the mere possibility of being confronted.

Therefore, before attempting to question a person regarding an investigation, the guard should determine how a person responds to non-accusatory questions. To meet this end, the guard should make the person feel as comfortable as is possible. He or she should ask non-offensive questions such as "Do you have any hobbies?" or "Do you like sports?" During this period the alert guard will pay attention to the non-verbal responses, eye contact, posture, breathing and so forth. Once he or she determines the usual responses, he or she can move into the investigative mode, paying more attention to the responses.

One other point regarding false statements. If a person is asked if he or she acted wrongly, the usual, truthful response will be, "No, I did not do that!" Any other response may indicate that the person acted as the guard suspected. False verbal responses include: "Are you accusing me of this, if so, I'll sue!" or "It is wrong to do that, I would never try and hurt someone." or any other vague answer. The reason is simple, again, they are avoiding the necessity of lying.

Written Communication

Written communication is an essential aspect of security officers' functions. The issues of time, date, location, who, what, when, where, why and how must be addressed in incident reports or they are incomplete. The security officer must make certain that he or she completely and accurately documents activities such as theft, fire, vandalism, trespass, vehicles, people, accidents, injuries and so forth. A written record aids memory and can facilitate managers or other agencies for a variety of reasons, including planning. To meet this end, reports should be neatly written and completed as soon as is possible after the incident. To help the reader understand, all reports should be simple, short and to the point. As was noted earlier, plain English is better than complicated wording. Remember, there is no room in a written report for personal opinions unless they are totally based on facts. Supposition and conjecture should not be included in these documents. The topic of written communication will be addressed in detail in the chapter on report writing.

The security officer will be responsible for the completion of several reports. They include notes, activity logs, daily reports, incident and accident reports, memos and the newly developed electronic E-mail.

Statements and Interviews

Security officers engaged in recording or listening to statements must remember that statements must be freely and voluntarily given. Threats, promises or intimidation can negate the value of any statement.

All interviews must be planned in advance and the objectives must be established. One objective might be to determine what exactly did a particular witness observe. To meet this end, security officers must ask the appropriate questions at a location favorable to gaining the needed answers. For example, interviewing a witness who is cold and uncomfortable will be less productive than interviewing that witness in a warm, dry location. Security officers should consider planning their methods of recording interviews. Regardless of the method of recording, they must realize that some people are reluctant to talk if notes or other recording methods are employed.

Interviewing is a skill that must be developed. There are a variety of resources that can teach interviewing techniques. If security officers are interested in developing those skills, the public library is a good starting point.

5-5   OBSTACLES TO EFFECTIVE COMMUNICATION

Any effective communicator knows that skills, attitude, prejudice and knowledge of what is being communicated are important to the process. He or she also knows that obstacles can occur in any of the three communication mediums. Before communicating verbally, the sender should consider three aspects of language skills. One, what skills are required in the work place. Two, what language skills does the security guard possess. Three, what are the language skills of the people the guard will be dealing with.

The sender must possess a positive attitude. He or she must communicate in a neutral, calm and controlled way. The communication should not be delivered with emotion or in a degrading fashion. If a guard is angry or excited, he or she should calm down before sending the message or restrain from showing that condition when communicating. Shouting at someone or demeaning them will stop the process, anger the receiver and may result in a confrontation.

Displaying prejudice is a sure way to thwart the communication process. Prejudice can be displayed through non-verbal body language or verbally through slurs. Overt prejudice can, at the very least cause listening failure or at the worst, cause confrontation. There are very few people who are not prejudice to some degree against some human condition, be it against race, gender, ethnicity, creed, age or religion. Most of us are able to put the prejudice aside and deal positively with other people. It is absolutely essential that security officers realize their shortcomings in this area and put them aside when dealing with others. In today's multi-cultural climate, the display of any prejudice is frowned upon. A security officer who openly displays prejudice in this service industry may find his or her career path obstructed.

Knowledge of the subject matter is important for effective communication. In the security officer's case this knowledge should include knowing his or her duties and responsibilities, post orders, employer policies, rules and regulations, laws and ordinances. For example, if a guard is assigned to access control, he or she must know who is allowed entry and under what circumstances. This information is gained from knowing the post orders and company policy. Post orders may inform the guard that a particular person has been terminated. If that person attempts to enter, the guard must communicate that the entry is forbidden. If the guard does not know the post order, he or she could not communicate to the person entering the facility that his or her access should be denied.

Message Breakdown

There are several ways in which communication can break down. The message may be delivered poorly due to speech or language difficulties. Psychological barriers may be present during the process. The receiver may have any of a variety of other problems such as stress, mental illness or cultural differences, including a language barrier.

Poor delivery is a common problem. The communicator must select the words, phrases and jargon properly. Another problem in this area is that the messenger may not understand the message. In that case the message will seem jumbled. Security officers should make certain that the delivery is coherent and not awkward. They should organize their ideas before attempting the delivery. To avoid vagueness, the message should be clear.

Psychological barriers can interrupt the process. Prejudice, as was mentioned earlier, is an excellent example of a psychological barrier. Personal bias can be included into this area. Panic, fear and threats to personal safety preoccupy both the sender and the receiver. The results of these conditions negate the communication. Extreme emotional stress will shut down the process because the person is preoccupied with a severe problem. Some of these problems could include financial problems, health problems and marital stress to mention a few. Status can add to the problem. A person of high rank can easily communicate downward, however, a person of lesser status may find it difficult to communicate upwards. Self-confidence is a psychological factor. People who lack this find it difficult to communicate and may be easily offended when receiving a communication.

Miscellaneous barriers could include external barriers such as noise, temperature, weather, the condition of the facility where the communication occurs, mental illness, physical problems such as being hearing impaired, cultural and language barriers, to name a few.

5-6 COMPONENTS NECESSARY TO BE AN EFFECTIVE COMMUNICATOR

Five components have been identified as being necessary for effective communication. They are as follows: proper attitude, understanding of duties and environment, sensitivity and compassion, listening skills and interpreting the message.

Proper attitude has been discussed earlier and means being professional.

It is difficult to communicate if one does not understand his or her duties, responsibilities and environment. For example, if a hazardous material accident occurred, how would the guard know how to communicate the response procedure if he or she did not know what that procedure was or where the hazardous material was stored?

Sensitivity and compassion can be categorized as being part of having a proper attitude. Gruffness, callousness or disinterest serve only to inhibit communication and can anger the sender or receiver. One must be sensitive and compassionate to a range of situations including: age and gender differences, patience with attempting to understand foreign accents or cultural differences, dealing with frustrated individuals, attending injured people or listening to disgruntled co-workers, to name a few. By opening the communication process in a courteous, sensitive manner, the guard will gain respect and successfully communicate. An old saying applies here, "You catch more flies with honey than you do with vinegar." The guard should also realize the security business is a service business. This usually means that there is much contact with other people. An insensitive, uncompassionate security officer may draw complaints from co-workers or the public. Employers do not need this bad publicity. The result may be termination of the guard's services.

Hearing the message or using a third ear is probably one of the most important aspects of being a good communicator. If one does not listen, one cannot properly respond. Listening is a developed skill. People tend not to listen for a variety of reasons. Lack of interest is one. The security officer may not think that another person's problem is important enough to deserve a response. The guard should realize that if the other person thinks that he or she has a problem, then resolving that problem is important to that person. He or she deserves to be heard. Lack of interest will quickly become obvious and the sender will stop communicating and leave frustrated. That person will have a low opinion of the guard and the guard's employer. Thinking of a response is another listening problem. This occurs to often and happens when people are thinking about an answer before the sender is finished communicating. If a person is thinking about an answer, he or she cannot be listening. Then, of course, there is jumping to conclusions. Once a person jumps to a conclusion the listening process is over and the message probably was not understood. False conclusions can be harmful. They can lead an investigation on the wrong course or cause an improper action to occur. The better security officers will train themselves to listen.

Interpreting the message can be a difficult task. As was discussed earlier with the word "work," many words have different interpretations. To add to this confusion, one must realize that many words have more than one dictionary definition. One must also remember that non-verbal communication can alter the meaning of the verbal message. Improperly interpreted messages can lead to confusion or the wrong course of action. The best way for a sender to know that the message was properly received is to seek feedback, ask questions. The best way for a receiver to understand is to ask questions when there is a doubt as to the message's meaning. The receiver should understand that there is no such thing as a stupid question. Any question that can help the receiver understand a message's meaning is a valid inquiry.

The rate of speed with which a message is delivered is important, too fast and the message will not be received. People can only absorb so much information in a given amount of time. To help others understand, it is recommended that the speaker pace the words. Slow down! At times, particularly in emergency situations, people tend to speak fast. They must condition themselves to slow down.

During face to face conversations all parties involved should acknowledge each other through non-verbal communication. This includes maintaining the appropriate eye contact. Remember some cultures look away or down during conversation. If that is appropriate cultural behavior then one must accept it. Other ways to acknowledge other participants is to use gestures, facial expressions and nodding of the head in acknowledgement. These non-verbal forms of communication show that there is an interest in what is being communicated. Non-verbal gestures and so forth can assist the sender in making his or her points because they reinforce words with actions.

One recurring theme in this chapter is *keep it simple*. Simple language is the easiest language to understand particularly when the receiver must rely on memory to carry out a direction, order or utilize the contents of a message at some future time.

Repetition is also an important aspect of communication. The more a theme is repeated, such as the *keep it simple* theme, the more likely it is that the message will be understood. Repetition also reinforces retention. Hopefully through repetition the message is received and retained as well. Repetition is useful in feedback situations. If the feedback seems weak, re-word the idea and check for understanding. Analogies and examples during this process can help clarify the idea.

Command presence, the displaying of confidence and control in emergency situations is important. One who displays command presence should also ensure that the communication is crisp, clear, understandable and concise. This communicator must know the procedures used in each emergency.

5-7 COMMUNICATION MEDIUMS

In modern society security officers will be called upon to accomplish a variety of tasks. Some will be assigned to fixed posts where they will answer telephones, enter data into computers, communicate through two way radios and utilize public address systems. They will work at the hub of the communication center. This segment discusses the procedures used with the various communication mediums available to today's guard.

Telephone

The telephone is one of the most frequently used communication devices available today. Telephones are an essential aspect of a base station and because they are portable they can be used in cars and on foot posts.

When communicating via the telephone, the guard should follow certain routine procedures. When a guard answers the phone he or she should give the name of the business, his or her title and name. The guard should then ask how he or she may help the caller. The guard should bear in mind that the telephone call may be the caller's initial encounter with the agency that the guard represents. Because first impressions are lasting impressions, the guard should be courteous, calm and helpful. When making a phone call the guard should start the conversation with a greeting, announce his or her title, name and identify the company which he or she represents. Any security officer who has the responsibility of answering or making calls would be wise to keep a note pad and pencil available. Notes should be taken because the information received or imparted may require other action. Note taking will help in passing along accurate information. It is unwise to rely solely on memory when giving or receiving information.

Security officers will receive and make calls in two broad categories, emergencies and non-emergencies. Emergency phone calls demand immediate attention and action. When receiving an emergency call, the security officer should seek and record the following information: name and address of caller, call back phone number, nature of the emergency including the extent of injury, location and the name of the nearest cross street, if applicable. The guard should realize that people panic during emergencies and the caller may be in that state of mind. The guard must remain calm and have patience in those cases. When making emergency calls, the guard should be prepared to give that information described above. Information from emergency calls should be taped or recorded on a log.

Non-emergency calls consist of calls for information or assistance, complaints regarding the operation and administrative calls such as phoning another security officer to give an assignment. When receiving a call for information, assistance or a complaint, the guard should provide the information, arrange for a service or record the complaint. If he or she cannot accomplish the objective a referral to a source that can is advisable.

When handling complaint calls, the guard should consider the fact that the caller may be angry. It is ill advised to argue with the complainer, regardless of the merits of the complaint. Perhaps the best course of action is to attempt to calm the complainant, record the information, assure the person that the incident will be investigated and pass the complaint along to a supervisor for further action.

Radio

Two way radio is the main form of communication between base stations and patrols, and between patrolling officers. Information received at the base station which requires fieldwork is relayed via two way radio and back-up calls between patrolling officers are examples of the many uses of two way radio.

When using radios, security officers should follow a procedure. The messages should be coded. Any guard who uses the radio should know the code and its translation. Coded messages reduce time spent on the air. All radio transmissions should be brief, therefore the message should be thought-out before being transmitted. Lengthy conversations or transmission of sensitive information should be avoided. In these cases guards should use telephones. Security officers should know that only one person can speak into a radio at a time. Lengthy transmissions stop others from transmitting during that time. The reason sensitive information should not be broadcast on a radio or cellular phone is that other people may possess radios or phones of the same frequency. Criminals, in particular, can use the sensitive information to their advantage. Guards who are not involved in the transmissions should listen to be aware of the activity around them. Profanity should not be used on the radio. It is unprofessional and if the station is licensed by the Federal Communication Corporation the offender can be fined.

Public Address Systems

Occasionally security officers may utilize public address systems, including loudspeakers. These devices are certainly valuable when large groups need to be addressed or directed. All messages should be thought-out before engaging the device. The communication should be concise. To avoid confusion, the message's meaning must be clear. When the device is engaged a clear, calm voice should be utilized. It is not necessary to yell into the public address microphone. Yelling runs the words into each other, making them garbled. A normal tone, spoken at a slower pace, allows for clarity.

Communication Centers

Security officers may be assigned to three types of communication centers. They may be assigned to public information posts, command posts or base stations. Public information posts may be established in lobbies of corporate headquarters, government buildings, airports and shopping malls. While functioning in a public information post, security officers will be required to respond to questions from the public. To meet this end, guards should be knowledgeable with every aspect of the post and the information which he or she is responsible to dispense. There will be times when security officers will not be able to furnish the requested information. When this happens security officers should research the information or refer the seeker. In the capacity of information giver, it is important for guards to present and maintain a professional image. They should be pleasant and courteous, bearing in mind that the impressions they leave with the public are the public's impression of their companies' as well.

Command posts are base stations set up close to an emergency situation. In these cases, security officers may be required to notify emergency responders, describe the emergencies and give directions. They may also be required to communicate via radio and telephone with other guards at the scene. Under these circumstances guards should make field notes regarding what agency was communicated with, who was spoken with and at what time this occurred.

A base station can be the hub of a security operation. Security officers may have a variety of tasks to perform. They may be responsible for monitoring closed circuit televisions (CCTV), maintaining a variety of logs and communicating with other officers and other agencies. Regardless of which types of communication centers guards are assigned to, they should make every effort to develop excellent communication skills, follow telephone, radio and public address system procedures.

Computer Networks

Computer networks are important in today's security industry. To be an effective computer communicator, security guards should know how a computer operates. A computer is an information storage and retrieval system. It can be seen as an electronic filing cabinet. The filing system inside the computer is software known as a program. A person puts information into the program and later takes that information out. Basically, a computer contains three components known as hardware. Hardware consists of an input device such as a keyboard, a processing device called a computer and an output device such as printer or a television screen. The input device gives the processor the information. The program within the processor files and stores the information. The output device calls up the data for the computer operator. Computers can be very small, such as an arithmetic calculator, or large enough to fill an entire building floor.

Computers can be operated alone or can be connected to others in what is known as a network. Through networking information is shared with other computer operators. Networks can be local or they can be global. Local networks can be confined to one floor of a building, such as in a small business, or as in larger companies, connected to other computers miles away. If a computer has a device known as a modem, information can be sent to other modem equipped computers anywhere in the world. The data is sent through telephone cables.

The uses and functions of computers are only limited by man's imagination and technology. Today, computers can keep track of cargo, program hotel key cards and otherwise control access, communicate post orders, gather background information on people, produce reports and perform many other security related tasks.

The key to computer function is in the program. The program will dictate what information the processor will accept. There are many programs available and they do a variety of jobs. Some programs are data bases. Data bases store information and can compile statistics. For example, if a security guard needed to know how many alarms rang in two years, at a particular location, a data base could rapidly furnish that information. Other programs are word processors. They allow an operator to type, edit and spell check documents, including reports. Some programs are both data bases and word processors. Additionally, computer programs may dictate who has access to it. This is accomplished through a password or pass numbers. Without knowing the proper password or numbers a person will not be able to operate the computer. The procedure to be followed in computer networking is determined by the program and company policy.

5-8   COMMUNICATING WITH A DIVERSE POPULATION

Culturally Diverse Groups

The trend in contemporary America is to be sensitive to the customs, traditions and needs of the various diverse groups which make-up our society. A prejudicial or bigoted attitude is offensive and can lead to a strained or non-existent communication process and hostility. Bigotry and prejudice should be buried when security officers communicate. Understanding that others have dignity and pride in who they are is the key to sensitivity training. He or she should be objective, that is impartial, not partial or subjective when dealing with others. A good rule to follow is to "treat others as you would have them treat you."

Security officers must be aware That the United States is a country comprised of immigrants. Within the main culture there are ethnic cultures from all over the world. The ethnic cultures possess norms and customs that may differ from the mainstream. Some sub-cultural behavior may seem odd, strange and insulting. For example, the mainstream culture dictates that eye contact should be maintained during conversation. If a person does not maintain eye contact then he or she is either lying or is not interested in the other person. In some cultures looking into a speaker's eyes during conversation is impolite and disrespectful. Even though they have moved here, those people will maintain their former country's custom of not looking into the speaker's eyes. They do not mean any disrespect nor are they lying.

Language is often a barrier to communication. We communicate with words that both the speaker and the listener know. When another language is spoken the words are unknown to the receiver. If this barrier is encountered, the best alternative is to secure a bilingual person or guard to interpret. Often the communicator knows how to speak English, but he or she pronounces the words incorrectly because of an accent. In these cases security officers should possess patience and attempt to understand the communication. Eventually the message will be received.

Religious Orientation

The constitutions of both the United States and New York State guarantee religious freedom. It is against the Security Officers' Code of Ethics not to uphold the constitution. Therefore, security officers must respect the right of others to practice the religion of their choosing. We are as religiously diverse as we are ethnically diverse. We are so diverse that two security officers working together may have different religious views. One may pray in a church on Sunday, the other in a synagogue on Saturday or pray on a shawl, facing east. One may hold cows to be sacred, the other may not eat pork. Furthermore, there is one thing we can be sure of, each view is held sacred and the holder will defend that view. Bearing this in mind, security officers should be objective in dealing with religiously diverse people. A person's religious position should never be an issue in the decision making process, whether that process involves handling a complaint or rendering assistance.

Physically Challenged

Security officers must be sensitive to the needs of physically challenged people. Guards must understand that the disabilities create challenges in life that unchallenged people take for granted. Challenged people are not seeking sympathy, but are seeking as fulfilling a life as is possible. At times, when trying to pursue that life, the challenged person, like anyone else, may become frustrated with the situation. Frustration can convert into anger and may be directed at the guard. Professional security officers should realize that these circumstances occur. They should maintain a professional attitude during those times and not respond in anger. Whether frustration is present or not, guards should communicate that they are there to assist the challenged person when the need arises. In rendering that assistance, they should be courteous and understanding, not condescending or demeaning. They should also know that laws exist to accommodate Americans with disabilities. Therefore, guards should know and be able to communicate the location of accommodations such as wheelchair ramps, modified toilets, parking spaces and special elevators, to name a few.

Elderly

Older residents of this country require understanding. With age the human body changes. Some changes affect hearing and sight. They are slow to take place and because of this, we may not realize that our hearing and sight have been reduced. This reduction hampers the communication process and causes frustration for both elderly people and security officers. Other changes affect movement. Older people react and move about more slowly than younger ones. The slowness that accompanies age can cause impatience in younger people, security guards included. Guards must understand that older people may suffer diseases, such as Alzheimer's Disease, which cause them to act confused, disorientated, or become forgetful. They may also behave in a bizarre manner. Older people also fear crime more than younger ones. This fear can show itself in paranoid behavior because the older person thinks that most strangers may be criminals. By being aware of these problems and possibilities, security officers should take steps to overcome poor communication through patience and consideration.

Sexual Orientation

Homosexuality is a controversial issue which should not affect the way security officers interact with people. Another person's sexual preference is none of a guard's business. Security officers should be aware that the homosexual community is striving for equality. One strategy in achieving that goal is to protest. Protesters often form picket lines to draw attention to their cause. Protestors feel strongly about their beliefs or they would not be there. If assigned to these situations, security officers should maintain an attitude of neutrality and objectivity. They must understand that those who protest have this right under the First Amendment of the United States Constitution. Security officers who abide by the code of ethics have pledged to uphold that right. Whether on a picket line or in everyday situations, guards should deal with people as people. They should realize that communication will be hampered if verbal abuse or body language indicates a displeasure at another's choice of sexual activity. This applies equally to homosexual guards when dealing with the heterosexual population or for that matter, with any guard when dealing with another whose sexual tendencies vary from the mainstream. Guards' priorities should be to firmly and fairly protect the interests of their employers and not be concerned with another's sexual preferences.

Gender

Today, men and women are considered to be equal. Women do not want to be treated in any manner which portrays them as second class citizens. Men do not want to be treated as second rate citizens either. However, because of the history of discrimination against them, women are sensitive to this and other issues involving male dominance. Security officers should be aware of the equality and domination issues, particularly if the guard comes from a culture where females are held in less esteem than males. This awareness should foster better communication between the genders. By treating someone as an equal, he or she is being treated with respect. Respect fosters communication.

Sexual Harassment

As recent litigation has shown us, sexual harassment can be committed by both sexes. The Civil Rights Act of 1964 has forbidden sexual harassment in the work place and the Equal Opportunity Employment Commission (EEOC) enforces that law by bringing civil actions against offenders. Sexual harassment can occur in the work place in a number of ways: by unwanted sexual advances, either verbally or physically, by sexual remarks that discriminate or degrade. Harassment has occurred when the targeted individual feels offended, takes objection, feels discomfort or is humiliated. Sexual harassment also occurs if employment, transfer or promotion is based on the giving or withholding of sexual favors. Examples of sexual harassment could include: continuously asking someone for a date after he or she has repeatedly refused, using gender based slang such as "bitch," making comments about the genitals or breasts or touching the private areas, to name a few. Sexual harassment may be committed against members of the opposite sex by supervisory personnel. However, the law also forbids coworkers from creating a hostile environment by engaging in sexual harassment. Sexual harassment may constitute the crime of sexual abuse if the advance involves sexual touching. Harassment is a lesser offense and occurs when the actor engages in a course of conduct or repeatedly commits acts which seriously alarm or annoy the victim.

Sexual harassment is a confusing topic because people react differently to the same situation. One recipient might feel flattered and enjoy the attention, another might become upset or angry and consider the conduct harassing. One deliverer may be joking, the other may be attempting to annoy, gain an advantage or make sexual relations a condition of employment. Because there are no hard and fast rules, each case is based on its own merits. The key to this issue is that the actions or words are unwanted by the recipient. The safest course of action is to avoid making the advances or remarks, even if they are meant as jokes and treat others with respect. Many companies have policies regarding this issue. Wise guards will be familiar with them. More than one security officer has been terminated for violating company policy regarding sexual harassment.

5-9   INFORMATION DISSEMINATION TO THE PUBLIC AND THE MEDIA

A newsworthy event will draw attention from both the media and the public. Due to the nature of security work, guards may be involved in those events. At other times plain curiosity will bring inquiries from the public. Whatever the situation, security officers must be mindful of company policy when responding to questions. The rule of thumb is that any information that is not readily available to the media or the public should be treated as confidential information.

At a major event security officers may be approached by the media for information. Security officers are not generally authorized to release information. Subsequently, unless otherwise stipulated, professional security officers should courteously refer the inquirer to a company official. Many companies have a designated public relations staff, inquiring people should be directed to them. If no company official is available, refer them to a supervisor. Guards should bear in mind that their part of the action is limited to their immediate vicinity and that they do not have a full understanding of the total situation. Therefore, the information which they might offer may be partially true or in error. They should also realize that reporters can be very aggressive in seeking information. Security officers should not surrender to pressure and give the requested information. They should politely insist on referring.

There are many motives for curiosity during the day to day operations of an organization. One might be espionage. Security officers must be mindful that passing confidential information can cause serious harm to the employer or client. He or she should never give information regarding: confidential information, customer information, pricing and client billing. Security officers should not give information contained in security reports unless the release is approved by a supervisor.

5-10 CONCLUSION

Communication is an essential aspect of human existence. We communicate through signs, symbols and words. These take three forms, verbal, written and non-verbal. When communicating verbally both the sender and the receiver must understand the meanings of each word. Non-verbal communication includes body language and symbols. Non-verbal communication is often the real communication and if studied will give information the sender or receiver may be trying to hide. To make sure that the communication was received, the sender should always seek feedback. A good communicator is a good listener as well.

Security officers must develop the art of communication. They must communicate in a courteous, professional manner through a variety of mediums including telephone, radio, public address systems and computers.

Sensitivity to our diverse population is an important aspect in the communication process. Prejudices to race, creed, color, national origin, gender, age and religion should not enter into the process. Sensitivity training is the key to understanding. Understanding and patience are crucial aspects in the process of communicating with diversity.

6-1 INTRODUCTION

Access control is one of the most important functions of the security industry. The main objectives of access control are the prevention of crime and loss due to theft or injury. Security relies on restrictions and the control of traffic. Access control is controlling the movement of people, vehicles and at times property, into, within and out of an employer's property. A vast amount of time, money and effort is dedicated to this task.

The amount of control an employer needs is determined by the threat level. Some employers have very little threat level and, therefore need minimal access control. Perhaps a sign which reads "employees only" is all that is required to control access. Others, such as the United States Government, have different access levels because the threat levels change.

Access control is comprised of natural and man made barriers. It also includes specific procedures such as wearing identification, logging-in visitors and enforcement of company policy. Every security officer assigned to access control should know the employer's policies and expectations regarding this function. No system will work unless the guard is alert and aware. Through the use of barriers and equipment, security officers assigned to access control will provide a beneficial service to the employer. The benefits will be realized through the reduction of loss and injury.

6-2 BASIC ELEMENTS AND IDENTIFICATION

The first two questions a security officer should ask him or herself when assigned an access control post is "Who and what is allowed into this place?" The answer will be found in the company policy and may include: employees, vendors, visitors, delivery people and certain cargo.

The next question is, "How will I know who to let in?" Again the answer will be found in the company policy. Certainly employees will have access. In very small companies with a minimal turnover rate visual recognition may be acceptable. In those companies all of the employees know each other and each other's business as well. If a person is terminated the word is quickly passed along.

Visual Recognition or Personal Knowledge

In companies where the turnover rate is high or there are enough employees to make name-face associations difficult, written documentation such as photo identification cards should be required. In these instances visual recognition is the least reliable form of identification. Familiarity can make security officers complacent. Complacent guards will fail to ask for photo identification cards when allowing access. Access by recognition may allow terminated employees to gain entry when they have no authority to do so. At the access control post security officers should have the following lists: current employees, vendors, contractors and new terminations. Guards at these assignments should be aware of the hours of operation, who has access to what areas of the facility and what identification card codes allows access to what areas. It is important for a security officer to know, for example, that a red coded card allows access to an airplane hanger, a blue coded card allows access to a guided missile storage area. If a person wearing a red coded identification card is in the missile storage area, an investigation is in order.

Written Documentation

Since many organizations are not isolated from the outside world other people may require entry. Written documentation will allow them access. Employees should display identification badges. Visitors, such as sales people, can be issued visitor passes. Vendors who service copy or soda machines should have identification from the companies which they represent. Vendors and other people who provide services may be required to have work orders describing the service that they are to perform. Cargo arrives with delivery manifests. These are printed sheets of paper which may identify the carrier, describe the cargo being delivered, give an item count and state the destination of the cargo.

Written documentation may be the determining factor that allows visitors to enter the facility or a specific area within the facility. Entry decisions do not have to be based strictly on the presented documentation. There is a bigger picture that should be considered. If the presented document is inadequate, the guard could consider checking an employer-issued work order, delivery manifest, request for service or a permit before allowing entry.

Written documentation should always be checked for authenticity. Each document should be checked for fraud or alteration. The expiration dates should be noted. In cases involving batches of newly issued identification cards, guards should be alert for outdated cards. If there is a doubt as to the authenticity of written documentation, security officers have several options. They can ask for additional identification which names the person in question, preferably one with a photograph. If a problem arises during operational hours, the guard can contact a supervisor assigned to the area the visitor requests access to. During off-hours, the security officer can contact a company official assigned to the area of the requested visit. The company official can then determine if the visitor has clearance to enter. If there is a doubt regarding a vendor or delivery service, security officers can contact the vending or delivery company to verify the identity of the person. If possible, the security officer should check the contents of any packages or utility bags attempted to be brought into the facility by the vendor or deliverer. In cases where a delivery person attempts to deliver an item to the guard which is meant for another employee, the guard should refuse to accept the item unless company policy provides for the guard to accept it.

Should a doubt persist regarding the purpose or validity of the visit, the guard should deny access until he or she can confirm or verify that access clearance is authorized.

Third Party Authorization

Third party authorization occurs when someone within the company asks the security department to admit another person into the premises. They may make the request by phone, but a written request detailing the date and time of the visit is preferred. Once the person arrives at the premises, the security officer should verify the identification by contacting the employee who authorized the entry. This also serves to inform the employee that his or her guest is present and that he or she should respond to the security post to escort the party to the work area.

At times security officers may be requested to escort a visitor to a work area. If this is formal company policy, security officers should escort the visitor to the work station and monitor the visitor's activity until relieved by the employee who requested the escort. This method allows the visitor little freedom of movement until the guard is relieved by the employee who authorized the visit.

Log-in Procedure

Log-in procedures serve several purposes. Logs document who visits whom. To some degree they hold both the employee and the visitor accountable. For the purposes of emergency preparedness, logs can keep security officers abreast of all occupied areas within a facility. The larger the facility, the less reliable this method will be regarding knowledge of occupied areas.

Logs regulate security guidelines. If policy requires certain visitor information be recorded by directing guards to follow a pre-printed format, the requirement is met. If, for example, a guard is assigned to access control and the supervisor explains that he or she is required to write the following visitor information: name, company represented, nature of business, time arrived, time departed, whom visited, vehicle registration tag number and make of vehicle and once on post the guard forgets to record some of the information, company policy has not been followed. However, if this information is pre-printed at the top of the log, the guard need only to fill-in the correct box and the guideline has been followed.

Logs discourage unauthorized entry because they require certain, personal information from visitors. People with doubtful motives may not want their names recorded on business records for later examination.

Log-in procedures encourage interaction between security and visitors and between security and other employees. A professional, courteous security officer seeking visitor information enhances the image of the security operation. When using that same attitude to notify an employee of the guest's arrival, confidence in the security operation is enhanced from within the company.

It is very important to monitor and maintain electronically or manually recorded logs at the various access points. By daily monitoring, security officers can determine if a breach has occurred. For example, if a card-key is required to gain entry into a sensitive area, by interrogating the lock, it can be determined if an unauthorized entry has been attempted and by whom. Irregularities can be discovered by monitoring. If, for example, a vendor usually visits the facility once a week, but recently has stepped-up the frequency of his or her visits, then an inquiry may be needed to determine the reason. By daily monitoring, the alert security officer will know who is, or has been where in the facility. This can be important if, for example, a systematic theft has occurred at the times when a particular non-employee has appeared at the facility.

Monitoring can narrow the investigation to that visitor. If monitoring uncovers any discrepancies or unusual incidents, the security officer should document and report those situations.

All documentation, whether it consists of identification cards, visitor passes, permits, logs, manifests and work orders, should be considered vital to the employer as official and legal documents. They should be maintained, retained and safeguarded against misuse. The guard should follow company policy in these matters.

Repetition reinforces retention. Again, when a doubt exists regarding the validity of an access request, deny it until a supervisor or company official authorizes entry.

6-3 THREAT POTENTIAL AND NEEDS ASSESSMENT

As was noted in the introduction, access control is determined by threat potential. In determining threat potential and therefore, the resulting access control, one must answer the question "What is the risk of injury or harm to employees, property and information ranging from secret formulas to business accounts?" In answering this question one must consider several points. One, the demographics of the area. Demographics is concerned with population. Factors to be considered include: population density, many people or few people; city, suburban or rural areas, poverty and crime history. Because crime is higher in poor neighborhoods, the threat potential is higher there. Two, the type of industry must be considered. They include: government facilities, retail merchants, manufacturing plants, residential neighborhoods, health care facilities and warehouse storage buildings. A marine-radio warehouse has a lower threat potential than a warehouse that contains nuclear bombs. Three, occupant function is a concern. Within the facility each employee has specific duties. These duties may confine him or her to certain areas. Other areas are off limits. For example, a nuclear physicist would have access to a plutonium storage room. A secretary would not have that access. He or she would be the subject of an investigation if he or she was found there alone. Four, the level of security is a consideration. This includes physical security, locks, alarms, closed circuit television, perimeter fencing, security personnel and the response by local police.

Once the threat potential has been analyzed and all of the factors given consideration, an access control plan can be formulated. The plan can be simple such as, posting signs and locking exterior doors at closing time. The plan could be sophisticated, involving the posting of guards at access points and installing gates, CCTV and alarms. The analysis will determine the needs.

6-4   THREE THREATS TO INDUSTRY AND GOVERNMENT

All organizations are subject to overt threats to security and stability. The threats come from both within and without of a given organization. Security and staffing address the issues of fire, theft and other crimes, accidents and emergencies. One could say that overt threats are the normal order of the security business.

Covert threats are also issues in the security business. The security industry is concerned with three covert threats: sabotage, espionage and terrorism. Loosely, these threats cover a variety of actions.

Sabotage is the intentional destruction or disabling of property. In its true sense sabotage is criminal mischief. Criminal mischief is a crime under the New York State Penal Law. Generally one violates that law if one intentionally damages the property of another person. In addition to its ordinary meaning, the word "person" includes corporations and the government. There are many reasons for sabotage. Employees may commit those acts for overtime benefits or because of frustration with management. Unscrupulous competitors may derive a business edge through sabotage. Revenge is a powerful motivator and sabotage can serve as a vehicle to meet that end. These deeds are accomplished through treachery and subversive tactics. Security officers should be alert for suspicious situations and disgruntled workers. Unauthorized access into or within a facility can result in sabotage. Areas of concern include assembly equipment, computer programs, electrical closets and administrative offices. Unauthorized people in those areas should be investigated.

In the broad sense, espionage is stealing. The ultimate goal of a spy is to steal. When the goal is to steal company secrets the crime may be grand larceny if the secrets are classified as secret scientific material. Secret scientific material is loosely defined as an item or any record that represents a formula, invention, scientific or technical process or any part thereof and the item or record affords an advantage to the owner superior to that of the competition. Spying is not limited to stealing secrets. They might be interested in stealing the product for analysis, client lists or other administrative records. Today, espionage is a major concern of both American business and the federal government. Spies accomplish their goals through surveillance and infiltration. Security officers should pay attention to suspicious people and vehicles at the perimeter of the property. Attention should also be devoted to unauthorized people in administrative officers, computer rooms, laboratories and other areas where sensitive information is stored.

The third threat, terrorism has no universally accepted definition. The definition really depends upon political beliefs and affiliations. Some consider a former President of the United States to be a terrorist, some don't. Others believe that Timothy McVeigh was a terrorist, others don't. Chapter 10 offers the Federal Government's definition of terrorism.

According to the FBI there are two varieties of terrorism, international terrorism and domestic terrorism. Title 18, section 2331(1) of the United States Code (USC) defines International Terrorism. Basically this form is conducted outside of the United States or initiated outside and having results inside the U.S. Title 18, section 2331(5) USC defines domestic terrorism. This form occurs within the borders of the United States.

Until recently terrorism, per se was not a specific crime. The underlying crimes committed by the terrorist were the issues, multiple murders for example. Terrorism was the motive for the crimes. The terrorists would generally be charged and tried at the State level for those murders. If the crimes violated Federal law the criminal would be charged and tried by the United States Government. Today terrorism itself is a crime. In New York State the terrorist laws are set forth in Articles 470 and 490 of the Penal Law. The Federal Government also has statutes regarding this topic.

Terrorism can be rooted in political, religious or social beliefs. These beliefs may be extreme. At times special interest groups engage in this activity as well. The international community has approximately 200 countries with great diversity amongst the various governments. Some of these governments oppose each other and engage in terrorism. Other terrorists have agendas they want implemented yet are not affiliated with any political entity such as Osama bin Laden's Al-Qaeda. On the national level political terrorists can be aligned with the extreme left or right of the two political parties, liberal on the democrat's side (left), conservative on the republican side (right). There are also special interest groups who champion various causes such as animal rights, environmental issues and the right to life. People have destroyed property and killed for their causes through bombing, burning, vandalizing and shooting. Few acts are of the magnitude of the 09/11/01 incidences. Many targets of the special interest terrorists are small to medium businesses, organizations and clinics.

Security personnel should be aware that terrorism has a small side as well as a large side, that small, medium and large organizations could be targeted. No venue is invulnerable. The question is, what is this organization all about? What one is asking is how vulnerable are we. Once this issue is settled one can go about making policy as to how best to protect the organization against an attack or to determine a response if attacked. Security officers may be able to protect their employers against terrorism by following the procedures outlined in the sections that discuss sabotage and espionage. They should also consider following the bomb threat procedure discussed in chapter four.

6-5 TYPES OF ACCESS CONTROL

Access is controlled by three broad concepts. They are barriers, physical security and security personnel. Barriers include natural barriers and man made barriers such as environmental design.

Environmental design refers to barriers that are designed to control the movement of people and vehicles. This design includes building construction, landscaping and illumination. When constructing a facility, the employer should consider and analyze the threat potential. The use for which the building is intended is an important consideration when dealing with threat potential. A warehouse for example, may store valuable items or they may house invaluable items. For security reasons, many warehouses do not have ground level windows. This helps prevent burglaries.

Landscaping can play an important role in access control. For example, if the employer does not want easy visual access to the building's interior, yet wants an open feeling that windows provide, he or she can provide positive access control by placing large evergreen shrubs at strategic locations. The shrubs will prevent visual access. This is a common concept in landscape design. Many homeowners use trees and shrubs to prevent neighbors from having visual access. Likewise, rows of thick thorn bushes which surround a facility will provide some measure of physical access control.

Lighting is an effective method of curtailing criminal activity. Many criminals prefer to work under the cover of darkness. Illumination removes that protection. By lighting the parking areas, entrances and exits, the employees are provided with a measure of positive security. Likewise, by illuminating the exterior walls of a facility, burglars may be discouraged from criminal activity. Interior lighting is an effective deterrent against crime. One advantage to interior lighting is that security officers can see into a building yet, often those inside cannot see out.

Physical security plays an important role in the inner defense. Technology in this area is progressing at a rapid rate. Computerized card keys provide electronic access control. By programming a credit card type key, access to an area is controlled. Some card-keys may access the entire building while others are limited to only certain areas. By checking with the computer, security personnel are able to interrogate locks to determine what card-keys were used to enter an area, how many times each was used and on what date and time each was used. One advantage to card-keys is that if an employee was terminated and he or she has not returned the card-key, that card-key can be de-programmed, thereby being rendered useless as an access device. Other, more traditional forms of physical security include: tamper resistant locks, burglar resistant doors and frames, local and central alarm systems and closed circuit television cameras with remote monitors.

Security personnel play a pivotal role in access control. Environmental design and physical security are limited insofar as the protection which each provides. They can facilitate security personnel in the providing access control, but they alone cannot provide total protection. Security officers are the backbone of access control. They can be assigned at entry points on fixed posts or on patrol within the premises. On fixed posts, guards can authorize or deny entry in accordance with post orders and company policy, complete visitor logs, monitor CCTV screens, communicate with patrol and check for the proper identification. While on patrol, they can secure breached areas, such as open doors, make certain that physical security devices are functioning properly, question suspicious people, respond to alarms and perform perimeter patrol. The best method of providing access control is to employ environmental design, physical security and security personnel.

6-6 BARRIERS AND CONTROLLED ACCESS POINTS

As was mentioned earlier, physical barriers, both natural and manmade, aid security officers in controlling access. Natural barriers make use of the terrain and geography to achieve the goal. A mountain, for example, can be a natural barrier if it is bored-out and the interior converted into rooms. Add some security officers and physical security and the end result is a rock fortress that even atomic bombs may not be able to penetrate. Other natural barriers include: lakes, rivers, islands, such as Plum Island at the end of Long Island where animal disease research is being conducted, deserts, swamps, such as that which surrounds Paris Island, South Carolina, where the Marine Corps holds basic training, and scrub oak forests to name a few.

Manmade barriers can be installed to reach the three security objectives of outer, middle and inner defenses. Outer defenses secure the premises and can include: walls, fences, razor or barbed wire, gates, fixed guard posts, landscaping, illumination and alarms. The middle defenses include building construction and the types of doors and locks used for controlling the flow of people and property. Inner defenses include: enclosed lobbies, interior doors, card-key entry, close closed circuit television systems, turnstiles, signs and safes to name a few. The more sensitive the work area, the more devices will be used to control access.

Access control points vary depending upon the size and scope of the facility. For a small firm, with a minor threat potential an enclosed glass lobby with a buzz-in door lock system is sufficient to control access. The area will contain non-employees until the visitor's business can be established and the proper employee notified. Other facilities may require a fixed post at a gate guardhouse. This may be beneficial where large numbers of employees have access to a large, somewhat sensitive premises or where trucked cargo is heavy and the potential for theft is high. In the former category, security officers may be required to check photo identification cards, in the latter, inspect incoming and outgoing loads. Sensitive areas may require access control to thwart espionage efforts. This can be accomplished through a fixed post, an alarm, keyed access and CCTV.

6-7   ACCEPTABLE FORMS OF IDENTIFICATION

Employee Identification

A common access control device is the employee identification card. Identification cards not only authorize entry into a facility, they can control movement within. By incorporating features such as card-key codes and expiration dates on the cards, access can be limited or expanded, depending on the status of the employee. The usual card has several features, all serve a purpose. At the very least, cards should contain: the name of the employer, the photograph, name and signature of the employee, an employee number, a unique logo or other symbol difficult to duplicate and possibly an expiration date. Identification cards should be laminated to make alteration of the card more difficult.

Keys are often the only access control device for a given business, particularly in small companies. The issuance should be controlled and terminated employees should be required to turn the key in before making a final exit.

Parking stickers are frequently used to gain access to parking areas. They usually have expiration dates and/or are color coded during a given time frame. Parking stickers can be permanent or temporary depending upon who requires access. An employee requires a permanent sticker, a contractor is an example of a person who needs a temporary one.

Non-employee Identification

Non-employee access can be controlled in several ways. The visitor pass is common in many industries. They are issued to authorized visitors ranging from sales people to delivery service people. Each visitor pass should be conspicuously marked as such and be returned at the conclusion of the visit. If visitors are given dated passes which need not be returned, then upon entry each pass should be inspected for expiration. Temporary passes can be issued to contractors, temporary employees and other people who need to perform extended services at the site but are not permanent employees. These also should be checked for expiration dates. Every delivery should be accompanied by a cargo manifest. Depending upon the company policy, the manifest may serve as the means to gain access.

Governmental Agency Identification

Government agencies issue identification to their employees. Law enforcement officers, at all levels, are issued identification cards, numbered badges or both. Other agencies may issue identification cards. Unless there is an emergency, a search warrant or other legal grounds which void an access control program, the governmental agent should be treated as a visitor. The employee which the governmental agent has business with should be notified that the agent is on the premises. He or she should respond to escort the agent or the security officer should escort the agent to the work area.

Counterfeiting

A wise security officer should realize that entry documentation can be counterfeited. To avoid allowing an unauthorized entry, security officers should be thoroughly familiar with entry documentation. By becoming familiar with normal documentation, the guard should be able to realize the counterfeit. He or she should look for any alterations, white-out areas, smudged areas, loose lamination, type character change or misaligned lettering and over imposed pictures.

Controlling Mechanisms

Whether the guard is controlling access of employees, deliveries, contractors, vendors or visitors a controlling mechanism should be employed. The usual controlling device is a log. Logs can be maintained to control the issuance or receipt of all of the variety of passes, stickers, identification cards, keys and deliveries. Regularly kept logs serve as business records. Business records, as one security officer can testify to, can be used in court. In this case, the guard's entry into a security log of a person's name, helped convict that person of murder. The log entry showed that the person was at the facility during the time of the homicide. Generally each log will be set-up according to the access control needs of the employer. Logs may be established to record vehicular traffic, pedestrian traffic, truck activity, contractors, vendors and visitors.

6-8 THREATS OTHER THAN SABOTAGE, ESPIONAGE AND TERRORISM

Larceny and Criminal Mischief

By controlling access of individuals, other threats to the employer and fellow employees can be averted. Two exterior threats are larceny and criminal mischief (vandalism). Employee vehicles can be the target of both crimes. The cars themselves could be stolen or items from within, such as the radio, can be the target of a thief. Those same vehicles can be subject to criminal mischief ranging from punctured tires to smashed windows. The employer's vehicles are subject to the same hazards. This may be particularly true in case involving labor disputes or the revenge of a terminated worker. The building itself may become victim to graffiti artists, a form of criminal mischief.

Within the inner defenses larceny and criminal mischief can be committed against both employer and employees. Larceny of the product, warehoused merchandise and employees' private property occurs regularly. Vandalism, other than sabotage, can be committed by authorized and unauthorized people. Some theft and vandalism will be diminished if security officers make certain that perimeter doors and gates are secure. They should also look for suspicious activity in areas where access is available. Remember, crimes are generally committed when the opportunity is present, by diligently performing access control the opportunity will be reduced.

Violence

Two types of violence can be avoided if the security officer diligently performs access control. One is domestic violence, the other is work place violence. A spouse, boyfriend or girlfriend may demand access to the facility with intent on engaging his or her spouse, boyfriend or girlfriend in an altercation. If the entry is not authorized then the case is closed and access will be denied. However, if company policy authorizes visitation by spouses, then the security officer should look for and be aware of any agitation in the visitor before allowing access. As far as access control is concerned, work place violence would occur between employees and non-employees. A terminated employee, for example, might want to gain entry to settle the score with a current employee. To avoid this problem, all security officers assigned to access control should know who has been terminated and deny them access.

Special Problems

Some special circumstances will strain an access control program. These include special events, media events, accommodations for handicapped individuals and maintaining access control equipment. Special events are causes for celebration. Outside guests may be invited to participate. Usually rules are relaxed for the event. Therefore, it is necessary for security officers to closely monitor people at the event. Media coverage may attend the event or be present after a newsworthy incident. The media should always be accompanied about the facility. Security officers should never divulge information to the media unless they have authorization to do so. The security concern is always the protection of the employer, fellow employees and property from harm. Adverse media coverage can harm any of the above. The law requires that handicapped people have certain accommodations, such as wheelchair ramps, a special parking area and toilet facilities to name a few. These may breach an access control program. If the accommodations do breach the program, it is security officers' responsibility to close the breach as soon as it is possible to do so. To be effective, equipment such as remote alarms, CCTV monitors, fences and such should be in operating order. Defective equipment can cause breaches in the system and open the employer to litigation. All equipment should be maintained for maximum efficiency. Defects should be reported immediately.

6-9 CONCLUSION

Access control is an important aspect of security officers' duties. They must protect their employers, coworkers and property from the results of unauthorized entries. Those results could included sabotage and other forms criminal mischief, espionage and other forms of theft, violence, assault and local terrorism.

In aiding the security professional in accomplishing this objective he or she can rely on environmental design, barriers and physical security. They have other tools such as CCTV, alarm systems, access control via computers and dogs to reach this end.

Documentation is an important aspect of this effort. Security officers should not become complacent when checking entry documentation. They should become familiar with the obvious because that familiarity will enable them to identify counterfeit documentation. In addition to reviewing documentation, security officers should maintain various visitor, vendor, contractor and delivery logs. Logs controlling who has what access device should also be kept. Logs should be monitored daily to determine if security breaches have occurred.

CHAPTER 7

ETHICS AND CONDUCT

7-1 INTRODUCTION

Professionalization of the security industry is one of the objectives of New York State and the executives in the security field. All professions have a code of conduct including the professions of medicine, law, military and law enforcement. In many of these one can lose his or her license for violating the ethical code. By adhering to the ideas embodied in the code of conduct, security officers will gain the respect and confidence of their coworkers and the public alike. New confidence and respect will enable security officers to shed the sometimes poor public image associated with their profession.

7-2 DEFINING A CODE OF ETHICS

A code of ethics is a statement that incorporates moral and ethical principles and philosophies. Moral principles are beliefs that deal with "right" and "wrong." They are opinions we form about what is right. For example, most people would agree that it is not morally right to steal. Ethics are concerned with conduct, our actions. Ethical conduct involves moral principles because the actions we take should be morally correct. Ethics involves a choice between choosing the value of one thing or idea over the value of another thing or idea. For example, a security guard in a given situation may have a choice between accepting a bribe or reporting the incident. If he accepts the bribe, he is acting without ethics. If he reports the incident he is acting ethically. Ethical conduct should lead to the highest good. Philosophy, in this concept, is a value system consisting of moral beliefs and ethical conduct. The philosophy is to think and do what is right. The code of ethics is based on this philosophy. The code of ethics sets the standard of correct behavior. If the code sets the standard, it then can measure a person's actions against that standard. The highest mark a person's actions can receive is based on strict compliance to the code, without deviation. Realistically, however, right or wrong is judged and measured by the average person within a given profession. This professional is usually of ordinary intelligence, judgement and experience.

A code of conduct is a measurable standard beyond basic ethics. One of the responsibilities of society is social control. This is accomplished through moral principles, ethics, laws, regulations and norms. Our society has established a basic morality. It also has defined ethical conduct. The basic standards of behavior apply to the general population. However, a code of conduct targets a particular profession and demands more than the basic ethical behavior. For example, the idea of accepting a gratuity is not generally unethical. Waiters and waitresses, doormen and women and a host of others expect gratuities. However, it is unethical for a security guard to accept gratuities. The reason is simple, by accepting the gratuity a door is open for other unethical behavior, like looking away when someone parks a motor vehicle in an unauthorized spot.

Defining Professional

Since this discussion is focused on defining a code of conduct for professional security officers, it might be appropriate to define the word professional. At the very least, a professional is a trained individual who adheres to the technical and ethical standards of a profession. By conforming to the Security Guard Code of Ethics, security officers are taking the first step toward professionalizing.

7-3   WHY A CODE OF ETHICS FOR SECURITY GUARDS

There are six reasons why security officers should have and adhere to a code of ethics. One, because their duties revolve around protecting people and property from harm, the employer, co-workers and the public have a higher expectation of them in performing those duties. Two, this higher expectation is also caused by the position they hold in society and the trust placed on that position. Three, their actions or non-actions could possible be the cause of serious harm, injury or loss. Four, security guards represent their respective employers. In the public's eyes their actions, attitudes and demeanor are the employer's actions, attitude and demeanor. Five, security officers derive their power via the employer's authority. In the course of accomplishing their objectives, they control and direct others, including situations involving arrest and detention. Six, the employer, co-workers and the public expect security officers to respond correctly to situations ranging from emergencies to requests for directions.

7-4   THE CODE OF ETHICS

The code of ethics embodies principles and standards of conduct which characterize the duties and responsibilities of the security professional. The code is derived from the codes of ethics of the American Society of Industrial

Security, the International Association of Chiefs of Police and Private Security Management and Security Employees (Private Security Advisory Council).

There are ten elements to the code of ethics for security guards. The code is as follows:

In my capacity as a security guard hired to prevent, report and deter crime, I pledge:

A- To protect life and property; prevent and reduce crime committed against my employer/client's business, or other organizations and institutions to which I am assigned; abide by the constitution of the United States.

B- To carry out my duties with honesty and integrity and to maintain the highest moral principles.

C- To faithfully, diligently and dependably discharge my duties, and to uphold the laws, policies and procedures that protect the rights of others.

D- To discharge my duties truthfully, accurately and prudently without interference of personal feelings, prejudices, animosities or friendships to influence my judgements.

E- To report any violation of law or rule or regulation immediately to my supervisors.

F- To respect and protect information considered confidential and privileged by my employer or client, except where their interests are contrary to the law or this code of ethics.

G- To cooperate with all recognized and responsible law enforcement agencies within their jurisdiction.

H- To accept no compensation, commission, gratuity, or other advantage without knowledge and consent of my employer.

I- To conduct myself professionally at all times, and to perform my duties in a manner that reflects credit upon myself, my employer and the security profession.

J- To continually improve my performance by seeking training and educational opportunities that better prepare me to carry out my security duties.

7-5   BENEFITS OF A CODE OF ETHICS

Business's greatest asset is its employees. People who are competent, skilled and who perform their duties in a morally correct manner benefit the employer and subsequently themselves. Dedicated, competent people build confidence, respect and pride. They also enable business to survive in competitive environments. Obviously, dishonest people can have the opposite affect in the business world. They will encounter disrespect and distrust. Dishonest employees serve only to hurt both business and the public alike. Many a business has folded because employees lacked ethics, leaving other coworkers to seek unemployment benefits and subsequent new employment . All residents of this country pay in one form or another for the dishonesty of others. The toll may be taken in the form of higher taxes or the purchase price of merchandise.

Adherence to a code of ethics fosters professionalism. The more reputable security units or agencies prefer to hire competent, dedicate, positive people. They are aware that security officers are entrusted to protect and honest people protect honestly, with integrity. Security officers are often at posts far from the overseeing eye of the agency's management. Management realizes that guards who are diligent and dependable will create a favorable image for both the company and the guards themselves. They will appear as scheduled, in a neat uniform and conduct themselves professionally. They are also aware that serious, career minded guards will seek to better themselves through training and education. The company also benefits because trained guards are more effective and competent. These guards can help diminish the probability of successful litigation.

Because of their roles in society, security officers should be, as police officers are, held to higher standards of conduct than the average person. Security officers are provided with a measurable standard of conduct outlined in the code of ethics. By adhering to that code, security officers are elevated to the higher standard of conduct.

Both employer and guard benefit by adapting and adhering to the code of conduct described above. By following the code a particular guard's effectiveness is increased. Increased effectiveness is better performance. Better performance means closing in on the goal of professional performance. The better one performs, the higher the degree of trust that person gains. The combination of effectiveness and trust can lead to an expanded role. As proficiency increases, assignments will become more diverse. The guard will gain more responsibility and increased authority. The guard's satisfaction level will also increase as the assignments become more challenging. Because of the increased diversity, challenging assignments, and expanded role, the security unit or agency can provide a higher level of service and enhance its professional reputation.

As the industry professionalizes a better caliber of personnel will be attracted to the field. The Security Guard Act of 1992 supports the code of ethics by restricting employment. The law prohibits certain convicted criminals from working in the field. A professional environment, void of these disreputable characters, fosters esprit de corp, job satisfaction and self-worth. Satisfied employees tend to remain on-the-job thereby reducing the high turnover rate in the industry. A low turnover rate increases the experience a guard needs to make correct judgements.

At times there is undisputed tension between members of the security field and law enforcement officers. The law enforcement agents tend to view security officers as untrained amateurs. Dedicated security officers resent this negative attitude. Security officers can change this view by adopting the code of ethics and by presenting a professional image. This is accomplished through increased training, appearing neat and clean, and acting in a manner which reflects a positive, eager and dedicated attitude. The positive image should enhance cooperation between the members of both fields. However, regardless of the possible friction, section "G" of the code mandates that security officers "cooperate with all recognized and responsible law enforcement agencies..." Failure to cooperate with a law enforcement officer can result in criminal charges. If a guard obstructs an investigation, he or she can be charged with Obstructing Governmental Administration. If a guard fails to aid a peace officer or police officer in effecting an arrest or preventing an arrested person from escaping, he or she can be charged with Failure To Aid a Police or Peace Officer.

Public cooperation with security officers will be enhanced by professionalization. When dealing with the public, a courteous, attentive security officer will leave people with a favorable impression. Guards must remember that, if approached in a positive manner, people are cooperative by nature.

7-6 UNETHICAL PRACTICES

A code of ethics is a code of conduct. It is a measurable standard of performance. Section "C" of the code states, "[I pledge] To faithfully, diligently and dependably discharge my duties, and to uphold the laws, policies and procedures that protect the rights of others." Some of the performances expected here are obey the law and respect the rights of others. The rights of others include legal rights and moral rights. Legal rights are those which are granted through legislation and the constitutions of both the United States and of New York State, such as freedom of speech. Moral rights are those which society bestows such as the right to reasonably discipline a child in public. At times both conduct may be distasteful, yet it must be condoned.

Unethical conduct which would violate section "C" and other sections include: excessive use of force, false arrest and detention, illegal search and seizure, impersonating a police or peace officer, bribe receiving and falsifying reports. Excessive use of force is using more force than that which is necessary to arrest a person or to protect life and property. The key word is "necessary" which means use just enough force to do the job, nothing more. The deliberate use of excessive force is not only unethical, but can be criminal as well. Excessive force can result in an assault charge being brought against a guard who uses it.

False arrest and detention can occur when the arrest is unauthorized by the Criminal Procedure Law or when a person is found not guilty after trial. Most false arrests are mistakes by untrained security officers. A mistake of the mind is not unethical, but a mistake of the heart is unethical. A mistake of the heart occurs when the guard knows that the arrest of a person or custody situation is invalid, but continues in that course of conduct. False arrest or invalid custody is also illegal. Both criminal and civil litigation can result from these situations.

The constitutions of both the federal government and of New York State do not prohibit citizens from searching and seizing. They prohibit governmental agents from this conduct. However, this conduct can be illegal from a security officer's perspective when the right of privacy is being invaded.

Impersonating a police or peace officer is not only unethical, under certain circumstances it is criminal behavior. Unethical impersonation can take many forms. Security officers who wear uniforms with patches and badges that closely represent local or state law enforcement agencies may be seen as attempting to impersonate those police or peace officers. Imitation patches and badges are unlawful because they appear to simulate those worn by sworn police officers. The public subsequently views those guards as police officers and responds accordingly. The use of red, flashing grill lights or roof lights in pulling motor vehicles over may be impersonation as well. Under the vehicle and traffic law, those lights are reserved for emergency vehicle only. Outright impersonation occurs when security officers pretend to be public servants or falsely express by word or action that he or she is a public servant and induces another to act based on the pretended authority.

Bribe receiving is criminal if the money is accepted to influence some aspect of the employer's or client's business affairs.

Falsifying reports is criminal when the reports are business reports and there is an intent to defraud. Otherwise, this unethical conduct discredits a security officer's integrity and can be used later in court to discredit any testimony offered by the guard in either a civil or criminal trial.

Section "B" of the code states, "[I pledge] To carry out my duties with honesty and integrity and to maintain the highest moral principles." If this is the pledge, then any acts of dishonesty cannot be tolerated. Acts of dishonesty include: stealing information, property and time, lying, deceiving, cheating, falsifying reports, telephone abuse, unauthorized use of company property, sleeping on duty and a range of other unsavory conduct.

Failure to report criminal acts, procedural or policy violations is in direct violation of the philosophy described in section "E" of the code which states, "[I pledge] To report any violations of law or rule or regulation immediately to my supervisor." Security officers, consistent with company policy, are commanded to report those who violate rules to his or her supervisor. Failure to report the violators has negative impacts, such as the failure to fulfill the primary responsibility of protecting life and property, the appearance of favoritism, lax conduct on the guard's part, and inattention to duty. Failure to report violations also diminishes trust in the guard and can be seen as implied approval of the misconduct. As it is in the enforcement of the rules, failure to report violators creates confusion regarding what behavior is acceptable in the work place. A security officer who is consistent in this area gains the respect of his or her coworkers. They will realize that he or she is not out-to-get-them or that he or she is not a company informer, stool pigeon or rat, but rather a person doing his or her job.

Gratuities are given in anticipation of a job well done or as a reward for an accomplishment. Gratuities include compensation, commission or other advantage, such as a free meal. Accepting unauthorized gratuities places the security officer in a bad position. Firstly, rarely is anything given without some expected return. The expected return could range from loyalty to special treatment. Secondly, anyone witnessing the event may believe that the security officer is compromising his or her position and trust. Thirdly, accepting gratuities can lead to diminished effectiveness. A guard may hesitate on taking action against someone who has rewarded him or her. He or she may overlook rule violations and fail to report the violator. Finally, when accepting a gratuity for the administration of first-aid, the guard has received compensation and is no longer protected by the Good Samaritan Law. Section "H" of the code forbids acceptance of unauthorized gratuities.

Exhibiting favoritism is unethical and demoralizing. This conduct violates section "D" of the code which states, "[I pledge] To discharge my duties truthfully, accurately and prudently without interference of personal feelings, prejudices, animosities or friendships to influence my judgements." Favoritism can occur when a guard supervisor shows preference to one subordinate over the others. In these cases, the supervisor gives the better assignments to the favorite worker. This is demoralizing to other coworkers and produces less efficiency. Favoritism can be shown when dealing with other employees of the business. This conduct arouses suspicion regarding the motive for the favoritism. Security officers should treat people equally and fairly.

7-7 PROTECTION OF LIFE AND PROPERTY

The first tenet of the code of conduct is "to protect life and property; prevent and reduce crime committed against my employer or client's business..." The protection of life and property is the number one objective of a security officer. For the safety of people and property, it is important for the guard to enforce rules, whether they are laws, regulations or ordinances. He or she must remember that rules are in place for reasons that may be beyond the guard's understanding. Therefore, he or she must enforce rules which he or she might consider trivial. Overlooking some violations and taking shortcuts in enforcing others shows people that the guard is inconsistent or lax. Inconsistent behavior is confusing to others. They become unsure as to what is acceptable behavior and what is not acceptable behavior. Negligent behavior on the guard's part, can encourage criminal activity. A professional security officer will set an example by making every effort to obey the rules him or herself. In order to accomplish this objective a security officer will be completely familiar with his or her employer's policies, rules, regulations and other laws which he or she is charged with enforcing.

Security officers should report for duty sober. Intoxicated security officers are not alert to their surroundings. They may miss seeing potential hazards, rule violators and criminal activity. Intoxication, whether by alcohol or other substances, reduces a person's ability to think and speak clearly and act rationally. Alcohol and many drugs slow the nervous system and reduce reaction time.

Security officers must maintain a professional image. This means they must have an attitude consistent with first rate performance. They must be firm, fair and courteous when dealing with people. They should report to work with a clean appearance and uniform. The professional image and attitude protects people and property in a number of ways. An obviously dedicated guard is alert to his or her surroundings. The would be criminal is deterred because his or her opportunity to commit a crime is diminished. This guard is more apt to discover hazards which can cause injury or damage. The professional will know where fire fighting and decontaminating equipment are located. He or she will know how to use the equipment as well.

According to section "F" of the code of ethics, security officers must protect company information unless the activity of the employer is illegal. Information should only be passed to people who are authorized to possess it, or as they say in the military service, "on a need to know basis." As was mentioned earlier in this text, passing information to unauthorized people can constitute espionage, a crime, or otherwise damage the employer's business.

7-8   DISCHARGE DUTIES WITHOUT PREJUDICE

Section "D" of the code of ethics states, "[I pledge] To discharge my duties truthfully, accurately and prudently without...prejudice..." Prejudice means to pre-judge someone. It is an adverse opinion formed beforehand or based on a lack of knowledge. These unfavorable opinions are formulated against people for a variety of reasons which include, but are not limited to: race, creed, color, national origin, religion, gender or sex, sexual orientation, age, homelessness, physical disability, and personal appearance. In today's society prejudice in the work place will not be tolerated. Prejudice practiced in the work place may result in litigation against the guard and his or her employer.

Guards should perform their duties without prejudice, bias or bigotry. All decisions and determinations should be reached based on the facts of the case, not by jumping to conclusions based on prejudice. Subjective, personal feelings can interfere and create hostility, contempt and disrespect. Hostility disrupts the work place and can cause injury to coworkers or damage to property. Contempt and disrespect can hamper a security officer's effectiveness. Fair and impartial security officers who show some sensitivity are better able to lead, control and direct. Therefore they are better able to protect. For these reasons, it is important for security officers to develop an awareness and tolerance for cultural diversity.

Security officers should be aware that many people have special needs, such as the physically challenged. It is necessary to make allowances for those needs, indeed, the allowances are often required by laws, such as the American With Disabilities Act.

7-9   TRAINING AND EDUCATION

The professional in any field will continuously improve his or her performance through training and education. The professional security officer will follow the tenet in section "J" of the code of ethics by seeking training and education.

Education is an important aspect of the professionalization process. Most professionals are educated. Training and education minimizes the effects of litigation, instill confidence and self-respect. Confidence and self-respect produce an outward appearance of leadership, pride and esprit de corp which are a positive influences on other people. We respect and are influenced by people who genuinely know what they are doing or talking about.

This influence can affect people within and outside of the security organization. From within, the influence can lead to promotions and leadership responsibility. People outside of the organization will respect the educated security officer, therefore he or she will be more able to achieve the objectives of the security organization.

In today's climate more and more litigation is brought to court because of training or the lack of training. In the future an untrained, uneducated security officer and the organization that employs him or her will be vulnerable to civil litigation.

We are in an era of rapidly changing technology and social conditions. To stay abreast of these changes guards must constantly update themselves regarding new technology and the ensuing procedural changes. The change from standard brass keys to card-keys is an example of a technical change. This change may result in a procedural change from hand written logs to electronically kept logs. Failure to update can result in wasted resources and the loss of a competitive edge. The result could lead to company failure and the loss of jobs. Failure to keep abreast of the changes in the legal system such as the addition of law, changing laws and new court decisions can result in unwanted litigation.

Education can be attained in a variety of ways and is a definite attribute to the career minded security officer. There are several ways in which a guard can be educated. He or she can contact the New York State Board of Cooperative Education (BOCES) to determine if they are offering courses in security administration.

There are scores of community colleges within New York State, some, such as Nassau Community College, offer courses in Security Administration. Security administration programs are often offered through the criminal justice department. An interested guard should contact that department. Community colleges offer open enrollment. Anyone can apply even if he or she does not have a high school diploma. If a community college in a guard's area does not offer security administration courses, other courses are beneficial. In the criminal justice field, courses such as criminal investigation, criminalistics, supervision, administration and criminal law can help a guard professionalize. Human study course can help a guard understand people. Some relevant courses would include: psychology, sociology, criminology and anthropology. These colleges also offer writing, business, computer and electronics courses. In addition to the community colleges, some four year and graduate schools offer degrees in security. To determine which schools offer the program, one need only to respond to a public library and ask a librarian to help find one of the college course-offering books.

Security officers in New York City should consider becoming Fire Safety Directors. To accomplish this goal, a guard must take a fire safety course at John Jay College, pass a written New York City Fire Department test and pass a New York City Fire Department practical field test.

The American Society for Industrial Security known as ASIS is a professional security organization with local chapters in New York State. They publish informative magazines regarding security and offer certificates in the Certified Protection Professional program, also known as CPP. CPP status is highly desirable and recognized in the security industry.

Security officers can seek informal education by reading the various books and magazine articles on the topic of security. See the reference list at the end of this publication for a start.

7-10 PROFESSIONAL CONDUCT: FITNESS FOR DUTY

Throughout this book and indeed through out this chapter one of the significant points addressed is professionalism. If one adheres to the tenets of the code of ethics discussed thus far, one will fulfill the requirements of tenet "I," the pledge "To conduct myself professionally at all times, and to perform my duties in a manner that reflects credit upon myself, my employer and the security profession. One aspect of professionalism is fitness for duty. Fitness for duty includes being alert, reporting to work unimpaired by alcohol or drugs, being mentally and physically prepared and possessing the right attitude and demeanor. Many of these topics have been discussed at various times within this volume. To fulfill the requirements of the eight hour in-service course further review of this topic is in order.

Alertness

Alertness is one of the major ways the security officers accomplish the mission of protecting his or her employer, coworkers and property. He or she must take a proactive approach and actively seek out potential or actual hazardous conditions. A guard must be alert for those who violate rules, regulations and law or ordinance. By being alert the active guard can deter criminal conduct. He or she would recognize suspicious people, activity and situations such as merchandise stacked near trash dumpsters. Security officers should also be alert for changing conditions. In areas of high activity the scene can change many times during a tour of duty. During these times, situations can arise that can compromise health or safety. Security officers should train themselves to be observant. By observing and being alert security officers will be able to read situations and determine a course of action prior to the eruption of a problem.

Impairment by Alcohol

Impairment by alcohol was discussed earlier in this chapter under the heading of Protection of Life and Property.

Mental and Physical Preparedness

Security guards should be mentally and physically prepared for the expected as well as for the unexpected. Mental preparation includes current knowledge of the rules, whether they are regulations, procedures, policy or law. Security officers should mentally note conditions on the post, determine what is normal and what is abnormal. They should play if-then situations in their minds. For example, if a fire starts in place "A," then I will use the ABC fire extinguisher located at place "B" to extinguish it. Mental alertness is the ability to think clearly and foresee potential problems. This means reporting to work without being preoccupied with life's other problems.

Security officers can do many things to be physically prepared for work. They should eat healthy meals and avoid the fast food which supplies empty calories. They should attempt to maintain the proper weight and exercise both the muscular and cardio-vascular systems. They should report for duty adequately rested. Physical preparation includes making sure that all of the equipment needed in the performance of duty is in operable condition.

Appearance and Demeanor

It has been said that "clothes make the man." To some degree this is a true statement. When dealing with a security guard, his or her appearance is an important consideration of the public, coworkers and the employer. A security guard who reports for duty in a dirty, wrinkled uniform will receive less respect and have less influence on those people he or she is expected to direct, control and protect than one who reports in a clean, pressed uniform and polished shoes.

The initial encounter with the public and coworkers will determine how the security officer will be received. A guard who has not shaved, has unkempt or dirty hair, poor dental hygiene, or has overpowering body odor may be perceived as undisciplined. This officer will be less effective in gaining compliance to company rules and directing people. Security officers who present a neat, clean image at the first encounter will encourage further encounters and will be more able to direct, assist and gain compliance to the rules.

Demeanor means behavior. A dedicated security officer will behave in an alert, attentive manner. He or she will show concern when people bring problems his or her attention. The guard must remember that there are no trivial problems. When a person explains a problem to a security officer it is a real problem to that person. In appearing alert, a security officer should maintain an erect posture. This military bearing instills confidence and gains respect. A guard with the proper attitude opens the communication process. He or she should realize that non-verbal communication, such as a disinterested attitude can counter-effect verbal communication. An inattentive guard who passively listens will shut down the communication process.

A career minded security officer should be proud of his or her profession. Pride can bring self-respect and dignity. These are important aspects of behavior. If, it is obvious to people that the guard acts with self-respect and dignity, then people will gain respect and comply with the guard's directives. First impressions are lasting ones. A sloppy, inattentive, disinterested career minded guard, when first met, will give a negative impression. He or she will be hard pressed to overcome that image. His or her job will be difficult because people will not take him or her too seriously.

In addition to the sloppy appearance and inattentive behavior, three other aspects of attitude have given the industry a negative image. They are: arrogance, belligerence and bullying. Ideally, all guards should be even handed when dealing with others. One can always start an encounter politely then get stronger as the situation demands. One cannot start out strong then move towards politeness. When starting strong, the guard should expect confrontation and a deteriorating situation. This is not to say that some situations do not demand strong action. Breaking-up a fight, for example, requires immediate and perhaps aggressive behavior. This is not to say that a guard should approach a situation weakly either. This is to say that a guard should attempt to control the situation with a firm, fair, even handed attitude. Guards must remember that the public generally knows that security officers have no more authority than the public itself. He or she must accomplish the objectives by gaining cooperation. Cooperation will not be gained through a poor attitude.

7-11 CONCLUSION

By adhering to a code of ethics, security officers are taking steps to improve their profession. They are providing better services and are more effective. Adherence to the code promotes self-confidence, esprit de corp and dedication to the profession. These security officers are gaining the confidence of the public, coworkers and employers alike.

If the industry demands that security officers adhere to the code, management will be rewarded with a higher caliber of employees. They will be assured that their employees will be performing their duties diligently, with a minimal amount of supervision. The industry's turnover rate will be lower. The longer a guards remains with an employer, the more experience he or she gains. Experience, coupled with continuous training should reduce the negative impact of litigation and improve efficiency. Improved efficiency is a competitive edge. By demanding compliance to the code management can reasonably believe that sloppy, inattentive, belligerent or bullying guards will be weeded from the industry.

CHAPTER 8
REPORT WRITING

8-1 INTRODUCTION

During the course of a tour of duty, security officers may be required to complete several types of reports. They may be responsible for maintaining daily activity logs, field note books or access control logs. They may be required to write memorandums or complete extensive, comprehensive reports. These forms range from filling in the blanks to grammatically correct, multi-page documents. If the reports are a regular part of the agency's business, they are legally considered to be business records and can be introduced as evidence at either a criminal or civil trial.

Reports are retrievable records of activity, incidents, situations or observations. Reports provide an historical record of past events. When properly completed, reports can serve to document future needs of the organization. For example, they may show an increased workload which may require an increase in personnel or they can reveal that a policy change is required. They are also valuable in risk analysis. Reports can back-up the verbal testimony of a security guard at a trial. They can also discredit that testimony. Reports can document misbehavior and serve to validate an employee's termination. On the other hand, they can document reasons for promotion. They may be used to help prove or disprove an insurance claim. Reports fed into a computer data base can pick-up patterns of behavior, such as criminal methods of operation, including systematic theft or fraud.

Because reports are a necessary aspect of the security industry, every guard should make an effort to develop a clean, clear, concise and understandable writing style. For example, it is better to write, "He who lives in glass houses should not throw stones," than to write, "He who abides in edifices of crystal should not indulge in the hazardous hurling of geological objects." Everyone understands the sentence regarding "houses," educated people understand the sentence regarding "edifices of crystal." Whenever possible, make the report simple, objective and accurate.

8-2   THE BASICS OF REPORT WRITING

All reports should contain the six basic elements of "who," "what," "when," "where," "why" and "how." Of these elements "who" is the most complex. There may be many people who fall into this category. They include who: reported, owned, witnessed, was involved, was victimized, said what, had a motive, was notified, handled the case and took action to name a few. What happened is the most obvious question when dealing with the element of "what." Others include: What crime was committed? What action was taken? What was damaged? What evidence was recovered? What time did the incident occur and so forth. "When" can be cast in many roles as well. When can include: When did it happen? When was it discovered? When did the guard arrive? "When" should be included in the report when ever time is a concern in dealing with an incident. "Where" is a factor to be considered. The most obvious "where" is the location of the incident. Otherwise, "where" can include: Where was it discovered? Where was the guard? Where was the evidence found and where was the evidence and any reports sent? "How" can be answered by examining the following points: How did the incident occur? How was access gained? How was the incident discovered? How was the guard notified or the victim discovered? The sixth element, "why" is the answer sought during an investigation into the cause of a situation, the reason a situation did not occur or in seeking to determine why an incident was reported.

Some reports, such as the fill in the box type, will have these elements incorporated into them. All the guard has to do is supply the requested information and the report is complete. When a report is in the narrative form, a written account, the guard must remember the elements and make sure that each is answered thoroughly. A handy memory retrieval mechanism is the pneumonic device or code word, "NEOTWY." This code word takes the "N" from when, the "E" from where, the "O" from who, the "T" from what, the "W" from how and the "Y" from why. By remembering "NEOTWY" and associating each of the code word's letters with the proper letter from each elemental word, a guard should be able to recall the elements of who, what, when where, why and how. He or she should make sure that each element is present in the written account of an incident or memorandum.

Well written reports must fulfill seven requirements. By taking the first letter of the word that describes each requirement, the code word "ACCOUNT" is formed. The words that describe each area are: accurate, complete, concise, organized, understandable, neat and timely.

All reports must be accurate. They are based on facts, not opinion or speculation. They must truthfully record the event or situation.

For a report to be complete it must show the total picture. By filtering or leaving information out of the report, misunderstanding and false conclusions result. Future actions, based on false conclusion may result in failure to achieve future organizational objectives, such as policy changes. In the courtroom an incomplete report may cast doubts on a security officer's credibility.

A well written report is concise, meaning brief. The report should contain only relevant information. It should not ramble on. The best way to be brief is to record just the facts. They are the keys that support a conclusion or set the groundwork for future recommendations.

Reports should be organized. They must have a certain structure. Fill in the blank reports are already structured. Narratives should also be structured. Once the structure has been established, the format should be the same in every narrative each guard writes thereafter.

Understandable means that the words used are simple. For example, "house" should be used as opposed to "edifices of crystal." Understandable also means that a sentence should flow and its meaning is clear. Each word should have a relationship to others in the sentence. Each sentence should have a relationship to others in the paragraph. For example:

> Frank Furter did his hand get stuck in the machine which metal grinds in the back of the shop with gears. To the hospital he went. Once the gears were cleared. In their his fingers were broken.

The paragraph explains an industrial accident. However, the words and sentences do not have the proper relationships. Therefore, the paragraph is not easily understood. It is more easily understood when the relationships are proper, such as:

> Frank Furter's hand became caught in the gears of the metal grinding machine. The machine is located in the rear of the shop. His hand was removed from the machine. He suffered fractures of the fingers and was sent to the hospital.

An alert guard will also notice the first paragraph contains the misuse of a word and both paragraphs are incomplete because they fail to describe certain things. What are these two errors?

All reports should be neat. They should be printed legibly or typed. Neatness aids in the understanding of a report. Sloppy reports reflect poorly on the author.

The final category requires timely submission of the well written report. This must be done as soon as is possible after the incident is investigated. If the report is in regards to a faulty electrical outlet, for example, quick submission will alert others to the potential danger and, hopefully, bring a quick response.

Timely submission should result in timely action, regardless of the nature of the incident.

In addition to the basics noted above, generally reports contain other specific information. They are the date, time, location and name and signature of the assigned security officer.

Dates are recorded in a number of ways, such as 03/06/95, 06 March 95, March 6, 1995 and so forth. The company policy will describe how dates are recorded.

Time can be recorded by the common A.M. and P.M. method or by using military time. Military time assigns each hour a number based on its relationship to midnight. One A.M. is the first hour past midnight. It becomes 0100 hours, two A.M. is 0200 hours and so on. 2300 hours is eleven P.M. because it is the twenty-third hour past midnight. The minutes are recorded according to their relationship to the hour. One minute past one A.M. is 0101 hours, fifteen minutes past one A.M. is 0115 hours, fifty-nine minutes past one A.M. is 0159 hours. By keeping time in the military fashion, there is less room for confusion. The time should be recorded whenever a noteworthy situation occurs. The time of the situation's occurrence should be entered into a report.

Location can mean incident location, post location or a combination of both. Some reports will require a specific incident location. Where an accident occurred, for example. Others, such as logs, will only need information regarding the location of a particular post or work station. Some reports may contain a variety of locations. For example a report may contain the location of a specific incident and the post or zone where the incident occurred.

Reports usually require the name and signature of the author or the name or some other identifier of the person making an entry. The bare minimum would be the person's last name, first and second initial or position title. However, this could cause confusion because many people have the same surnames. Smith, Brown, Diaz, Rodriquez are common last names. To avoid confusion, the writer should include his or her full name, position title and employee number. In log entries a simplified identifier would be position title and employee number.

8-3 THE NARRATIVE REPORT

A narrative report is usually produced after an investigation of an incident. The report details the investigation. This type of report can also be filed to explain why an action was or was not taken. They should be based on field notes, a topic that will be discussed shortly. Narratives can be as short as one paragraph or as lengthy as a book. Reports of this nature should start with a unique case number. Any other report related to that particular case should also bear that unique case number. As was mentioned earlier, narrative reports must be structured. The same structure should be followed by all security personnel to ensure uniformity and consistency. Each report should flow in a logical order within the structure. Describing how the situation unfolded in a time sequence is probably the easiest logical order. This is referred to chronological order.

Unique case numbers are assigned for several reasons. Unique case numbers allow for retrieval of all documents filed regarding an incident even if the documents are filed in separate areas. They can be recorded on evidence to show that the item is connected to a particular case. By citing the case number, one can track the progress of a case and determine what stage it is in. Case numbers can reveal the identity of other people who worked on the case and the results of their investigation. Case numbers aid in the coordination of the effort.

The newspaper style of reporting is probably the simplest structure for the narrative report. This style has three components, an introduction or topic paragraph, a body and a conclusion. The introduction or topic statement is a brief explanation of what the rest of the report will contain. The body contains the facts of the case, in a chronological order. The conclusion sums-up the report, draws conclusions based on the facts and may make recommendations for future actions. For example:

(INTRODUCTION)	On July 16, 1995, at 10:00 hours, a hazardous material was spilled in the M Building located at 125 Carl E. Flower Drive, East Podunk, New York.
(BODY)	At 10:15 hours, the writer responded to the M building. He or she was directed to the southeast corner of the facility. At that location he or she learned that sulfuric acid had spilled onto the arm of Mike Rophone.
	Mr. Rophone reported that at 10:00 hours he was using the acid to clear a drain. As he was pouring the acid into the drain the acid splashed onto his left forearm. The spill was decontaminated by rinsing the arm with five gallons of water. He suffered an acid burn to the arm. At 10:35 hours he was transported to Podunk Hospital in the security car by the writer. Mr Rophone received emergency room treatment consisting of an application of a burn ointment. He was released at 13:00 hours. He returned back to work in the M building at 13:15 hours.
(CONCLUSION)	This is a valid case of a hazardous material accident. The victim received treatment and is back at work. No rules or procedures were violated. It is recommended that any employee of the M building who uses sulfuric acid should wear rubber gloves when handling the acid. This case remains active, pending a review of the recommendation.

This narrative is based on the assumption that the report is pre-formatted to include fill-in boxes which include Mike Rophone's, date of birth, home address and home phone number. Witness accounts of the incident would follow the narrative after Rophone's return to work. If notifications are required by law, then they should be included in the body after the narrative regarding Rophone's return to work or after all witness's accounts have been added.

8-4   REPORT FORMS AND LOGS FOR THE WORK SITE

Daily Activity Logs

During a tour of duty security officers may be required to maintain a daily activity log. These are chronological logs of the happenings and activity for each shift. In many cases all of the happenings and activity are recorded, even routine activity is noted. Daily activity logs should begin with the date, shift, post and can include the weather conditions or other information required by the employer. Each activity is entered chronologically in either standard or military time. For example:

> July 18, 1996, 3-11 tour
> Post: Turnip Grove School
> Weather: clear, dry, 80 degrees
>
> 3:00 P.M.   On duty at school relieved Guard Frank N. Stein
> 3:10 P.M.   Checked exterior of school, all secure
> 3:40 P.M.   Checked interior, found leak in northwest bathroom sink
> 3:45 P.M.   Notified janitor Mort Tician of leak
> 4:20 P.M.   Mort Tician responded, fixed leak
> 5:00 P.M.   *Suspicious person, Steve Adore, DOB 7/18/58 of 12 Corn Stalk Drive, East Podunk, NY found sleeping near northeast door, awakened and left premises*
> and so on and so forth until
> 11:00 P.M. Off Duty, relieved by Guard Bennet
> Guard's signature

Any suspicious or unusual activity should be underlined so other guards' attention will be drawn to the entry. At shift change the oncoming guard should be briefed by the outgoing one regarding unusual activity.

Parking Stickers

Many Firms, businesses, municipalities and schools require parking permits for automobiles. The permits themselves may be cards placed on dashboards or stickers affixed to windows, bumpers or rear view mirrors. Some are temporary. Some are permanent. Many have control numbers. By checking the sticker number against the control number on file in a log, data base or filed form, security officers can determine who is registered to park at the facility with what vehicle.

It may be the security department's function to issue parking stickers. Security officers may be required to complete a form for each vehicle needing a sticker or the sticker itself may require certain information. The information recorded should include the date each sticker was issued and an expiration date. Expiration dates are important, particularly if vehicles with expired stickers are subject to parking enforcement regulations. Vehicle data such as the year, make, model, color, vehicle identification number (VIN) and license plate number should be included. This helps identify the vehicle and discourages switching stickers from authorized vehicles to unauthorized ones. If the vehicle is an employee's vehicle, the information required may also include personal data about the owner or operator. This includes name, address, home telephone number and work station.

Visitor Logs

Visitor logs record the coming and going of people into and sometimes within a facility. Passes may be issued to show that the visitor has clearance to be on or in the premises. Visitor logs should include: The date and time a person entered the facility and the time that he or she left. The visitor's full name and the company or department which he or she represents. Who the visitor intends to visit or what function the visitor has within the facility, such as a vendor who has responded to repair a copy machine. No visitor should be allowed entry until the security officer has been shown the proper identification. If a visitor pass is issued and its returned is required at the end of the visit, the security officer should note in the log that the pass was returned. If pass return is not required, then the date of the visit should be recorded on the pass to prevent unauthorized entry on another day. All visitors should be required to sign-in and sign-out of the premises.

Safety Violation Reports

There may be a company policy that requires security officers to report safety violations. Because safety violations can cause injuries, safety violation notices deserve priority handling. To distinguish these reports from routine reports, they should be color coded. Color coding will draw attention to those reports for immediate action. The report should contain specific information regarding the violation: the date and time of occurrence, the rule number violated, the wording of the rule, a description of the violation, the name and work station of the violator and the signature of the guard, attesting to his or her observation. For example:

> On July 18, 1996, at 10:00 hours, Lou Esseana of G department violated rule # 6, which states, "No person shall smoke tobacco in the gunpowder room." On that date, time and location Lou Esseana did smoke one filter tipped, brand name, cigarette in the gunpowder room in violation of rule # 6.

These reports should be accurate and documented. They may be involved in litigation cases because of injury or termination. As a result of the violation, the violator or a co-worker could suffer an injury. Either can bring a civil action against the employer. By recording and documenting the incident, the effect of the suit might be lessened against the employer and shift the responsibility to the violator. In some instances a rule violation could be automatic grounds for dismissal or repeated violations are grounds for dismissal. The employee or possibly the union that represents him or her can initiate litigation for job reinstatement. Accurate and documented reports will assist the employer in asserting his or her right to terminate the rule violator. The reports can be documented through scene photographs and evidence collection. In the example noted above the cigarette would be evidence.

Property Logs

Property logs and passes are used to control the movement of property to, from or within a premises. The property can be company owned, privately owned, lost and found property or evidence. Generally, property should not be moved from the premises without the authority of management or a manager's representative, such as an inventory clerk. Logs are used to control movement by showing who has the property at what location and for how long. Property passes are issued to show that the movement is authorized. A library is a perfect example of an operation with this type of set-up. The log is stored in a data base, the date imprinted card is the pass that allows a book to leave the library.

Generally, the log and or pass should contain an accurate record of the property to be moved, including a description of the item and a serial number when applicable. Attaching company inventory numbers to the items makes this process easier. Inventory numbers also make property identification and tracking simpler. The dates of the loan period should be noted in the log and placed on the pass as well. The person who authorizes the movement of an item should be identified in the log and sign the log and pass. Security officers are responsible for verifying the signature.

Lost and found logs are appropriately kept in security offices near where the public congregates or has access. Articles are lost daily in shopping malls, on public transportation and at colleges to name a few places. Lost and found logs should contain the following additional information: Name, address and home telephone number of the finder, name, address and telephone number of the claimant. Security officers should not release property without the approval of a supervisor. When considering the release of property, the security officer should make an effort to verify the claim by asking for a description of the property, including any unusual markings.

Evidence Logs

Evidence logs are essential to security agencies that make arrests. In addition to the general procedures regarding property, these logs should fully identify who brings the evidence in for storage, state where and how the evidence is stored. The log should also fully identify who removes the evidence for processing or for court appearance and when he or she returns the evidence. The case number must appear in the log and on the evidence. For further information regarding evidence consult with Chapter 2 of *New York State Criminal Law For Security Professionals*.

8-5   FIELD NOTES

The more complicated an investigation becomes, the more there is a need for field notes. Even simple investigations require some field notes. Field notes are brief written descriptions of the facts attending an investigation, at the time of the investigation. Field notes supplement and trigger the memory. They include: names, addresses and telephone numbers of anyone connected to the investigation, including witnesses, victims, complainants, suspects, responding security officers and emergency units to mention a few. Notes should be recorded when any action is taken. They should describe what action was taken, by whom and at what time the action occurred. Remember, logical reports are written in chronological order. Field notes should be taken regarding the guard's observations and the observations of witnesses, victims and complainants. They should be taken when detailing the descriptions of property or people. Security officers are better off if they record more information than they need, than to record too little and be at a loss later when writing their reports. Sometimes, after the initial investigation, it might be too late to gather other needed information.

Field notes serve several purposes. They are needed to assist in preparing the formal narrative at a later time. The serve to refresh the memory before follow-up investigations occur. During the follow-up investigation, security officers can determine if the information gained in the second interview is consistent with the information gained during the initial encounter. The refreshed memory gained by reviewing the notes is essential when interviewing or interrogating a suspect. It is difficult to question a suspect without knowing the detailed facts of the case. If the suspect committed the offense, he or she knows those details. Inaccurate speculation will tip the suspect to the fact that the questioning guard is not prepared. The suspect will gain confidence and be more resistant. Finally, the guard can review the notes before offering testimony in court.

Security officers should be aware that any notes which he or she brings to court can be viewed by the defense attorney. The notes should not contain information that can discredit the guard, such as racial slurs, sexual comments, et cetera. He or she should only bring the notes that will help him or her testify and no other notes. Additional notes can be viewed by the attorney and attacked to discredit the officer.

Field notes should be recorded in loose leaf type books or pads. Some agencies prefer bound pads with sequential page numbers. Loose sheets of paper are undesirable because they can be easily lost. The entries should be clear, legible, concise and understandable. The notes should be organized in a logical order. The notes should be complete enough to trigger the full memory of a particular aspect of the investigation. Finally, notes should be complete and, above all, accurate. Names should be spelled correctly. The notes should reflect the case's facts and details.

When conducting the investigation, the note pad and pen should be handy. If the person offering the information is concerned about the notes, he or she should be assured that they are recorded only to aid the guard's memory. It is unwise to take notes when talking to a suspect. He or she might be reluctant to talk. Take those notes immediately after leaving the suspect's location.

The best way to conduct an interview is to plan the questions in advance. However, at the scene advanced planning may be limited to a few seconds. Think before asking. The questions should be open ended questions, not leading questions. The objective is to find the truth, not lead the interviewed person to a predetermined conclusion. Security officers conducting investigations should control the conversation. Do not let the conversation wander from the objective. When asking questions, use plain, simple, every day language, not security officer jargon or codes. While questioning witnesses, complainants and victims, security officers should be considerate. Many people are reluctant to give interviews, because of this the approach should be courteous and open. The guard can become firmer and more insistent as the situation dictates. If one starts off strong in the beginning, becoming softer is more difficult. If resistance to the questioning develops have another guard resume the questioning. Sometimes the change will bring about a cooperative attitude.

After the information is gathered and recorded in the field notebook the security officer is ready to prepare the formal report. Initially, he or she will review the notes and prepare an outline of what has to be written. The outline should contain the main points of the report. Each main point should be supported by facts contained in minor points. The outline should be adjusted and readjusted until a logical order emerges. For example:

Investigation of Smoking Incident

I-   Received report of smoking incident in gun powder room

    A- Date, 7/18/96

    B- Time, 10:00 Hrs.

    C- By: Frank N. Stein

    D- Suspect: Lou Esseana

II-   Personal investigation

    A- Responded to the gun powder room

        a- time

        b- with guard James

    B- And so forth

Once the outline has been completed, the guard can begin writing the formal report. The formal report expands each point and sub-point written in the outline. Once the report is completed, the security officer should put it aside and rest for a while. The rest time allows the guard to clear his or her head. Once the mind has been cleared, he or she should return and evaluate the report by proofreading.

8-6   PROOFREADING

Proofreading is important for several reasons. The reader may not understand the meaning of a sentence and probably will not have the opportunity to question the writer for a better understanding. The quality of the report may impact upon the safety of the coworkers. A sloppy report may be misunderstood and disregarded. The report, being a business record, can be used as evidence in court. If it is sloppy, the credibility of the writer can be questioned. The ability to write may be a condition for promotion. Supervisors and managers must write memorandums, post orders, rules and regulations, instructions and so forth. They must be clearly understood.

Proofreading involves editing or changing the report to make it clear, flow easily and be grammatically correct. When editing a report the first question is, "Does this sentence or paragraph say what it is supposed to say in a clear manner?" If the sentence or paragraph does not express what it is supposed to, or if it is not clear, then it must be reworded until it does express the thought and is clear. To meet this end each sentence should express one thought, each paragraph one idea. Syntax, as was discussed earlier, involves how the words are linked together. They should be linked in a way that makes the report flow smoothly (refer to the earlier example regarding Frank Furter). Among the many rules of grammar, consideration should be given to pronouns, punctuation, spelling and tense. Once the writer has proofread the report and is satisfied with the results, he or she should have another person read it. A second reading may disclose some confusing points or grammatical errors.

8-7 GRAMMATICAL CONSIDERATIONS IN PROOFREADING

Pronouns

Pronouns are substitution words for nouns. Nouns are proper words that describe people, places and things. A proper name for a person might be John. Pronouns that describe John are: he, him and himself. Pronouns can be singular, plural or possessive. They can be masculine (he), feminine (she) or neutral (it). John can be described by the pronoun "him" because "him" is a singular pronoun that describes one person. If the pronoun describes more than one person, place or thing, it is a plural pronoun. For example, " After Mary and Betty discussed the case, they decided to arrest John." The pronoun "they" describes Mary and Betty, two people. Pronouns can also be possessive pronouns. Possessive pronouns show that someone owns or has control over something or someone. For example, "Jane owns a new car. The car is her toy." In the second sentence, "her" is the possessive pronoun. Improper use of pronouns can be confusing. For example, "The guard saw him enter the room and then he left." The question is, who left, the guard or the person the guard saw enter the room? That sentence would be much clearer without the pronouns. For example, "The guard saw a person enter the room, then the person left the room." When writing, it is important to make sure that the pronoun is referring to the right person, place or thing.

Punctuation

In grammar punctuation covers a lot of territory. It ranges from the marks left at the end of a sentence, to comma placement, to quotation marks, to brackets and parentheses to mention a few. Here the concern is with basic punctuation. Generally, sentences end with a period (.). If excitement is being expressed, the sentence ends with an exclamation mark (!). If a question is being asked, it is closed with a question mark (?). Commas have many places in grammar, however, security officers should avoid using them. Commas tend to make a sentence more complicated. One of the objectives of report writing is to keep the report simple. By not using commas, security officers can concentrate on the idea of one thought per sentence. Commas allow more than one thought per sentence. Quotation marks are used when the writer is writing exactly what another person said or is copying exactly what another has written. Examples for each are, John said, "I plan on becoming a career security officer." Petit Larceny reads, "A person is guilty of petit larceny when he steals property." Notice the periods are within the quotation marks. Punctuation should be kept simple and consistent. Security officers must remember that misplaced punctuation can change the meaning of a sentence.

Tense

Verbs can show the time an action occurred. This is called verb tense. There are six verb tenses. Generally, security officers' reports will deal with two of them, past and future. When writing of an incident that has already occurred, the tense will be past tense. When making a recommendation for a future action, the future tense will be used. It is confusing to the reader when tenses are mixed. For example, "The writer writes the report last week." The verb "writes" is a present tense verb. The question is, how can a person do something today and last week at the same time? The correct tense is, "The writer wrote the report last week." When the writer is in doubt as to which tense is correct, he or she should consult a dictionary. A dictionary, for example, will state that "wrote" is the past tense of write. Some present verb tenses are: is, am, are and see. The equivalent past tenses are: was, were and saw.

Spelling

Spelling is crucial to a report. Some misspellings can change the meaning of the report or confuse the reader. For example, an officer once wrote, "The complainant reports the theft of a fir coat." The word "fir" is defining an evergreen tree. How can a person report the theft of an evergreen tree coat? Do sixty foot pine trees wear coats? Is the writer referring to the needles of the tree? Can a person steal pine needles? The word this officer should have used is "fur." This fur is the hair attached to an animal's skin. The skin and the hair are used in coat making. Now the reported incident makes sense. Misspelled words reflect poorly on the writer and reduce the quality of the report. The easiest way to correct this problem is to consult a dictionary. If security officers use word processors, the processor can spell-check the report. The spell check will not pick-up misspelled words such as "fir" for "fur." The reason is that "fir" was spelled correctly, but misused. Unfortunately, many people misuse words. The way they are misused constitutes a misspelling. Some common errors are: "their" for "there," "hear for "here," "roll" for "role" and "weather" for "whether," "effect for affect" and "accept for except." The best way to overcome the misuse problem is to have another person proofread the report. When writing about people, it is important to spell their names correctly. Misspelled names indicate low performance level. When in doubt ask people how to spell their names.

8-8 MISCELLANEOUS INFORMATION

When writing a report a concrete, active, third person narrative should be used. Concrete means be specific not vague or abstract. For example write, "He was six feet tall" not "He was a tall person." An active report shows what action occurred. "The writer arrested the perpetrator" is preferable to the passive phrase, "the perpetrator was arrested." Reports should be written in the third person. First person narratives use the words "I" and "you." It is writing about what is happening from your own, personal perspective. When writing in the third person the author takes him or herself out of the action. It is as if someone else was writing about the action you were involved in. Instead of writing "I arrested the perpetrator." It is written as "The writer arrested the perpetrator." or "The undersigned arrested the perpetrator."

Reports should express facts, not opinions. To write, "A person looked drunk" is an opinion. To write, "A person slurred his speech, had glassy eyes, staggered when he walked and smelled of an alcoholic beverage" are statements of fact. The reader can draw his or her own opinion based on those facts. By recording only the facts, the report will be objective not subjective.

Reports should not contain industry jargon, such as, "The writer responded to a 10-17 at the above location." People outside of the industry will not be able to understand the meaning of that jargon. If the jargon changes, future readers within the industry will not understand the jargon or may misunderstand the report.

Mistakes in writing can occur when one completes a report by hand. The method of correction is simple. The author should draw a single line through the mistake and place his or her initials at the end of the line. It is improper to erase, cover or white-out the error. By totally obliterating the mistake, questions can be raised in court as to the contents of that portion of the report. The single line method allows for examination of the words.

8-9 CONCLUSION

Since ancient times man has been recording and storing information in the form of reports. The reports have been filed for future retrieval and analysis. Reports can help plan the future direction of a company, be used to cause an action such as a termination, control inventory and access, report daily activity, be used as evidence in court and in insurance claims.

Security officers should make every effort in developing the essential skills of report writing. He or she should write accurate, clear and concise reports. All reports should be based on fact, not speculation or assumption. The wording used should be simple and understandable. Low quality reports reflect poorly on the author can impede advancement in the organization and cause embarrassment in court.

Mistakes occur when one writes. Few reports are perfect because most people are not trained editors. By following the basic rules of grammar, a security officer can turn in quality reports. To meet that end security officers should possess a dictionary and an inexpensive grammar handbook.

CHAPTER 9

INCIDENT COMMAND SYSTEMS

9-1   INTRODUCTION

In the summer of 1996 a jumbo jet crashed off the Long Island coast in the Atlantic Ocean. More than three hundred people perished. Countless police officers responded, fire departments were on the scene, ambulances were dispatched, so too were the FBI, the ATF and the Federal agency responsible for handling such incidents. Other organizations responded as well. The airplane had to be plucked from the sea piece by piece. The medical examiner was overwhelmed with the dead. The entire effort needed coordination, etc. Various command posts were established.

Today the phrase command post has been incorporated into a structure known by the acronym ICS (incident command system). One of the objectives of this volume is to make security officers aware its definition. A second objective is to bring about knowledge of the three goals a guard must have when responding to an incident. The third objective is to bring about an awareness of the six tasks of a first responder.

Think about that jumbo jet crash for a moment. Who would be in charge of that disaster, the police, the FAA (Federal Aviation administration), the Coast Guard, who? With no structure in place confusion, disorganization, lack of both coordination and communication between agencies, poor planning reigned.

9-2   INCIDENT COMMAND SYSTEM (ICS)

Since that fateful day in September, 2001 the Federal Government recognized a need for a structured approach to dealing with disasters. A review of past incidents has revealed that failure was due to poor management. Two questions brought confusing answers and poor performance. They were who is running the operation at what point in time and who is responsible to whom? Thus, in 2003 the Federal Government set a policy that required all federal, state and local public agencies to implement NIMS (National Incident Management System). ICS is incorporated within NIMS.

ICS is a specific organizational structure used in various emergency and non-emergency situations. It is designed to command, control and coordinate all responders in those situations and to facilitate recovery. Responders are from different agencies with different duties, responsibilities, rules and structures. ICS melds those various responders together to achieve a unified approach to an incident. ICS is also flexible. It can be used in small operations or large operations. It can be enlarged if an incident expands or it can be scaled back as an incident becomes resolved or diminishes. For example, there is a large building fire. Five fire trucks respond. One person has to take control and coordinate fire fighter response. Usually this person is a supervisor. Once the fire becomes controlled four of those trucks may no longer be needed and they leave. One truck remains. The person in charge of the personnel assigned to that truck is now in control.

The structure of ICS is set up through a line chart. The person in charge is from the first responder group on the scene and is referred to as the IC (incident commander). The severity of the situation determines the rank of the IC. If the situation is minor one security officer may be the incident commander as well as the officer assigned to handle the incident. In a more serious situation the incident commander may be a security supervisor assigning tasks to a group of security guards. In the most serious scenarios the incident commander will oversee a group of subordinates and will usually be a high ranking officer from a management position. This individual will have a staff for dealing with public information, safety and liaison to other responders. Others directly overseen by this person will include lower level managers assigned to supervising personnel in the following sections; operations, planning, logistics and finance/administration.

In the building fire example noted above there is a fire department response only. Suppose it is determined that there are other needs such as the police to control traffic and injured people who need medical attention and transportation to the hospital. The incident commander, a fire department official, would be charged with controlling and coordinating those activities as well as dealing with the fire.

The incident commander is a member of the response group assigned the case. The group may be one of local, state or federal jurisdiction. The incident commander could change if the jurisdiction changes. For example, a local agency would handle the fire noted above. If the fire is later determined to have been a terrorist attack then the FBI would relieve the local jurisdiction of command of that case.

ICS is involved in the process of response and recovery through goals and objectives, delegation, empowerment and collaboration. The structure of most organizations includes several layers of management and one layer of workers. Top managers are responsible for setting achievable goals. Creating goals is referred to as strategy. In many ICS situations those goals are to create a response and achieve a subsequent recovery. Mid level managers are responsible for implementing those goals. This is accomplished by creating objectives. Objectives are the how-to-do plans and are referred to as tactics. When objectives are reached the goals get accomplished. Operational level supervision achieves the objectives established by mid level managers by creating work plans. The workers follow those plans to accomplish tasks which achieve objectives that fulfill the goals.

Work is delegated. That is the official business word for assigned. The working level is usually delegated work by their immediate supervisor. This means the organization has given the worker the authority to accomplish an assignment. It also means that the worker has the responsibility to complete the job. Technically, the supervisor is responsible for getting the job done but because that supervisor cannot possibly complete all of the tasks he/she passes the jobs to the subordinates for accomplishment.

Empowerment embodies the idea that when a person is delegated a job that person should have some flexibility in deciding how that job should be accomplished. Empowerment may also encourage group participation when it comes down to discussing how to achieve, goals, objectives and work plans. Empowerment, of course does not apply to jobs which require strict adherence to a procedure or policy. The concept is based on the idea that empowerment is a morale booster. The employee has a better sense of self-esteem and believes that he/she is a valued employee. The employee may also find a better means to accomplish the task.

Collaboration basically means cooperation. One of the main objectives of ICS is to bring the responders together in a focused and concerted manner. For the response to be effective the effort must be a joint effort with each responder knowing his/her rehearsed part and executing their roles on cue.

Resources

ICS is an on scene standardized structure and personnel resources may include members of the security staff, police, fire departments, emergency medical services, utilities and other groups as deemed appropriate. Other groups, for example, might include, but is not limited to, the National Guard or state militia.

Security personnel must be totally aware of their roles in an ICS situation. Those officers must know the policies, rules and regulations of their employers. They must know if the incident is to be handled in-house or are official agencies such as the police to be brought in. They must be aware of their roles if an outside agency becomes involved. They must be aware that an incident commander change may be required.

Resources also include equipment and machinery. Each piece of equipment or machinery must have a specific title or label. This is necessary to fulfill the common terminology requirement applicable to ICS. When common terminology is used all responders know the meaning of what is communicated.

Efficient and Coordinated Use of Resources

Efficiency means getting the most out of the resources available with a minimum amount of waste. One of the goals of ICS is to combine efficiency with a coordinated approach to handling an incident. This approach is beneficial because personnel know their roles relative to the roles of others. Awareness and attentiveness increases safety.

Coordination enables management to consolidate control over large numbers of single resources. The most common single resource in an organization is the employee. When placed into work groups consolidation occurs. Each person in a work group performs similar tasks to others in the same group. Each group has a leader or supervisor. This facilitates the communication process because information is passed down from supervisors to lesser supervisors then to the work groups. This is referred to as the line of communication and is part of what is known as the chain of command. As a result of this process each person at every level in the organization who needs to know the communication is aware of the contents of that communication. In the chain of command each employee is responsible to one supervisor. This relationship is referred to as unity of command. When an employee is delegated a task or set of tasks that employee is accountable to the supervisor for the proper completion of that task or set. Because each person knows his or her role in the scheme of things and operates under the control of the chain of command, freelancing, going out and doing one's own thing, is reduced.

Utilization

ICS can be applied to planned occurrences which are referred to as "events" as well as to emergency situations which are know as "incidents". The difference is that events are pre-planned and incidents are not. Planned events include: exhibits, meetings, outings, events, parades and so forth. The agendas are set forth in advance. Take a parade for example, the starting point, route and ending point are established. Road blocking measures are considered and determined. A medical emergency station is created with an accompanying ambulance and so forth.

All incidents require a response. As was mentioned in an earlier chapter each possible incident that could occur should have a general response plan. All managers, supervisors and responders must know their parts. Incidents include the following situations: Terrorist attacks, natural disasters such as hurricanes and flooding, man made disasters i.e. industrial accidents, motor vehicle accidents, hazardous material spills and building collapses.

ICS Functions: Command

The highest function of ICS is to manage. One aspect of that management is to command, getting other people to complete assignments. The IC (top manager) is responsible for the overall management of the incident. That manager must determine the priorities a response team needs to address. Those rank from life safety, to incident stabilization, to property conservation. Note: life will always take priority over property.

The next function is to determine strategic goals, the overall game plan, and tactical objectives, the direct game plan based of the strategic goals. Consideration should be given to not wasting resources. Remember a majority of organizational resources are people. They must be deployed as and when they are needed with the equipment required. Effort should not be duplicated. Initially there is no such thing as too much. An old adage states, "Never commit a force to small too do the job." Excess personnel can always be returned or sent to a staging area for future engagement. Too few people deployed can result in physical danger to those who are engaged in fighting the disaster.

Personnel safety is a primary consideration in these situations. It must be made clear that procedures and deployment must follow the established order. Again, the proper amount of personnel should be used in achieving the desired ends. There is no place for recklessness, carelessness or heroics. Employees should be advised to act as they were trained to act and not to exceed the scope of that training.

Transforming goals into objectives was touched upon earlier. To alleviate possible confusion perhaps a little clarification is necessary. Most people would agree that goals are strategic and are broad based. They describe a desired outcome. Objectives describe the means to achieve those goals. Objectives are tactical in nature. Then there are work plans. The State's curriculum describes work plans as the tactical aspect of incident action plans. To get a feel for how this works follow this example; a person enrolls in a college. The goal is to get a college degree. This is the outcome. To achieve that outcome the student needs to fulfill objectives. The objectives needed to get the degree are the courses the student is required to pass. The work plan or the tactical aspect of the incident action plan involves the daily activity which occurs in the classroom, taking notes, passing examinations and participating in class. The daily activity during class should result in a passing grade for the student and thus the completion of one objective. Each completed class fulfills another objective until the goal has been reached.

Every situation that involves ICS requires a plan. This plan is referred to as incident action plans (IAP). IAP provides a clear means to communicate the objectives of the mission to both the operational and support staff. The plan is in part designed to make sure all are working together toward the same goals for a specified time. The plan must contain four aspects; where are we, who is responsible for doing it, how do we communicate with each other and what is the procedure if someone is injured? The IC is responsible for creating the plan. The operations chief is responsible for implementing the plan through his or her chain of command.

Plans are created as the situation dictates. Most ICS situations do not require a huge multi-organizational response. There may be one unit each of three different responders. The basic plan for that incident has already been established. Take a multi-car crash for example, security, police, fire department and an ambulance respond. Each responder knows from established procedure what the baseline plan is and assumes the role as is outlined in that plan.

The magnitude of an incident determines the complexity of the IAP. A major incident requires a complex plan. If an incident becomes more complex so also does the IAP. The IC has the responsibility of creating the plan. The plan must focus on management by objective. This includes a directed effort to obtain the tactical objectives required for reaching the strategic objectives (goals). In creating the plan consideration must also be given to creating and issuing assignments, plans, procedures and protocols. At the top of the organization these plans should be disseminated in writing. At the incident level they should be given as verbal orders.

The organizational structure is a top down structure. That is communication starts with the person in charge and flows downward through the organization until the communication reaches the operational level. In a small organization there may be only two layers in the process, the boss and the worker. As an organization grows so also do the layers. This situation applies to ICS incidents as well. The more complex the incident the more layers there will be in the command structure.

One must also consider resource management, where and why the available resources fit into the organizational structure. As was discussed earlier, most resources are human, security, fire department personnel and so forth. Some resources involve machinery and equipment: planes, bulldozers, helicopters, boats and such. It must be determined how the resources are to be used. Once that is established it can be determined where they fit in the structure. For example, the operations section is responsible for executing the tactical aspect of the engagement, getting the job done. To accomplish this, a bulk amount of the resources are required. The liaison section would probably get by with the least amount of resources. Liaison's function is to deal with other organizations and that requires a minimum amount of resources.

Incidents are generally fluid, that is they are constantly changing. Incidents must be constantly monitored for those changes. Change requires constant reevaluation of the situation. Change in the incident will often require that goals and objectives need revision. Change will require altering the IAP. Alterations may necessitate the need to redeploy tactical personnel to meet a new or growing threat or because they are no longer needed at that place and time. So, changes in the incident require flexibility in the ICS's organization.

A major responsibility of IC is to coordinate all the activities at the incident. There may be a variety of organizations participating in the event. Their activities must move in a synchronized manner, not willy-nilly. Willy-nilly creates confusion. Coordination creates cohesion. All assigned personnel know their duties and responsibilities at the incident and will perform them as directed.

The command staff is also responsible for scene safety, liaison with other agencies and the dissemination of incident information. Of course the IC does not personally get involved with the actual duties in these areas. The IC delegates them to others in the command staff. The positions of safety officer, liaison officer and public information officer are directly below the IC on the line chart of the organizational structure. The safety officer is responsible for human safety at the incident. That officer must monitor safety conditions at the incident and make safety adjustments when necessary. In many incidents there are hazards to human safety and life. There is no avoiding those conditions; however mitigating them deserves attention and effort. The liaison officer is the go to person for communications with other organizations that will or may become involved in the incident. The public information officer is responsible for news dissemination to interested parties official and unofficial, internal and external. This individual keeps operational personnel up to speed as well as informing the media of the circumstances. The information officer may also be required to inform elected officials of the unfolding events.

Operations

The operations section chief is a member of the general staff. Like the command staff, the general staff answers directly to the IC. In a major event the ICS command structure would be implemented. An established line chart would be put in place. Once the position has been established, this chief would be responsible for implementing the plans that would achieve the mission goals. Operations personnel are responsible for the bulk of the actual work. They will accomplish the tactical objectives through work plans. These plans constitute the completion of assigned tasks that will result in a recovery.

The ICS grows and shrinks as is needed. Much of the expansion or reduction is based on the concept known as span of control. Simply put, the span of control is the number of people a supervisor can effectively supervise at one time. The acceptable range is between three and seven subordinates per supervisor, with five being the best number. If there are more than seven people who require supervision then a new section should be created and a second supervisor should be brought in to supervise the new section. If there are less than three, they can be supervised by the next higher level of supervision or assigned to a supervisor with five workers or less who have similar assignments. The span of control is based on the magnitude of the incident. The more layers the organization needs, the more spans of control will be required. An incident that requires five security guards to cause a recovery, for example, will not require the implementation of an operations section. One operation level supervisor will become the IC and that should suffice in coordinating and controlling the work tasks. The span of control operates at all levels of the organization from the top to the lowest level of managing.

Planning

The planning section chief is a member the general staff. At an incident this person is responsible to gather and display incident data consisting of the status of all resources and the status of the incident.

In the broader sense this person's job is to answer the questions where will the organization be in a future state regarding goal accomplishment and how will we get there. In the immediate situation the goal is recovery. Consideration must be given to answering the following questions, where were we, where are we and where are we going? In the past goals were set based on the mission of the organization or of a subdivision such as security. It should be certain that those goals included plans for disaster recovery and how to achieve successful conclusions of planned events. One must look to the past to see how well the organization fared in handling those events. In after the fact conferences each prior incident should be evaluated for performance errors and missteps to prevent those problems from reoccurring in the future. Time changes situations. Yesterday there was little concern regarding terrorism. Emergency responders were not thinking about handling incidents involving WMD (weapons of mass destruction). Nor were they contemplating the effects of global warming on natural disasters, rising tides and more severe hurricanes, potential problems of the future. Plans must be made to deal with those futuristic events.

A major concern for the planner is resource status. During an incident resource status means, what resources are assigned, what resources are available and what resources are out-of-service. Resources are kept track of through resource status cards referred to as T-cards. These cards are placed in racks according to status. It is essential that all resource, both physical and human be tracked and accounted for. Without these requirements confusion and disorganization would occur.

Two aspects of planning are to determine what resources are needed and where they are needed. In this situation the planner must consider the availability of those resources whether they are people or things. That manager must also consider in what capacity they can be used and how rapidly can they be deployed to the incident.

Planning is determined by need. Understanding the need is based on the need required for recovery of past events under similar circumstances. If there were no similar situations to fall back upon for handling techniques then planning and execution are based on an analysis of possible event scenarios. If-then statements must be proposed and answered. Alternative plans are also essential.

From a larger perspective, resource status boils down to money and its allocation. Planning for incidents, recovery and practicing work plans is continuous. These activities are necessary especially in an era where the Federal Government has taken charge of preventing and subsequently investigating terrorism. To facilitate this activity increased FBI staff is required. The government has established the department of Homeland Security with its duty to protect. Thousands of jobs have been created for that department. As the federal budget expands fewer resources can be filtered down to local agencies. These situations have put more of a burden on local agencies regarding their ability to increase or at least maintain local resources. In today's climate, as it has been in the past, local responders will be the first on the scene responders. If there is a shortage of local, public responders, security personnel will necessarily be called upon to take action and pick up the slack.

The application of the planning process is simple. The process facilitates the operation section. It determines what resources are engaged, what resources are in the staging area ready to be deployed and what resources are unavailable. In short, resources are tracked and set-up so they can be quickly deployed or moved as is necessary.

Logistics

The logistics section chief is a member of the general staff. This person is responsible for the coordination of a complex operation. He or she is the supply officer responsible for securing the resources, services and support for the operation. This chief manages the flow of personnel, equipment, supplies, food, water and shelter to the incident.

Finance

This chief is also a member of the general staff and tracks the incident's cost. These costs include the price of resources such as payroll, including the possible cost incurred by overtime and equipment. They may also factor in expenses for food, drinks and peripheral costs such as shelter, sanitary measures and so forth. This person is also responsible for personnel records, requisitioning supplies and obtaining contracts for required outside vendors. This individual oversees the future payouts for services, equipment and incidental expenses. The finance chief is responsible for future budgeting. In most cases future budgeting is based on past incident costs of similar circumstances. In many incidents recovery funds are available from various sources including the Federal Government's disaster relief fund, State Governments and other sources. This officer is charged with obtaining those funds when available.

Security as IC

Security officers are often the first responders to incidents within the jurisdiction of their employers. Those officers will be the initial ICs. They may remain the ICs through the duration of the events or may be required to turn command over to supervisors, police officers, fire department officials or emergency medical technicians.

9-3   ICS UNIFIED COMMAND

Simply put the sum of unified command is people working together to achieve specific outcomes. Top management sets the goals, middle management implements the objectives and operational management makes sure the working level stays on target regarding objective achievement. The chain of command shows the lines of communication and who is answerable to whom. Incorporated in that chain is the idea that each person is accountable to one supervisor and each supervisor is accountable to one supervisor of the next highest level in the organization. There is less likelihood for confusion if a person answers only to one person as opposed to answering to more. The span of control limits the amount of people one supervisor oversees. This idea enables that supervisor to stay focused and maintain necessary control.

ICS command system is unique because it may involve multiple organizations pulling for the same outcome at a particular incident. Police departments, fire departments, the US Government and a variety of other organizations have established unified commands for their particular organizations. Their command systems are setup for doing their things. Unlike ICS these organizations have established organizational structures that do not vary with changing situations. ICS is flexible and changes with each incident.

Security guards have been trained to know that some incidents can be handled at the organization level, known as in house. Other incidents may require additional help from the police, fire department or other emergency responders. When other organizations become involved cooperation is absolutely necessary between all who are assigned. Collaboration creates a smoother operation, minimizes duplication of work, is more efficient, effective and reduces freelancing. Not previously mentioned anywhere in the organization of this material, but worthy of consideration is the emotional aspect. Some people for whatever reason may become angered when other responders, "Step on their toes." Collaboration, the idea of working together may well reduce issues which stem from emotion because each worker should know his or her responsibilities through mutual consent or as assigned by a supervisor or IC.

The command post is a headquarters, a central location from which operations are overseen. The post should be close enough to the incident to facilitate control, unity, organization, coordination and direction of the mission but out of harms way. Command posts vary in size according to the needs of the incident. Posts can be as small as a security officer's patrol car, as large as a huge mobile home specifically outfitted for that purpose or a building. Whenever a situation may require a command post the security guard should establish one. A basic tool at the command post is the communication process. Whether verbally, electronically or both the officer should use that process to promote the objectives noted above.

If the incident requires supervisory personnel from several responder groups the IC should bring them together to collaborate and coordinate the response. Note, the IC should be from the initial first on scene responder group. Remember, this leadership position can change according to jurisdictional changes. The response should be made through consensus, mutual agreement between the supervisors. The incident will determine the primary responder, i.e. a fire, multiple hostage scene and so forth. Other responders would assume delegated support roles, for example, the police or security might reroute traffic at a fire scene and an emergency medical staff would establish a first aid station. It is also advisable to have the managers in a central location, usually the command post. This would facilitate the communication process between staff members from the various responder groups.

Remember ICS is scalable and flexible. As an incident increases in intensity more and a greater variety of responders are necessary. The more the incident becomes controlled the less the need for that variety and quantity.

Keep in mind the fire incident discussed earlier. The primary responder role can change as well. When the task of putting the fire out is the main goal, the fire department is primary. If it is determined that the fire was suspicious then the police assume that responsibility.

Three Major Goals of Security

When responding to an emergency the security officer must consider and act upon completing three major goals.

First – assess the situation.
Second – make sure people are out of harms way.
Third – alleviate or mitigate the problem.

One assesses the situation by using the senses, observing, listening, smelling and so forth. There also must be a communication process. In assessing the situation the number one priority is preservation of human life. The assessment must also consider the security officer's safety. If a security officer risks life or limb it must be because the situation has been properly assessed. The action should be calculated and viable. The action should not be a jerk knee, spontaneous reaction or be based on an inaccurate assessment. When in doubt, play it safe. A downed officer cannot accomplish any goal and becomes a liability. The assessment must be done quickly.

Once the situation has been evaluated, safety is the first objective. People in danger should be removed and sent to an area outside of the inner perimeter. The people removed should be sent to a predetermined holding area in the outer perimeter. Placement in that area enables an accurate head count of all who were in the affected area. If they cannot be removed due to injury or some other factor they must be protected from whatever danger is present. For example if an injured person is lying on the floor near an arching electrical wire then it would make sense to shut the electricity off in that area, not to go in and try to remove the arching line. Once the hazard has been eliminated remedy can occur.

Mitigating the situation means returning to a normal condition. There are so many possible incident scenarios out there. To be able to successfully deal with them a dedicated security officer would know company policy and procedures regarding incident management. Within the framework of those polices and procedures the security officer should know the emergency response plans. If none exist he or she should prepare emergency response plans. The officer can do this by creating "if" and "then" scenarios in the mind. The guard should ask him or her self what if this should happen. Then he or she would consider a variety of responses. After considering the alternative actions the guard could then determine the appropriate remedial activity.

Six Critical Tasks

When dealing with an incident of some proportion a security officer must complete six tasks. These tasks include; communication, inner and outer perimeters, command post and staging area establishment. The final task is the request for additional responders.

The security officer must open a line of communication free of clutter. This means clearing the radio frequency making its use exclusively for the current emergency. If available a separate frequency should be used for this purpose. All participants should be advised to tune in to the separate frequency. Do not overlook the cell phone. Its use may be necessary especially when communication is required between the security officer and the immediate supervisor or if the communication is sensitive in nature. The cell phone or land line could also be used to summons outside responders.

A security officer must be aware that in these incidents common termi-nology is used by all responders. Each word or phrase has the same meaning to all. For example, note the use of acronyms throughout this volume: IC, ICP, IAP and ICS. They are universally understood to mean what they have been described as in this text. Security personnel should become familiar with this jargon for a clearer understanding of the ICS process.

Perimeters must be established. There are two types, inner and outer perimeters. The inner perimeter must be as close to the incident as is possible and yet out of harms way. This area should contain those people who are directly involved with remedying the incident. They should be identifiable i.e. uniformed security personnel.

The outer perimeter should be at a safer distance than the inner one. This perimeter provides a safe work area for staff and other support services. It also serves as a barrier to keep unnecessary people away from the incident area i.e. crowd control. The media will also be controlled in this area. At the discretion of the incident commander the media may be given access to a specific area of this perimeter. Within this perimeter resources, human and mechanical are controlled. This area should be clearly defined and secured in some manner.

This can be achieved by roping the area with yellow tape, by uniformed security personnel, with the use of cones or the building itself.

Every major incident needs an ICP (incident command post). The security officer must establish one. The ICP should be as close to the scene as is safely possible. This is the location where the IC and his or her staff direct the operation. The command post is the hub of the communication network. All efforts at remediation emanate from this point.

The fifth task is to create a staging area. This is the location where unassigned but available resources are located. It should be in the proximity of the incident. The staging area must be large enough to accommodate personnel and equipment such as the required vehicles i.e. fire trucks, ambulances and other machinery.

The first responder security officer is also responsible for summoning the required resources needed to remedy the incident. This must be accomplished when practical after assessing the situation.

9-4 CONCLUSION

The incident command system is an organizational structure designed to recover from incidents through the use of command, control and coordination of resources.

Embodied in this response are five main ideas.

The *first* is unity of command, each person answering to only one boss.

The *second* area embodies the idea of span of control, the concept that each supervisor can only be responsible for supervising between three and seven subordinates, with the optimum being five.

The *third* area is management by objective where the IC sets goals and objectives and all involved do their parts to accomplish those goals.

The *fourth* area is flexibility; the ICS expands or shrinks as needed.

Finally, there must be common terminology. All responders, regardless of their affiliated agency, must know and understand the meaning of specific words and phrases.

Notes

10-1 INTRODUCTION

This chapter contains awareness level training only. People who are trained at this level are not qualified or certified to perform ongoing operations or support at the scene of a WMD incident. This text does not discuss philosophy or address terrorist ideology. That information can be found in chapter six, access control. As a matter of fact, much information found in the previous chapters can be applied to aspects of this chapter. For example, the procedure for dealing with explosions can be found in chapter four. The concept of deterrence is located in chapter two.

This chapter is primarily concerned with creating an awareness of the government's definition of terrorism and discussing the various WMDs (weapons of mass destruction). The reading opens with a discourse regarding prevention and deterrence. It is followed by a dialogue of the five WMD, namely chemical agents, biological agents, radiological materials and nuclear weapons and finally, explosive devices.

In the first segment, prevention and deterrence, emphasis is placed on defining terrorism and WMD, listing actions indicating potential terrorist activity, list potential targets, define precautions to protect one's self if involved in a WMD situation and define the elements of RAIN.

Terrorism Defined

As has been previously stated there is no universally accepted definition of terrorism. The United States Government has defined terrorism in a manner to meet its needs and objectives. Terrorism is defined as, "The unlawful use of force and violence against persons or property to intimidate or coerce a government, the civilian population or any segment thereof, in furtherance of political or social objectives." This definition can be found in 18 U.S. C., Chapter 113B, Section 2331. Included in this concept are the ideas that these acts must violate the criminal laws of any political subdivision or that they affect the government through mass destruction, assassination or kidnapping. Originally, there were no specific terrorism laws in place. The crimes that were committed during the attack formed the basis for criminal prosecution, often at the State level. Since Sept. 11, 01 New York has adopted terrorism laws (see Criminal Laws for Security Professional, Looseleaf Law for details).

WMD

These are defined in Title 18, U.S.C. 2332a (Section 921). There are five categories of WMD. They are:

- chemical agents,
- biological hazards,
- radiological hazards,
- nuclear hazards and
- explosives.

CBRNE a commonly used mnemonic device is used to denote those weapons.

Chemical weapons are toxic, poisonous chemicals that are capable of causing serious injury or death. Sarin, an illegal chemical is an example of a chemical agent. This chemical was introduced into the Japanese subway system in 1995 causing twelve deaths and six thousand injured people.

Biological hazards result from biological sources such as viruses, fungi and bacteria. Anthrax, a form of bacteria is an example of this type of hazard. Beginning on September 18, 2001, this disease causing agent was sent through the mail to several people in the United States. The bacteria killed five people and infected seventeen others. The incidents caused a massive criminal investigation.

Radiological weapons, often called dirty bombs, do not reach the notoriety of nuclear bombs because there is no nuclear reaction explosion. These bombs rely on ordinary explosives to spread radioactive material upon detonation.

Nuclear bombs rely on a complex process which results in the splitting of atoms. The energy released from this process creates a massive explosion and radioactive fallout. At one time the bombs were relegated to super power governments. Today many nations possess this power. Additionally, the dismantling of nuclear weapons by the United States and Russia may see enriched uranium move into the hands of terrorists.

Explosive devices are not limited to bombs. They include grenades, incendiary devices, rockets, missiles and explosives.

Another mnemonic device or acronym used to describe those weapons is BNICE, B standing for biological, N for nuclear and so forth. This one flows easier and mentally can be more readily recalled than CBRNE.

Factors of Threat

The following factors may impact the threat of an attack. They are: surprise, method of attack, target, previous knowledge of the community's response and symbolic dates.

When attacking surprise usually is advantageous whether it is a military strike, police raid or a terrorist attack. Surprise is controlled by the fact that little intelligence is leaked by the lone terrorist or by the small cell group to which that terrorist belongs.

The element of surprise allows for a deeper impact of the attack due to the fact that the victims are caught off guard. Initially there would be shock and confusion causing a delayed response. This delay would in all likelihood contribute to an increase in damages and loss of life.

The means attack? That's an interesting question. The answer can be found in the mind of an attacker or the attacker's mentor. Since the beginning of terrorism we have seen some very ingenious delivery systems. IEDs (improvised explosive devices) the most common weapon to date have been delivered by suicide bombers, hidden in sneakers, placed in underwear and of late disguised as laptops. The means of delivery is limited by the ingenuity of the creator.

Targets, we have seen all types, the Pan American airliner blown up above Scotland, trains in Spain and Japan, and lately a car bomb in New York's Times Square designed to blow-up people. Targets could be people subject to assassination or kidnapping, members of the general population who happen to be at the wrong place, at the wrong time. Infra structure such as the World Trade Center was attacked twice. There are also symbolic targets that represent our heritage and culture such as Yankee Stadium. One consideration of the attacker is mass casualties; other considerations are disruption of life and the creation of fear and panic.

Intelligence or foreknowledge of the community and the community's likely response are basic considerations for anyone who wants to initiate an attack especially if the attack involves WMDs. The activity of gathering intelligence is essential for successful planning. Consideration should be given to the type of responders available; police, fire, ambulance and other first responder groups. Another concern would be how well the responders take action, including speed, effectiveness and coordination. Intelligence is gained by surveillance, secret observation.

Many of the terrorist attacks to date have been executed on special days. Timothy McVeigh bombed the Federal building in Oklahoma City, 4/19/95, the second anniversary of the FBI's attack on the Branch Davidian's Waco, Texas compound on 4/19/93. McVeigh made it clear that the date of his attack was significant and was correlated with the FBI's earlier attack The eleventh day of the month appears to have some significance with respect to terrorist attacks. The attacks in both Spain and New York occurred on the eleventh day.

Forewarned is forearmed. Communities should analyze and appraise the WMD threat. Is the threat viable? If so then contingency plans should be made to deal with each of the five categories of WMD attacks. Consideration must be given to ICS (Incident Command System). All responders must be thoroughly knowledgeable with the details of that system. The contingency plans should be practiced regularly and all participants need to know their particular roles in dealing with disaster.

Identifying terrorists is no easy task. Intelligence is a key ingredient in that effort. The community should be the eyes and ears in an effort to gather data. Members should be on the alert for unusual or suspicious activity and report what was observed to the proper authority. The community must also realize that gathering information regarding people's loyalties and dubious activities can be a delicate endeavor. One must be concerned with encroaching upon legal rights and civil liberties.

Most of us have a preconceived notion of what a terrorist should look like. A stereotypical image forms in our minds and these people bring our focus to them. But what of the Timothy McVeigh types? He was a man who was a loyal American. He served in the U.S. Army and was deployed to Iraq during the first American invasion. He attempted to become a soldier in our special forces. Then he blows up the Alfred P Murrah building in Oklahoma City killing one hundred and sixty eight people. In our concern for terrorism we must be mindful of this type of citizen. There are many people out there who love the United States but have an active disdain for the actual government.

Threat Levels

The risk of terrorism is of constant concern to the government. On any given day the administration wants all levels of government to be aware of two situations, the probability of attack and the potential seriousness of the attack. The Department of Homeland Security has devised a color code scheme to announce threat levels. The lowest level of both threat and impact is green. A guarded condition is indicated by the color blue. In this condition there is a general risk of attack. The elevated level is indicated by the color yellow. Yellow means that there is a significant risk of an attack. A high risk of attack is denoted by the color orange. The final color indicates that there is a severe risk of attack. This color is red. The different color levels cause various responses at all levels of government.

Threat Indicators

Watching people, their activities and behaviors is a key aspect of gathering intelligence. In the law enforcement community, this is referred to as surveillance.

An impending terrorist attack requires a process of activity beginning with planning. One cannot plan without a familiarity of the community to be attacked, without establishing achievable goals and objectives and without creating work plans to reach those goals and objectives.

Surveillance activities are conducted by law enforcement, security personnel and terrorists. What would a terrorist be looking for? The terrorist would be looking for the most appropriated entrance and exit routes, suitable targets, responder activity, population density and other strategic and tactical issues. The surveillance activity could take weeks or even months to gather the required information. The surveillances may establish a pattern of behavior and as a result catch the eye of an alert officer. For example, observing a person who repeatedly is seen in the vicinity of a nuclear reactor but with no apparent legitimate reason for being there.

Surveillances allow the plan to develop. The next step is to acquire the necessary supplies. One must remember that the community has the ability to supply the terrorist unwittingly. As Timothy McVeigh and Terry Nichols so clearly demonstrated locally acquired nitrogen based fertilizer became a WMD. In the attempted Times Square bombing in New York City the terrorist filled his motor vehicle with propane cylinders and gasoline.

Weapons must be prepared. Nitrogen based fertilizer by itself is generally not capable of detonation. Other ingredients must be added. These devices must be containerized. Many chemicals that can be used in WMD have unfamiliar odors. Security personnel should be alert for suspicious containers, for example a fifty-five gallon drum seen in an unusual place. They should be alert for unusual odors discovered in inappropriate locations.

Once the terrorist has completed the preparation phase he or she is ready to execute the actual attack. The terrorist must gain access to the target and deliver the device. Security personnel should be aware of unusual activities in and around potential targets. For example, in July 2010, alert street vendors noticed smoke spewing from a sport utility vehicle parked in Times Square, New York City. These alert vendors notified the fire department which responded. The firefighters discovered that the vehicle was an explosive device. Fortunately the device was disabled before a horrific crime would have been committed.

Suspicious People

Regardless of the situation, whether one is observing a person, vehicle, action or object one must know what is normal for that situation before one can make a determination that suspicion should be aroused. The following circumstances should be considered worthy of further examination if the observations are not within the realm of normalcy; arriving and departing at unusual times, exiting and entering places where the public does not usually have access i.e. tunnels, restricted areas of bus and train depots, people who do not fit into the environment because they seem out of sorts and people who exhibit unusual behavior for the time and place, i.e. avoiding eye contact, turning away when approached and staring where inappropriate.

Suspicious Vehicles

The Times Square incident noted earlier exemplifies a classical suspicious vehicle, a vehicle that was out of place and smoking. A vehicle parked for extended periods of time in inappropriate places with occupants or mobile vehicles continuously frequenting the same area should arouse suspicion. In these cases surveillance activity may be in progress. Vehicles with altered frames or removable signs or decals should draw attention. Remember the beltway snipers who crippled the Washington, D. C. area a few years ago? They altered their vehicle to facilitate their sniping activity.

Suspicious Actions or Objects

Security officers should always be on the look out for suspicious packages, luggage or backpacks placed in unusual places. The unusual place could be a crowded shopping area or near a ventilation system or electrical closet. Unattended packages regardless of where they are found should arouse suspicion. These packages may contain bombs or other WMD. As was noted in chapter four bombs can and have been delivered through the mail, remember the unibomber. Experience has demonstrated that the bacteria anthrax reached several people via the post office. Fires with unusual colored smoke or smell should bring attention to themselves as should disagreeable odors not associated with fire. Those odors may have toxic chemical origins. Security officers should be suspicious of unusual stains in motel and hotel rooms, in apartments and in storage containers. Rural folk should be curious about and report any unusual explosions. Blueprints often are guarded company secrets and anyone, other than an authorized person, who requests them or attempts to purchase them illegally or purchases those legally available to the public should bring an awareness to themselves. Heavy unexpected packages with excessive postage should raise a red flag. These are but a few thoughts on suspicious objects and actions. The bottom line is keep alert for any unusual situation or activity and remember, know what is normal because if a guard does not know that then the guard will not know what is unusual.

10-2 POTENTIAL TARGETS

Critical Infrastructure

Infrastructure is defined as the facilities and equipment needed for the functioning of a nation or an area. These facilities and equipment include; telecommunication systems, electrical power, gas and oil, banking, finance and the commercial sector, water systems, emergency responders and other governmental operations.

Telecommunications systems include facilities and equipment that support both the transmission and exchange of electronic communication. These include, but are not limited to, telephone, radio, cable and computer communication.

Electrical power includes generation of electricity. Once generated that power must be transmitted through power lines and distributed through out the nation or local area. Finally the power reaches end users who utilize the power for various applications.

In regards to gas and oil concerns are with production, storage and delivery of those products. This ranges from drilling, to refining, storage and the massive network of delivering those products, first to providers and then to end users.

Banking, finance and the commercial aspects of the infrastructure include a host of organizations. These organizations are interested in the flow of assets within and outside of the nation. They are involved in monetary transactions at all levels and in many applications from savings accounts, to loans, investments and in the exchange of money for products and services. The World Trade Center was the symbol of this infrastructure and the power that structure represented.

Transportation systems are often taken for granted and little thought is given to them. Our highway systems, some of which were built for national defense, do not only facilitate daily commutes but are predominantly responsible for the movement and dispersal of goods. Some were even designed for the rapid deployment of the military. Included in this category are the railroad systems used for passenger and freight service, aviation with all of its applications and shipping. These systems are essential at all levels of society from the individual doing errands, to facilitating commerce by moving goods and government at all levels for a myriad of purposes.

Water is taken for granted; however, nothing is more vital to human survival than this liquid. Additionally, water is used in all aspects of our society from domestic use, to industrial use, to fire fighting and recreation. Water comes to us from reservoirs, wells, aquifers and so forth. Water may be briefly stored before distribution or distributed directly via aqueducts, tunnels and pipelines. There is no doubt that there is serious concern about contamination of the water supply as well as damage to storage and delivery systems engineered for major cities and suburban areas.

Another potential terrorist target is our system of emergency services. Inclusive in this area are: the police, fire fighters, EMTs, rescue workers and other personnel where appropriate such as public health officers in an emergency situations requiring their expertise. Inhibiting these responders will most likely increase the loss of life, injury and property damage occurring at the original target.

Government is in our everyday lives, from delivering the mail, to running the subway systems and maintaining that infrastructure, to air traffic controlling, to caring for health, safety and welfare. All levels of government are involved in these efforts. Remember an earlier discussion regarding Japan's subway system attack or consider the consequences of the air traffic control mechanism being disabled. There are many possibilities out there.

Other Targets

Yes, there are many possibilities out there especially when it comes to targets.

Anyplace where there is a mass congregation of people is a potential target. These areas would include: concerts (the Times Square bombing attempt was executed during the opening of a movie), shopping malls, sports arenas, schools, high rise apartment dwellings, office buildings and so forth. Other targets selections may result from religious ideology. In these instances the targets may be places of worship where statements against those religious beliefs can be inferred.

Regardless of the initial target it would make sense to go multiple. Selecting multiple targets would initially create confusion, delay response and stretch responder capability. These issues would result in more extensive damage. For example, if the initial target was infrastructure in nature, i.e. the subway system, secondary targets might be responding emergency units such as a fire department's vehicles and personnel. Confusion, lessened response and stretched ability could give the public the impression that the government is not dealing effectively with the attack or terrorism in general. Deflated confidence is a morale buster.

10-3 IMMEDIATE ACTIONS

Unless otherwise officially qualified, certified and trained security officers, as was noted earlier, are not authorized to perform ongoing operations or support at a WMD incident. They may, however, conduct certain necessary tasks at the onset of an incident. The activities authorized are contained in the important acronym RAIN.

RAIN stands for *recognition, avoid, isolate* and *notify*.

When initially encountering an incident a quick and immediate assessment is required. In the process of that assessment the guard must strive to recognize the hazard or threat. This is accomplished through the senses, sight, smell, hearing and so forth. It would be a great advantage if the guard has had previous training in knowing what to look for in each major category of WMD i.e. chlorine gas has a yellow-green cloud and smells like laundry bleach. The guard should also be familiar with the hazards one is most likely to encounter as they are discussed in the Emergency Response Guide (ERG).

The second aspect of the acronym is to avoid substances that can cause health issues. One must avoid the condition whatever it may be, cloud, vapor, powder, liquid or suspicious box. Hazards include all types of WMD ranging from chemicals to explosive devices and so forth. Hazards pose threats to health and may very well cause illness or death upon exposure to them. Some hazards are capable of causing bodily injury, including death to people in harm's way. The message here is get out of the area in a timely manner and stay out beyond the perimeter recommended by the ERG until the area becomes safe again.

The third step in the acronym is to isolate the area. The guard should leave the location. People who are exposed or are in a position of potential exposure should be escorted away from the contaminated location. The area should be cordoned off, prohibiting anyone but first responders or authorized entrants to enter.

Notify is the final task of RAIN. After assessing the situation the security officer should notify someone. This person may be one of any different classifications of people. The guard may be required to notify someone in the employer's chain of command. The guard may have the liberty to call a public first responder such as the police or fire department. They guard should furnish as much information as is possible about the incident at hand, what action he or she has taken to this point and what future action is contemplated.

10-4 GENERAL PRECAUTIONS

General precautions involve protective actions. These are actions taken to preserve health and safety in emergency situations. Human life requires preservation first, including the security officer's life. Property preservation is secondary.

One must consider evacuation as a possibility. This activity should be accomplished in accordance with the employer's policies and procedures.

Ideally, this activity should occur as soon as it is determined that people are in or are about to enter a contaminated area and that evacuation is the proper action. Other people outside the immediate area may also be at risk and they should be advised to vacate too. Many WMD are heavier than air, move with the wind or flow downstream. Given these facts one must evacuate in the opposite direction, go upwind, uphill and upstream.

Isolation has been previously discussed in this chapter. This function goes hand and hand with evacuation. Get people away and keep them away.

In many instances it is not safe or practical to evacuate. In those cases one must create a shelter-in-place for potential victims. In this instance people should seek shelter inside a building and remain there until the situation is resolved. For better protection the ventilation system, windows and doors should be shut off or closed. One must always be aware that one device may not be enough and a secondary event might be at hand.

Sight is an important sense, but focused sight or seeing is a critical necessity for security officers. When driving a car, for example, one notes the back of the car in front. It's a blanket picture which includes the registration tag. A focused, concentrated effort would enable the observer to note tag's letters and numbers. In the initial overall assessment the officer should be in tune for out of the ordinary visual experiences. These would include: new visible corrosion, chemical reactions, pooling of liquids, condensation on pressurized tanks, clouds and vapors, explosive damage, fire and smoke. The officer should look for dead animals and wilted or dead plants.

If people are present the officer should look for multiple casualties and the common symptoms associated with various WMD. These symptoms might include: shrapnel wounds, blistering of the skin, burns, choking, difficulty breathing, spasms and convulsions, cramps and vomiting. The officer should also look for incontinence, lack of bowel or bladder control or both.

Sound is the noise that is translated into some form of logic via the hearing process. In an incident the security officer may be bombarded by noise. It is necessary to focus the hearing process on the noises which will help in an assessment. These noises will probably be unusual. Many WMP in the chemical group are dispersed through aerosol devices. When releasing its contents a hissing sound would be audible. Many chemicals when released are in liquid form which rapidly evaporates to poisonous gas. In this process the liquid may bubble. Explosive devices create a boom. If there is an evacuation it would be wise to query the evacuees to determine if they heard anything unusual.

Odors in the area of an incident may reveal the possible presence of a hazmat. These odors can emanate from fires, vapor clouds, gas leaks or weapons, usually chemical in nature. Many chemical weapons have signature odors. There is a potential problem in the area of odors if one can smell it one may be already contaminated. If one can smell it, leave! Remember the longer the time one is exposed to a contaminate, the greater the potential injury.

Never touch or taste any unidentified substance including suspected hazardous material. Additionally do not touch or taste any material which may have been contaminated such as food. As a reminder, this also includes any controlled substance or illegal drug.

10-5 (ERG) EMERGENCY RESPONSE GUIDE

The Emergency Response Guidebook (ERG) lists chemicals and other hazardous material. This volume is published every four years by the Department of Transportation. The guide is designed to facilitate quick identification of the hazards associated with specific chemicals, etcetera. The guide is applicable for a time period of the first thirty minutes on the scene. There are four colored sections in the book. They are in this order, yellow, blue, orange and green. The first section contains a yellow border. This section lists the material by a four digit identification number. That number has been previously assigned. This section records the ID number first, followed by a three digit guide number and then names the chemical itself. The blue bordered section contains an alphabetized listing of the material followed by the guide number then the ID number. The orange bordered pages contain the guide numbers. Under each guide number a section describes potential hazards, public safety measures, protective clothing to be worn and evacuation measures. The green bordered pages are concerned with isolation of the incident and protective evacuation distances. Finally, there is a colorless section used to describe material used for terrorism. The Department of Transportation has also developed placards for use on railroad cars and trucks. These diamond shaped cards show the ID number of the chemical the vehicle is transporting.

10-6 CHEMICAL AGENTS

Introduction

Chemical agents are not new to the scene. Chemicals, such as chlorine, mustard gas and phosgene have been here at least since the early nineteen hundreds. They were used in the First World War when and modern chemical warfare emerged on the scene. The objectives in this section are to provide the reader with knowledge of selected chemicals, TIC (toxic industrial chemicals) terms, definitions and characteristics. The reader will be expected to be able to recognize the physiological signs and symptoms of exposure. The reader should also be aware that the ERG will be referenced through out the rest of this work. He or she should apply the concept of RAIN as it would relate to each WMD type.

Recognizing Chemical Agents (The R in RAIN)

Security officers should be alert for changing conditions. To understand a change one must understand what is normal and what is not. When a chemical incident occurs change will happen rather quickly. In chemical incidents changes tend to follow patterns depending upon what chemical is used and what area of the body is affected. Security officers should be aware of the medical symptoms associated with the various and more common chemicals of terror. Medical symptoms can occur within minutes of a release, but then some may take hours. Chemicals may leave colored stains, kill insects, small animals and foliage. Chemicals often leave odors behind.

When trying to identify chemical weapons one must consider several points. Those points are: type of chemical, dissemination or how the weapon is disbursed, availability, volatility, vapor density, odor, routes of entry into the body and general signs and symptoms. For reporting purposes it might do well to format the body of the report in the following manner:

Type: Chemical's name

Dissemination: How disbursed

Availability: Available or not

Volatility: Non persistent or persistent

Vapor density: Heavier or lighter that air

Odor: Smells like

Routes of entry: Inhalation, etc

General signs and symptoms: Choking or whatever

The sources that would help identify a chemical agent could also help one in a RAIN situation, i.e. identity of substance, a yellow green cloud for example indicates chlorine gas (recognition). Once the substance is recognized exposure should be terminated by leaving (avoidance). One should keep others out of harm's way by setting up barriers or taking other appropriate actions (isolate). During this process the proper responder can be contacted and appraised of the situation (notify). The ERG is an excellent source of information for RAIN purposes.

There are several sources that can help identify hazardous materials. The ERG is a distinguished source and it is the one designated for security guard training. It should be noted that the ERG posts emergency response telephone numbers. It would not be a bad idea to program the appropriate number into a guard's cell phone. The US military classifies hazardous material by two letters such as GB for sarin, a nerve agent, CG for phosgene a choking agent and so forth. Another great source containing chemical identifying information is the NIOSH Pocket Guide to Chemical Hazards. That volume is produced by the CDC (Center for Disease Control). One can download the data from the web page, WWW.CDC.Gov/niosh/npg/. Remember the MSDS (material safety data sheets) discussed in a previous chapter? They are also a good source if the chemicals are already present at the job site. Finally, NFPA704 (National Fire Protection Association) has what is referred to as the "Fire Diamond." Within a large diamond four smaller diamonds are located. They are of equal size. One diamond is blue, one red, one yellow and a white one. The blue diamond is on the left corner and represents health issues, the red on the top corner represents flammability, on the right corner the yellow diamond represents instability/ reactivity and a white diamond on the bottom indicates a special notice. Located within each smaller diamond is a number which represents the level of posed threats.

Dissemination means delivery, how the chemical is disbursed. These chemicals can be delivered by the wind as was sometimes done in World War One. They can be delivered through artillery fire and missiles. Hazardous materials can be introduced via aerosol containers or sprayed. Chemicals can be introduced into ventilation systems, water supplies or by whatever creative means available. Dissemination is a major consideration factor in identifying an agent i.e. if an aerosol reveals a yellow-green cloud the agent may be chlorine. The direction of movement will also facilitate the direction of evacuation another consideration.

Many hazardous materials are commercially available. Chlorine, one of the first elements to be used as a lethal weapon has many uses. It is used to purify water, as a laundry bleach and swimming pool antibacterial agent. Phosgene, also used in WW1, is used in the manufacture of plastics and fertilizer. Ammonia is another chemical readily available. This chemical is a household staple used for cleaning. Propane and gasoline are two other commonly found substances, not necessarily chemical agents, but worth mentioning here. They were combined together creating a car bomb in New York City during the summer of 2010.

Volatility means the rate a substance evaporates, turns from liquid into gas. The more rapidly this occurs the faster the disbursement of a chemical, the more volatile the chemical is. Substances are referred to as persistent or non persistent. A persistent substance is one that stays around due to slow evaporation. A non-persistent substance is short lived because it evaporates quickly. Obviously the threat is impacted by the vaporization rate.

Vapor density, roughly speaking, is the weight of a substance in relation-ship to the weight of air. The denser a gas the heavier it is. Air has a vapor density of one. Any substance that has a vapor density of more than one is denser or heavier than air. Conversely, if the density is less than one that substance is lighter than air, i.e., a helium balloon rises, a balloon blown up by way of the mouth with carbon dioxide falls to the earth.

Odor, who does not know what chlorine bleach, gasoline and ammonia smell like? Many chemical agents have unique odors and those smells operate as red flags signaling a problem. Again, one must know what is normal. Again, if an odor is out of place, evacuate.

Chemicals affect the body in various ways. Some are designed to enter the body through breathing. Others enter the body by ingestion. In many instances this occurs accidentally after chemical residues were deposited on food and were not washed off. Chemicals can be absorbed through the skin, mucus membranes and open wounds. Yet others can be injected, a real stretch as a weapon of mass destruction.

If a person has been exposed to a chemical agent there will usually be signs of exposure and symptoms as well. A sign shows the presence of a disease. A symptom is a change from what is normal. For example, people are exposed to a yellow-green cloud and after that exposure they begin to choke. The choking is a symptom of chlorine gas poisoning.

Toxic Industrial Chemicals/materials (TIC/TIM)

These are chemicals that result from industry and many have application in a manufacturing process, a finishing process, result in final products such as fertilizer and insecticides and have many other uses. These materials include; anhydrous ammonia (ammonia without water), chlorine, phosgene and hydrogen cyanide. All are described in the ERG and other references. Each has a Department of Transportation placard containing the ID number of the chemical, which is found in the yellow bordered pages. Each is contained in the alpha listed blue pages, the orange bordered guide number pages for responder action and the green bordered evacuation and in-place-shelter information section. All of the chemicals noted above are available commercially therefore it would be advisable for security officers to know their particulars as they are described in the ERG. Remember, depending upon the circumstances, exposure to these chemicals can have negative consequences to living things.

The sources of TIC/TIM are varied and numerous. Note that many of these chemicals were invented for industrial, manufacturing and home purposes. Obviously then, chemical manufacturing plants are a source of chemical agents. Other sources include industries that use chemical agents in the production process. These include cyanide and mercury. Chemicals such as anhydrous ammonia are used in food processing and storage. They are stored in tanks at those facilities. Gasoline and jet fuel are held in large tanks at distribution centers. Compressed gas can be located at various terminals, in pipelines and pumping stations. These may be found at airports, barge terminals and propane filling sites. Pesticide and fertilizer manufactures and distributors are sources, too. Educational, medical and research laboratories use and contain hazardous agents.

Various Agents

Incapacitation agents are chemicals that are designed to temporarily incapacitate people. They are not designed to be lethal. The incapacitation can be physiological, mental or both. They can affect people for various times from hours to days after exposure. Tear gas is one of these agents.

Chemical warfare agents consist of choking agents, nerve agents, blood agents and blister agents. They are classified according to the impact they have on the body. These elements and compounds are lethal. Some of these agents were created for industrial use, such as chlorine and phosgene. Others were specifically created for use as WMD on the battlefield.

Choking agents attack the lungs and the victims respond as if they are choking. Two choking agents that have been used for military purposes are phosgene and chlorine. Both have industrial applications and are commercially available. They can be disseminated as solids, liquids and gases. In terms of volatility they disperse quickly and are therefore nonpersistent. The vapor density of these agents is heavier than air therefore they sink to the lowest point. From an odor perspective, phosgene may smell like new mowed hay and chlorine smells like laundry bleach. The route into the body is through inhalation. The signs and symptoms include damage to airways and lungs with irritation to the entire system. The lungs fill with fluid, a condition known as pulmonary edema. These conditions begin to commence immediately after exposure.

Blood agents are chemicals that stop the transfer of oxygen from the blood to the body's cells. The focus here is on hydrogen cyanide as the main agent. There other cyanides and there are other blood agents including arsenic and carbon monoxide. Hydrogen cyanide can be disbursed as either a liquid or a gas. Its volatility is non persistent. The substance dissipates rapidly. The vapor density varies. It ranges from heavier than air to slightly lighter than air. This cyanide has an odor resembling bitter almonds or peach pits. The primary route of entry is breathing. Signs and symptoms include; gasping for air, frothing at the mouth or vomiting, losing consciousness and dying. The signs and symptoms occur within seconds of exposure.

Mustard agents, lewisite and phosgene oxime are classified as blistering agents. Of this type mustard is the most likely to be used. Dissemination is accomplished by way of liquid which then vaporizes a double edged sword. Mustards are not commercially available. It is theorized that some countries may have them in stockpiles. Its volatility is persistent because the liquid evaporates slowly. The vapor density of these agents is heavier than air. Various odors have been reported. Mustard odors remind people of the spice mustard, onions, garlic or horseradish. Lewisite creates an odor reminiscent of geraniums. The odor of phosgene oxime is said to be intense and irritating. There are three possible routes of entry, inhalation, ingestion and absorption. The signs and symptoms of blister agents include a redness of the skin with water blisters, eye damage, respiratory discomfort and an accompanying severe pain in those areas. Other symptoms include: nausea, bloody diarrhea, vomiting and extreme weakness. Mustards manifest signs and symptoms four to six hours after exposure and skin exposure two to forty-eight hours after exposure. Lewisite and phosgene oxime pain symptoms occur immediately.

Tabun, sarin, soman and VX are types of nerve agents. In short these agents stop the nervous system from sending messages. They can be disseminated in both liquid and gas form. These chemicals are not commercially available. Some countries may possess illegal stockpiles. The volatility of the nerve agents tabun, sarin and soman is non persistent. VX is slow to evaporate and is therefore persistent. The vapor density of these agents is heavier than air. The routes of entry into the body are through inhalation and skin absorption. It is also possible to ingest these agents. The signs and symptoms are many. They include: miosis (pupil contraction), weakness, vomiting, diarrhea, sweating, disorientation, respiratory problems, slurred speech, drooling and trembling. These poisons begin working immediately.

Toxicity

Most people are familiar with chorine. It is used as a household laundry additive known as bleach. People keep their swimming pools free of germs with it. Most of us know what it smells like. To give the reader an idea of how toxic chemicals can be, a comparison between those previously discussed and chlorine will give the reader an idea of their dangers. Cyanogen chloride is twice as toxic. Phosgene is six times worse. Hydrogen cyanide is seven times deadlier. Mustard is thirteen times more dangerous. Sarin, the nerve agent, is two hundred times more devastating. Finally, at six hundred times more damaging sits the nerve agent VX.

Avoid: Chemical Agents (The A in RAIN)

There are three ideas at work in the isolation stage of RAIN. They are time, distance and shielding. First, avoid the obvious. If one comes across a suspicious substance spend as little time there as possible. Get out and do not return until authorized to do so. The more one is exposed the more likelihood of injury. In terms of distance, the further one is away the better. Distance lessens the chances of contamination. Not to be redundant but one must consider going upwind, uphill and upstream to the distance recommended in the green bordered pages of the ERG. Finally, when necessary a person must seek to shield oneself when shielding will reduce or eliminate exposure to an agent. One seeking shielding may find a shelter-in-place as was discussed earlier.

Isolate: Chemical Agents (The I in RAIN)

There are three zones involved in controlling the hazardous material and stopping its spread. They are the hot zone, the warm zone and the cold zone.

- The *hot zone* is the area immediately surrounding the chemical incident location. It should extend far enough away from the location to keep people protected from chemical contamination. This zone is also referred to as the exclusion or restricted zone.
- The *warm zone* is the area where personnel, equipment, decontamination and hot zone support occur. The warm zone includes access control points thereby reducing the spread of contamination. This zone is also known as the decontamination, contamination reduction or limited access corridor.
- The *cold zone* is the furthest from the scene. It houses the command post and other support required to control the incident.

Notify: Chemical Agents (The N in RAIN)

Inevitably, the security officer will be required to cause a notification of the incident. Who this officer notifies will be determined by company policy and procedure. In all likelihood an emergency responder will become involved and will bring in other emergency responders, investigators and federal agencies as they are needed. An ICS will most likely develop. The officer will be responsible for answering the who, what, when, where and how of the incident. They will include what happened, where it happened, when it happened, the identity of the hazardous material if known, special hazards associated with the event, the number of victims, protective measures taken and the facilities and locations affected.

Advantages and Disadvantages of Using Chemical Weapons as WMD

There are nine advantages to using chemical agents as WMD. One, they are easy to make or acquire. The cost and technology are low and assembly is simple. The second advantage is that the chemicals are available. They can be obtained through manufacturing process sources such as electroplating, metallurgy, metal cleaning, photography and pool supply outlets. Advantage number three, chemical weapons are cheaper than both conventional and nuclear weapons, the former costing $2,000 per square kilometer and the latter about $800. The fourth advantage is that they have an immediate effect. The closer one gets to the point of origin the higher the contamination and incapacitation. The fifth advantage is that chemicals are hard to detect. Many of them are odorless and tasteless too. The sixth advantage is that chemicals are easily spread. They can be spread by the wind, aerosol, through food and water supplies and by explosives. Seven, use of chemicals will tie up resources through the process of decontamination, aiding the victims, removing the deceased and restoring normalcy to the area. Many and varied types of responders, including the media, will be required to deal with the continuous and evolving problems created by the released chemicals. The psychological affect is the eighth advantage. This impact will go far beyond the initial attack. Confidence in our government's ability to protect us will be shaken. Also, many people do not know much about these weapons and are afraid of them. Finally, Use of these weapons, may lead to an escalation into the use of more potent and devastating weapons, an all out chemical war or heightened violence.

There are three major disadvantages. One, chemical attacks require large quantities of the poison to be effective as a WMD. Obtaining the required amount may be impossible due to the Chemical Weapons Convention, (www.cwc.gov/cwc_treaty.html). Two, production and deployment may be dangerous to the terrorists. There is an inherent risk in creating such weapons. Without the proper safeguards and protection the producer is at risk of becoming a victim. Finally, it is easier to prepare for a chemical attack than it is to prepare for a nuclear, explosive or biological attack. Most chemical attacks are non persistent, whereas the effects of the others linger and become more difficult to deal with.

10-7 BIOLOGICAL AGENTS

Biological agents consist of disease causing bacteria, viruses, prions, fungi and other microorganisms. They are also derived from mainly bacterial toxins. Many of these agents mimic naturally occurring diseases. Those diseases would usually occur sporadic in a community. If large numbers of people fall victim to the same disease, i.e. develop the same symptoms further investigation is necessary.

Recognize: Biological Agents

In recognizing the various agents certain criteria must be noted. The criteria are similar to the information needed with chemical agents with an additional two areas of commentary. Again, for reporting purposes it might do well to format the body of the report in the following manner:

Type: Name the agent

Dissemination: How disbursed

Availability: Available or not

Volatility: Non persistent or persistent

Vapor density: Heavier or lighter that air

Odor: Smells like

Routes of entry: Inhalation, etc

General signs and symptoms: Skin lesions or whatever

Mortality: Probability of death

Basic treatment: Prescribed medical treatment

Bacterium Infections

Bacterial infections are caused by single-celled organisms that attack plants, animals and humans. They also create poisonous toxins. Three bacterium of major concern here are anthrax, yersinia (plague) and tularemia (rabbit fever).

Anthrax is usually a disease of animals, mainly herbivores because the bacteria occur naturally in the ground. This bacterium is distributed to many laboratories. Humans can contract the disease through the skin or by inhalation. In the past humans became infected through contact with diseased animals or products of those animals, such as wool or meat. Efforts at curbing this disease have been very successful and contamination is very rare. If humans become infected it is through deliberate effort. The worst bio-terror attack in United States history began on 9/18/01 when several anthrax laced letters were sent through the US Postal Service. The anthrax was distributed in a solid form as a powder. Five people died and seventeen others were sickened. Some of the victims inhaled the powder others became ill after the germs entered their skin. Inhalation is the worst case scenario. Other routes of entry are: injection and consumption. Anthrax, like most diseases has an incubation period. Early symptoms are flu type symptoms, fever, chills nausea and swollen lymph nodes.

Early treatment of cutaneous (skin) anthrax is curable. Without antibiotics and treatment the mortality rate is 20%. Inhalation mortality is about 75% and for gastrointestinal (eaten) anthrax the rate is between 25%-60%. Antibiotics are the basic treatment for the ill.

There are two types of plagues of interest here. Yersinia bacteria cause both the bubonic and the pneumonic plagues. Most cases of bubonic plague are transmitted to people via fleas that have contracted the disease from rodents. In the US there are about fifteen cases annually. This plague cannot be transferred from person to person. Pneumonic plague occurs when the bacteria enters the lungs. Pneumonic plague can be transferred from one person to another if someone breathes in the bacteria passed along by an infected person, or as in a terrorist attack, by breathing in aerosolized bacteria. Both plagues are naturally occurring and are distributed to many laboratories. The bacteria enter the body through inhalation, ingestion, or injection. The incubation period is two to three days. Pneumonic plague symptoms include chills, high fever, headache and hemoptysis (spitting blood or bloody mucus). These quickly turn into more serious symptoms such as labored breathing, a harsh respiratory sound and a blueness of the skin. Death results from respiratory failure. The bubonic plague incubates for between two to ten days. The ill suffer from malaise, high fever and tender lymph nodes. This disease can possibly spread to the lungs. Without treatment the mortality rate is about one in seven.

Tularemia is a disease of animals, rabbits, hares and rodents, which can be transmitted to humans. Natural infections in humans are caused by insect bites. Many laboratories possess this germ. Terrorists may disseminate the bacteria though solids or aerosols. This bacteria enters the body via inhalation, contact, ingestion, injection, handling infected carcasses or ingesting infected food or drink. This disease cannot be transmitted between humans. Symptoms include fever, chills, headache, muscle ache, joint ache progressive weakness and pneumonia. The incubation period is generally three to five days but can take as long as fourteen days. The mortality rate in the US is very low. Early antibiotic treatment is recommended when exposure to the germ is suspected.

Viral Infections

A virus is small organic substance which can cause disease. They are smaller than bacteria. A virus needs a host to reproduce and spread. They do not respond to antibiotics. The best way to deal with a virus is through prevention of an infection via vaccination. This volume is concerned with three viruses, smallpox, VEE (Venezuelan Equine Encephalomyelitis) and VHF (Viral Hemorrhagic Fever).

Smallpox has been on the human scene for about three thousand years. The virus was recently eradicated through vaccination efforts. However, the vaccination has caused problems and its use was stopped. Today most people would be vulnerable to smallpox infection. Currently there are only two sources of smallpox, one in Russia and one in the United States. If a smallpox outbreak occurs it would be a deliberate act. Smallpox can be disseminated through aerosol, person to person or object to person. The most common distribution is through large droplets propelled via sneezing. Those droplets are inhaled. Smallpox is a person to person disease. No animals or insects are involved. The incubation period is generally between twelve and fourteen days. Symptoms include: high fever, extreme lethargy, severe headaches, severe backaches, severe abdominal pain and vomiting. Lesions form on the skin and fill with fluid. Smallpox can be confused with chicken pox because of the lesions. In chicken pox the fever is lower. There is a feeling of lethargy. The rash begins as red bumps then develops into blisters which are itchy. Most people who contract smallpox survive, about 30% do not. Those who survive bear pockmark scars, some become blind too. Vaccination will prevent this disease. As with most viruses there is no cure.

VEE virus is a naturally occurring organism which originally infected horses and related animals. It is spread to humans via mosquito bites or inhalation. As a WMD it can be disseminated via aerosol, liquid or solid. This virus is very potent and very infectious. It also can be produced in large quantities. A minute amount of it is sufficient to cause illness. For these three reasons this virus is considered a strong candidate as a WMD. The incubation period is between one and five days. The symptoms are flu like including headache, fever, malaise and soreness on the legs. The mortality rate for this disease is extremely low, around1%. There is no cure for this ailment. This virus would be used to incapacitate not to kill.

VHF infections can be mild or severe. Two of the most dangerous are Ebola and Marburg. The central source of these viruses is Africa. These organisms are naturally occurring and affect humans and primates. There has not been a reported case in the U.S. As a WMD this virus can be spread via aerosol, liquid or solid. They enter the body through contact, inhalation ingestion or injection. Signs and symptoms vary depending on the specific disease contracted. Initial signs and symptoms are flu like. Advanced cases would include bleeding from the internal organs, bleeding beneath the skin in bruise like fashion, bleeding from the nose, eyes, ears and other bodily openings. The mortality rate depends on the type of virus, some lower than 10%, some as high as 90%. There is no cure for these diseases.

Toxins

The word toxin is synonymous with the word poison. A toxin is a substance that can make a person ill or can kill. Toxins are produced from living plants or animals. For example, the toxin ricin is derived from the fruit of the Castor Plant, the castor bean. Eating upwards of twenty of those beans could produce death.

Ricin can be disseminated in any of the three major dissemination methods, aerosol, solid or liquid. This is a natural substance found in the Castor bean, the fruit of a virtual weed. Ricin is also available commercially. The routes of entry into the body are inhalation, ingestion or injection. The signs and symptoms of the poisoning vary but include: weakness, dizziness, dry mouth and throat, blurred vision and respiratory failure. Onset of the symptoms occurs between one and twelve hours. Low blood pressure and respiratory failure are the causes of death. Death generally occurs between thirty-six and seventy-two hours after exposure depending on the route. There is no antidote for ricin. The victim should receive routine medical care.

Avoid: Biological Agents

This is a difficult situation because of the incubation periods associated with most biological agents. One could have been exposed days ago and is now just realizing the condition exists. Where was the exposed person five days ago, where did the exposure occur, what routine was followed?

Consideration for avoidance should be given to gaining information about the source, tracking patients with unusual symptoms, prior immunization to the agent, protective clothing, purified breathing apparatuses and unbroken skin. It is not wise to eat or drink anything near the contaminated area because the ingested material may be contaminated as well. Items in the area may also be contaminated. It would be beneficial not to touch anything there. Wash exposed body parts with soap and water or use a sanitized wipe to clean those parts. Seek medical attention if illness symptoms develop.

Isolate: Biological Agents

The responding security officer should set-up control zones which are described in the isolation section of chemical agents.

Notify: Biological Agents

The responding security officer should follow the protocol described in the notify section of chemical agents.

Advantages of Using Biological Agents

These agents are readily available. They can be obtained from natural sources, hospital laboratories and other research facilities such as university and private research labs. These agents are hard to detect, a little goes a long way. These items are probably going to be used covertly, spread through large areas by weather conditions and as with VEE, mosquitoes. It is recommended that the virus be disbursed during mosquito season because they are carriers and distributors of that virus. These agents are easily spread. Building ventilation systems and transportation facilities can spread the material far from the original drop site. These agents can also be distributed from one person to the next and the next. Some of these agents persist long after the initial dissemination. Anthrax for example has stayed dormant for decades. This would require use of future resources for future decontamination clean ups tying up those resources. There of course would be the psychological impact as was discussed previously in chemical agent advantages. Preparing for this type of emergency is difficult. The magnitude of the incident may overwhelm the responders and support staff. Will the responders and support run short on staff and equipment? Will the hospitals and morgues have personnel, room and equipment to deal with the volume?

Disadvantages of Using Biological Agents

The delayed effects due to incubation can lessen the intended impact of the attack. Terrorists make political statements through their activities. The time required to determine if the incident was natural or intended would delay the political message. Production of those agents can be hazardous to the terrorist. Development of these agents requires difficult steps. Some steps would be hard to finish. Some problems which would be encountered are lack of expertise, difficulty in getting equipment and material, risk of detection and so forth. Unfortunately, these hurtles have remedies. Sometimes the climate works with us and sometimes not. Weather can foil the attack. Finally the predicable outcome cannot be determined as well as other forms of attack.

10-8 RADIOLOGICAL MATERIALS AND NUCLEAR WEAPONS

These are viable threats to our society. Security officers should realize the difference between the materials and the weapon. He or she should have a basic understanding radiation and radioactivity, the signs of exposure, identify devices and know the difference between nuclear explosions and conventional ones. As was previously done before the RAIN process is emphasized.

Recognize: Radioactive Material

The radioactive symbol consists of a rectangular box containing a yellow circle which contains a darker three bladed propeller with the blades spaced equally apart. Sometimes the sign reads, "Caution radioactive materials."

According to the World Nuclear Organization (www.world-nuclear org) twenty-million radioactive cargos of various sizes are shipped worldwide annually. This is an awesome amount of radioactive material on the move. Some of that material is dangerous, much of it is not.

Radiation is energy released by unstable atoms in the form of minute particles. Unstable atoms are ionized. Which means they do not have an equal number of protons and electrons, therefore electrically they are either positively or negatively charged. All ionized atoms or molecules are radioactive.

The objective of the atom is to be neutral, not to have any electrical charge. Subsequently energy is released in an effort to become neutral. This energy travels through the air in all directions from the source, including upwind. These particles are odorless, colorless and cannot be seen or tasted.

This chapter is concerned with four types of radiation particles released by radioactive material. They are alpha, beta, gamma and neutron radiation. Alpha radiation cannot penetrate a piece of paper. Beta radiation can be stopped by less than an inch of metal. Gamma radiation is powerful and energetic. That radiation can be stopped by lead. Neutron radiation is the only type that can make other materials radioactive and is used in all types of applications from medicine to industrial use. This radiation can travel great distances in the air and shielding consists of concrete or water. This type of radiation is used in nuclear reactors. Neutron radiation in an atomic explosion causes other substances to be radioactive.

Exposure to radiation by a person is referred to as a dose. Some doses are small and basically harmless to victims and responders. Others doses can be large and extremely dangerous to the health of both victims and responders. Symptoms to a harmful dose include: nausea, vomiting, diarrhea, burns and possible death. To this end there are two categories of radiation exposure, Type A and Type B. Type A exposure is exposure to non-injuring doses. This exposure is probably the most common type and according to Federal Law does not release radiation at a level dangerous to life. An example of a device that emits this level is a smoke detector. According to ERG guide number 163, Type B exposure can be life threatening. The locations of dangerous exposure possibilities are; hospitals and cancer treatment centers, industrial and construction sites, nuclear power plants and materials in transit. The sources would include: medical irradiators (X-rays and cancer radiation treatment), radiography cameras, food irradiators (radiation used to kill bacteria on food) and spent (used) nuclear fuel rods.

Exposure vs Contamination

External exposure means that the radioactive particles, those emitted from a radioactive source, reach a person or group of people not the source of radiation reaching the person or group. In This case there is no radioactive contamination. The individual is not radioactive. He or she was figuratively struck by miniscule bullets. This person is not a hazard to self or others. This can be analogized to sunburn. Exposure to ultraviolet radiation (sunlight) causes the burn to the person exposed but not to one who was in the shade. The sunburn does not rub off onto others.

There are two types of contamination, external and internal. Both can be disseminated as solid (usually dust), gas or liquid. External contamination occurs when the person actually has the radiological material on his or her body. If this is suspected or has occurred everyone and thing in the area of contamination must be decontaminated. It should be noted that in most instances of this type of occurrence the victims do not have enough contamination to reach levels dangerous to responders.

Internal contamination happens when the radioactive material enter the body. This can occur through; inhalation, ingestion, absorption through the skin, via a wound caused by a radiological device or through puncture or injection at the site of an external contamination. This type of contamination is usually more dangerous to the victim that external contamination.

Physiological Signs and Symptoms of Exposure

Victims who receive large doses of radiation poisoning may suffer from ARS (acute radiation syndrome). Most signs and symptoms of radiological exposure or contamination do not occur immediately. They manifest themselves hours later. Looked for symptoms should include the aforementioned nausea, vomiting and diarrhea. There are variables which should be considered. They include the intensity of the exposure/contamination, duration and closeness. These may impact the amount of time between exposure/contamination and the onset of symptoms, the arrival of the symptoms, i.e. the higher the dose the quicker the symptoms. A high dose may cause death, however if not high enough medical attention may stay death off. Victims who receive low doses may not exhibit any symptoms.

People who are exposed to high doses may receive radiation burns. They manifest themselves by appearing red and puffy. The skin may turn a bronze color. These, like the other symptoms may appear several hours after the incident. If they appear at the time of the incident or shortly thereafter they are probably another type of burn such as thermal or chemical burns. A lack of a burn does not mean the person has not been seriously contaminated. Initially burns are not painful. Once they develop pain may develop. Some burns appear to heal then return later with more intense pain, blistering and swelling. This is unlike other types of burns. From an investigative perspective if a suspect's hands have this type of burn it may indicate he or she was handling radiological material.

Recognize: Radiation Exposure Device

Radiation exposure devices, not contamination devices, take many forms. Any container that would allow radiation; rays, wave or particles, to pass through it would suffice. A good source for this device would be any of the previous sources noted earlier including industry. A few hundred of these devices are either stolen or abandoned every year. One possible scenario would be that a terrorist steals a device and places it in either a building or public place to allow high level radiation exposure to large groups of people. The device would continue to expose people until its discovery which could very well occur after people exhibited symptoms of radiation poisoning. These devices are rather small from less than an inch to about ten inches. They usually are shaped as cylinders or disks. Many are rather heavy because the devices are shielded by lead. Security officers should beware of heavier than expected courier bags, backpacks, brief cases, luggage or other packages particularly if they appear to be abandoned on their posts. Their suspicion should also be aroused if they observe someone laboring in the effort to carry one of those items.

Recognize: Radiological Dispersal Device (RDD)

This device is known as a dirty bomb, not a nuclear bomb. It is constructed with ordinary explosive material and is enhanced with any radiological substance. When exploded the device spreads the radioactive material. It does not cause a nuclear explosion. The Nuclear Regulatory Commission (NRC) has stated that the radiation from these devises would not present a major health problem beyond the initial explosion's affect. This device could be constructed from a common pipe bomb or could be attached to some radiological substance such as a radiograph camera. As was discussed earlier the sources for this material are many and these substances are readily available. A terrorist could steal the stuff, buy it or obtain it through deception. Remember, twenty-million radioactive items, of all sizes move through this world in any given year.

The effects of such a detonation would be psychological, contamination, the need to decontaminate and hindrance due to limited resources. The explosion would cause fear and panic. Many who would not be seriously contaminated would think they were. A few close to the scene and the scene itself would be contaminated. The situation may require regional sites for decontamination of thousands of people even though many would not necessarily require decontamination. Finally, lack of radiation detectors and trained personnel would inhibit the response.

Recognize: Nuclear Weapons

When one thinks of nuclear bombs thoughts go to Hiroshima and Nagasaki. One thinks of the loss of life and the devastation which occurred there. Two whole cities were all but destroyed. Those were big bombs. Both weighed about ten-thousand pounds. Both were about ten feet long. One, known as Little Boy, was twenty-nine inches in diameter the other, Fat Man, was five feet in diameter. Both bombs split atoms a process called fission. These bombs require highly processed, enriched uranium or plutonium. It would be unlikely that a terrorist would be able to deliver such an awesome device. If a nuclear device were to be detonated in this country it would be a much smaller bomb. A small device would not knock out a city, but would destroy some buildings or perhaps take out one city block. One might confuse the explosion with a massive truck bomb detonation. However, there is a difference. Both devices would create high heat and shock waves. In addition, the nuclear bomb would produce gamma and neutron radiation. Such a device would also produce radioactive fallout and contamination. Detonation of such a device would have a tremendous negative psychological effect in both the community where it occurred and in the rest of the nation as well. However, it would be more probable that a terrorist would use an RDD rather than a nuclear bomb.

Nuclear bomb devastation is measured in kilotons. One kiloton is equivalent to an explosion of one-thousand tons of TNT. In Japan the first bomb yielded the equivalent of fifteen-thousand tons of TNT. The second bomb yielded the equivalent of twenty-one thousand tons. Again, one can note the huge difference between a one kilo ton bomb and a large bomb.

Nuclear bombs also exhibit an observable difference than conventional explosives. After detonation a nuclear bomb produces a vertical smoke column whereas a conventional explosion spreads in all directions. The nuclear blast is usually light brown due to soil vaporization. The top of the column appears white due to water condensation. A mushroom type cloud may not necessarily form. The smoke from a conventional explosion will be dark brown or black.

Avoid: Radiological Materials

In avoiding radiological materials one must consider; time, distance and shielding. Minimize the time spent during exposure near the source or contamination. The more one is exposed, the more one is bombarded with the radiation. The quicker one leaves the area the smaller the dose. Each minute spent in the area increases the dose, for example, a two minute exposure would receive a fifty percent smaller dose than a four minute exposure.

Distance is important, the further away, the smaller the dose. If the distance away from the dose is doubled the dose is reduced by seventy-five percent i.e. if one moves from twenty feet to forty feet away the dose drops by seventy-five percent. The recommended distance, as was discussed earlier is eighty to one hundred and sixty feet.

Shielding is very important. As was mentioned earlier the various radioactive particles have varying penetration abilities. When practical one must keep as much protection between self and source. The more material one has between self and source the smaller the dose that person will receive. Consideration should be given to thick objects for protection. Thin materials offer little protection against radiation. Do not attempt to find shielding to place around the device. That would increase exposure by taking too much time.

Isolate: Radiological Materials

The three control zones, hot, warm and cold have been discussed previously and can be found in the section which discusses chemical weapons.

Remember, for a leak or spill, evacuate eighty to one-hundred and sixty feet. For a large spill or leak, something in the range of a fifty-five gallon drum or two-hundred liters in small containers evacuate to three hundred and thirty feet. If large quantities of radioactive material are involved in a fire evacuate to one-thousand feet.

Notify: Radiological Materials

This area has been previously discussed in the chemical weapons section. No additional information is required in the N aspect of RAIN

Advantages of Using Radiological Materials as WMD

Radioactive material is available. It can be bought or stolen. Use of such a device would tie up resources; responders, medical personnel, decontaminators and others for an extended time. The psychological impact would be devastating. These situations are difficult to prepare for. Use of this type of weapon would be the next level of escalation.

Disadvantages of Using Radiological Materials

The containers are heavy. In many cases there would be delayed health effects to victims, if any at all. The terrorist runs a risk of a radiation dose just by handling the substance. This could occur in the theft, manufacturing process or deployment of the device. Creating a device capable of mass destruction and death would take numerous difficult steps to create such an bomb. The material is expensive to procure.

10-9 EXPLOSIVE DEVICES

According to the FBI, explosive devices account for roughly seventy percent of all terrorist incidents. This type of attack is therefore the most likely method of attack. This fact is ample reason security officers should be very aware of recognizing, avoiding, isolating and notifying the proper authority. The RAIN principles apply in this section as well.

Recognize: Explosive Devices as WMD

Explosive Characteristics

There are three categories of rapid combustion material technically referred to as energetic material. They are pyrotechnics, propellants and explosives. Pyrotechnics are used to make sparklers, fire crackers and fireworks. They produce smoke, heat, light and a variety of banging and booming sounds. Sparklers can be contained in a device and will explode when properly ignited. However, generally these items are not used in suicide incidents. They can be used in arson and other type of bombings.

Propellants, also known as low explosives, are designed to create a release of gas for work purposes i.e. a nail gun using a twenty-two caliber cartridge. This material is also known as gun powder and is the source of power for firing bullets from guns. Gun powder is readily available. It can be bought as modern smokeless powder of as black powder used in cap and ball guns. Most any gun shop will sell gun powder. This type is not often utilized in suicide bombings. The most common unconventional use of propellants in the U. S. is in the Improvised Explosive Device (IED).

Explosives, also known as high explosives, are created to yield an almost instant release of energy. Often this energy is used for destructive purposes. This energy is released through TNT, the plastic explosive C-4 and dynamite. The dissemination of explosives is only limited by the mind of the creator. In 2010, for example, laptop computers were discovered to contain explosives. Remember, it does not take a large amount of explosive material to bring down the biggest airplane.

Stimuli (Insults)

There are six stimuli also known as insults which can result in an accidental detonation of a device. They are heat, friction, impact, electrostatic discharge, shock and radio frequency. Each category of energetic material has its level of sensitivity. Sensitivity is a category of classification. Some can be accidentally detonated by heat change. The heat change detonation might occur simply by an atmospheric temperature change i.e. going from an air conditioned room of sixty degrees to the outside where the temperature is ninety degrees.

The heat could also be provided by a fire. There are certain combinations of materials that when combined create heat and detonate.

Insults such as friction, impact, electrostatic discharge (electric shock) and shock (jarring impact) can cause accidental detonation. One can unwittingly introduce any of these stimuli into the environment containing the dangerous material and cause combustion or explosion. A person entering an area may not realize that there is energetic material there until awareness occurs. Once this happens care should be taken not to introduce stimuli into that location. Remember that electrostatic discharge can arc from a person to a device.

Many explosions are deliberately caused by radio frequency energy (RFE). It is therefore important to reduce radio transmissions to the bare essentials if not entirely when in a suspected area, otherwise they could accidentally interfere with a remote detonator and cause an explosion. If a device is suspected immediately withdraw all people to a safe distance. Also know that responder radios offer no advantage in these situations. A certified bomb technician should be contacted for guidance and assessment when suspicious packages or circumstance are discovered.

Categories of High Explosives

There are three categories of high explosives. They are primary, secondary and tertiary. They respond differently from each other to the various stimuli.

- *Primary* explosives are used to initiate the explosion of other energetic material. A blasting cap would be an example of this type of device. They are highly sensitive to the stimuli electrostatic shock, heat, friction, and impact. Because of their sensitivity they are very dangerous.
- *Secondary* explosives are less sensitive to the stimuli than are the primaries. These include the following explosives, TNT, the plastic C-4 and dynamite. Because they are less sensitive they can be safely handled and stored. Secondary material can be used in large quantities. They required a primary explosive as a detonator.
- A *tertiary* bomb is so insensitive to stimuli that it requires more power to detonate than a primary device can generally provide. This devise requires a detonation provided by a secondary explosive commonly referred to as a booster. One of the more common of this type of bomb would be an ammonium nitrate/ fuel

oil bomb. A device similar to this was detonated by Timothy McVeigh at the Alfred P. Murrah Building in Oklahoma City.

Recognize: Improvised Explosives

Most IEDs are made from chemicals handily available. They can be found in the home or easily procured in the community. They can be obtained in large numbers. Like military or commercial explosives they are a mixture of oxidizers and fuel. An oxidizer is a chemical, which when introduced to the fuel causes a detonation. These devices are exceptionally hazardous. IEDs can function as well as commercially manufactured explosives. Terrorists create these makeshift apparatuses in all shapes and sizes. Some of the more common materials terrorists use are: potassium chlorate, peroxide-base IED, ammonium nitrate and aluminum, urea nitrate and hypergolic devices.

Potassium chlorate is commonly used in firework displays and can be purchased in large quantities form chemical supply businesses. It has roughly eighty-three percent of the power of TNT. Potassium chlorate appears as a white crystal or powder.

A peroxide base weapon may be the explosive of choice in the future. In 2008 Fox News reported that a bomb was concocted from a powdered juice drink, hydrogen peroxide and a flash camera as a detonator. Other peroxide bombs include HMTD and TATP. Both of these compare to TNT, the former having sixty to one-hundred and sixteen percent of the power of TNT, the later having eighty-eight percent. Beware both resemble crack cocaine in the powdered form and will react violently when field tested chemically for cocaine.

Powdered ammonium nitrate and aluminum powder are easily found in the community. Ammonium nitrate can be found in fertilizers and cold packs. Aluminum powder can be located in paint supply stores or shaved off of a piece of aluminum. When combined these ingredients have seventy-five percent of the effectiveness of TNT. A simple blasting cap will cause detonation.

Another fertilizer based explosive is urea nitrate. Urea can be found in the granules used for melting ice on sidewalks and nitric acid is a commonly produced acid used in a variety of applications. This type of bomb has been widely used in the Middle East. This device is blasting cap sensitive and has the TNT destructive power similar to ammonium nitrate.

Hypergolic means spontaneous combustion or explosion when specific chemicals come into contact with each other. This can be a naturally occurring incident between acids and bases or it can be a contrived circumstance when two such substances are introduced deliberately to each other.

Preparing Improvised Explosives

Many of these devices require at least two ingredients. Some must be ground from granules to powders. These ends can be accomplished by commercial coffee grinders, grist mills and other types of mixing machines.

Recognize: Improvised Explosive Device (IED) Components

Most IEDs consist of five components. They are a power source, initiator, explosive, switch and fragmentation. The acronym for memory purposes is PIESF.

Most bombs use electricity as a power source because the initiators operate on electricity. Obviously, a battery will suffice for this purpose. Batteries come in all sizes, shapes and voltages. There are non-electric devises too. They can be set off by a spring under pressure.

An initiator is a gadget that causes the explosion. Often they are blasting caps. Sometimes initiators are flame producing products such as fuses. Hobby fuses, those used in pyrotechnic displays, can be purchased at fireworks wholesalers or on-line. Some other improvised initiators are flash cameras, as was noted above with the powdered beverage and hydrogen peroxide. Percussion primers, also known as percussion caps are used to ignite black powder in cap and ball firearms. This primer can detonate an explosive as well. Improvised blasting caps can be made with TATP a peroxide based explosive.

The explosive component has been previously discussed. However, one must consider that the explosive may not be connected to other components of the device. Many times those components will survive the blast. When located they must be considered as evidence. They may in fact indicate an M. O. of a specific bomber or organization or direct an investigation to a manufacturer.

Switches open and close electric circuits. A closed circuit allows electricity to flow, in this case probably to a blasting cap or other detonation device. Some devices have two switches, an arming switch and a fusing switch. The arming switch is a safety switch. When the switch is open it keeps electricity from reaching the fusing switch accidentally. When the arming switch is closed, the circuit is still open until the fusing switch is closed. When both switches are closed a detonation occurs (Note, the Federal lesson plan has open and closed reversed).

Fragmentation is the addition of material to an IED. The material is placed into the device to increase its maiming, killing and damaging effectiveness. These items could include geological objects such as rocks, nails, BBs, ball bearings and other hard items that could inflict injury. The IED can also be encased in a metallic container to increase effectiveness. These items can be referred to as shrapnel.

Recognize: Explosive Incident Response

In explosive situations there are three response modes. They are, pre-blast, post-blast and continuing incident modes. Each has its own approach to a solution. Remember safety of people is the first priority. An injured or killed responder adds to the problem, not to the solution.

Pre-blast situations when suspected of discovered will be reported to an agency such as the police. A responder reports to the scene and makes an evaluation. Perimeters should be established base on the Bureau of Alcohol, Tobacco, Firearms and Explosives (BATFE) distance table. Once a safe perimeter has been established search, evacuation and render-safe procedure considerations must be attended to.

In post-blast situations the decision making process will be based on the amount of destruction which is in direct proportion to the size of the device. The first decision and perhaps the most important one is where to establish the hot zone or inner perimeter. Next, treatment of the injured must be commenced. Collapsed building rescue may be required. In this case only those trained in that type of rescue and with the right equipment should carry out the effort to evacuate. One must also consider other hazards such as fire, exposed live electric lines, gas leaks, smoke and toxic fumes. A post-blast situation requires thorough assessment before action. Responders should not rush into the action without such assessment.

A continuing incident obviously poses the most danger to all at the scene, victims and responders alike. It is a difficult situation because of the many facets. The danger is ongoing and fluid until neutralized. This situation requires a tactical response.

Secondary Device

The phrase "secondary device" means the presence of another IED. Such a situation is commonly referred to as multiple devices. This device might be placed in an area near where the first device detonated but where people would congregate safely away from that ground zero. Then again, the people impacted by the second device might be responders and investigators. The second explosion could achieve one of the terrorist's objectives, the creation of panic and fear in those present and in the general civilian population. One should assume that if one device is present, a second one is there as well.

Avoid: Explosive Devices

Again, this involves the concepts of time, distance and shielding. The only addition to this topic involves distances. One should follow the recommended BATFE distance tables for all situations that do not involve shipment of explosive materials. This table can be found on the BATFE web page. The reader can go to the main page and in the search box type in "table of distances." If shipment is involved in the scenario one should follow the ERGs distance chart.

Isolate: Explosive Devices

In addition to the usual hot, warm and cold zones one must follow the distance tables noted above.

Notify: Explosive Devices

Follow local procedures and the procedures in the notification subtitles previously discussed in this volume. In addition other agencies may require notification. They are the FBI, FEMA, BATFE and perhaps a bomb squad.

Evacuations

This topic has been briefly discussed in chapter four, Emergency Situations. Further considerations on that topic would include the idea that an evacuation could lead people from one dangerous situation into another. One must consider the likelihood of a secondary device in the evacuation zone. The threat must be totally evaluated before considering evacuation. There are three possible scenarios to consider. They are; no evacuation and people continue their normal routines. A partial evacuation would leave essential personnel behind after all others have left. Finally, there is a full evacuation, when all leave the building or area.

Safety Considerations

If one suspects or confirms the presence of an IED everyone must move from that location to a safe place, period. Remember, if a person can observe the IED, the IED can if detonated kill that person. Once in a safe place contact the proper responder. Note a cell phone is a radio. Do not use one or any other radio within three hundred feet of the device. When calling the responder use a land line, the regular phone on a dedicated phone line.

When notifying a responder give as much detail regarding the device, real or suspected as is possible. The details should include location and the appearance of the device. Removal of the device should be accomplished by a trained bomb technician only.

The size and type of explosive device, plus terrain, shielding and other factors will determine the size of the area to be isolated. The distance from the device will influence the need for evacuation, staging locations, the placement of a medical treatment area and perimeter control points. Safely obtain as much casualty information as is possible. This would include; the number of victims, their location, condition and status.

Consideration must be given to the capabilities of the resources at hand, people and equipment. The IC will look to those resources to prevent loss of life. For example the IC may utilize equipment as shields to reduce shock waves, or consider opening doors and windows to reduce a blast's impact. Consideration must also be given to response time for key personnel such as bomb squad technicians. They may be on hand and come quickly or be from a distant jurisdiction and take hours to arrive. Finally, one must consider commitment levels of on-scene resources. There will be major decisions early on pertaining to the level of organizational engagement. The IC may commit personnel to dangerous duties such as searching for victims in weakened buildings. Prior to the commitment The IC must engage in a hazard-risk assessment and follow the agency's prescribed procedures.

Other safety considerations include notifying the proper authorities, staging areas for EMS, the police and fire department personnel and their equipment, prevention of further harm from explosive devices by establishing isolation zones and again do not use radios, radar or television transmitting devices.

10-10   CONCLUSION

The focus of this chapter has been on RAIN regarding the five categories of WMD; chemicals, biological, radiological material and nuclear weapons and finally explosive devices. The R in RAIN presents a major difficulty. In reality recognition of these agents and devises would be difficult if not improbable by minimally trained individuals. To overcome this handicap the guard should consider the ideas of suspicion and access control.

Suspicious is the operative word here. If it is out of place and does not belong it requires attention. Again, one knows what is out of place if one knows what is in place. If one cannot determine what is normal, one cannot determine what is not, know the post. Yes, this thought is repetitive. One must also rely on the senses, if the smell is not normal it deserves attention. If one observes a package out of place, it deserves attention and so forth.

Access control plays an important role when dealing with WMD. If the terrorist does not have access then he or she cannot deliver the agent or device. Strict attention should be paid to access control procedures.

In chapter four emergency situations were discussed. They still apply. Those situations present additional material for the reader to consider in response the WMD situations. They have also been retained in this work because they are still part of the original block of instruction.

Stay SAS (safe, alert and smart)!

Notes

GLOSSARY

Many terms listed herein many not be presented in this training course, however, they may be relevant in a CBRNE (Chemical, Biological, Radiological, Nuclear & High Yield Explosives) incident.

A

Alternate Light Source   Equipment used to produce visible and invisible light at various wavelengths to enhance or visualize potential items of evidence (fluids, fingerprints, clothing fibers, etc.).

Alpha   A type of radiation depositing a large amount of energy in a short distance of travel. Alpha radiation is an internal hazard only.

Ammonia   A commercially available, non-persistent chemical agent, usually disseminated in liquid or gas form. Has a very sharp, irritating, pungent odor, similar to cat urine.

Anthrax   A bacterial biological agent. It is naturally occurring and can be spread to humans by handling products from infected animals or by breathing in spores from infected animal products.

B

Bacteria   Single-celled organisms that cause a variety of diseases in animals, plants, and humans. They may also produce extremely potent toxins inside the guys body.

Beta   A type of radiation with a range of 10 to 30 feet. Beta radiation is an internal and external; however, one-quarter inch plastic or aluminum, or thick clothing will provide sufficient shielding.

Biohazard Bag   A container for materials that have been exposed to blood or other biological fluids and have the potential to be contaminated with hepatitis, AIDS, or other viruses.

Biological Agents

One of the following categories-bacteria, viruses, or toxins-used as a weapon.

Biological Fluids

Fluids that have human or animal origin, most commonly encountered at crimes scenes (e.g., blood, mucus, perspiration, saliva, semen, vaginal fluid, and urine).

Biological Weapon

Biological agents used to threaten human life (e.g., anthrax, smallpox, or any infectious disease).

Blister Agents

Military agents including mustards, lewisite, phosgene and oxime.

Blood Agents

Commercially available chemical agents, including hydrogen cyanide and cyanide and cyanogens chloride.

Blood-Borne Pathogen

Infectious, disease-causing microorganisms that may be found or transported in biological fluids.

Boundaries

The perimeter or border surrounding potential physical evidence related to the crime.

C

Chain of Command

A series of management positions in order of authority.

Chain of Custody

A process used to maintain and document the chronological history of the evidence. (Documents should include name and initials of the individual collecting the evidence, each person or entity subsequently having custody of it, dates the items were collected or transferred, agency and case number, victim's or suspect's name, and brief description of the item).

Chemical Agents

A chemical used as a weapon. Agents are further classified as Toxic Industrial Chemicals/Materials (TIC/TIM), Blister Agents, Blood Agents, Choking Agents, and Nerve Agents.

Chemical Threat

Compounds that may pose bodily harm if touched, ingested, inhaled, or ignited. These compounds may be encountered at a clandestine laboratory, or through a homemade bomb or tankard leakage (e.g., ether, alcohol, nitroglycerin, ammonium sulfate, red phosphorus, cleaning supplies, gasoline, or unlabeled chemicals).

Chlorine

A commercially available, non-persistent chemical choking agent, usually disseminated in liquid or gas form. Has a strong, offensive bleach smell.

Choking Agents

Military agents including phosgene and chlorine.

Clean/Sanitize

The process of removing biological and/or chemical contaminants from tools and/or equipment e.g., using a mixture of 10:1 household water and bleach).

Clear Text

The use of plain English in radio communications transmissions. No Ten Codes or agency-specific codes are used when utilizing Clear Text.

Cold Zone

Contains the command post and other support functions deemed necessary to control the incident.

Collect/Collection

The process of detecting, documenting, or retaining physical evidence.

Common Name

Each of the agents has a complex chemical name based on its composition and formula. They also have a common name that needs to be recognized.

Contamination

Term used when radiological material is physically attached to a person's skin or hair, or is ingested, inhaled, or received in a wound.

Control/Blank Sample

Material of a known source that presumably was uncontaminated during the commission of the crime.

Control Zones

The designation of the areas at the hazardous materials incident based on safety and the degree of hazard.

Cross-Contamination

The unwanted transfer of material between two or more sources of physical evidence.

D

Density   The mass per unit as a volume of substance under specified or standard conditions of temperature or pressure.

Dissemination   How an agent is dispersed.

Documentation   Written notes, audio/videotapes, printed forms, sketches, and/or photographs that form a detailed record of the scene, evidence recovered, and actions taken during the search of the crime scene.

Domestic Terrorism   The unlawful or threatened use of force or violence by a group or individual based and operating entirely within the United States and/or Puerto Rico, without foreign direction, and whose acts are directed at elements of the US Government and/or its population, in the furtherance of political or social goals.

E

Emergency Management Coordinator/Director   The individual within each political subdivision that has coordination responsibility for jurisdictional emergency management.

Emergency Medical Technician (EMT)   A health-care specialist with particular skills and knowledge in pre-hospital emergency medicine.

Emergency Operations   A pre-designated facility established by an agency or jurisdiction to coordinate the overall agency or jurisdictional response and support to an emergency.

Emergency Response Guidebook (ERG)   A guide to aid individuals in quickly identifying hazards of the materials involved in an incident.

Evidence Identifiers   Tape, labels, containers and string tags used to identify the evidence, the person collecting the evidence, the date the evidence was gathered, basic criminal offense information, and a brief description of the pertinent evidence.

Explosives   Also referred to as high explosives, explosives are designed to yield a near-instantaneous release of energy.

Exposure   Term used when radiation, but not radioactive material, reaches a person. The Source of the radiation (radioactive material) is not on or inside the person.

F
First Responder   The initial responding public safety official or service provider arriving at the scene.

G
Gamma   A type of radiation with a range of hundreds of feet. Gamma radiation is an Internal and external hazard, and shielding must be by very dense material.

General Signs and Symptoms   An indicator of disease, disorder, or exposure and how quickly one might detect these signs and symptoms.

H
History   Demonstrated terrorist activity over time or have a recorded, violent criminal history.

Hot Zone   The area immediately surrounding a hazardous materials incident, which extends far enough to prevent adverse effects from hazardous materials releases to personnel outside the zone.

Hydrogen Cyanide   A commercial available, non-persistent chemical blood agent, usually disseminated in liquid or gas form. Has a bitter almond scent.

I
Incident   An occurrence, caused by either human action or natural phenomena, that requires action by emergency service personnel to prevent or minimize loss of life or damage to property and/or natural resources.

Initial Action   The actions taken by the first resources to arrive at an incident.

Initial Responding Officer

The first law enforcement officer to arrive at the scene.

Intentions

Credible advocacy/threats of force or violence, or acts, or preparations to act, evidencing the intent to create a WMD, or carry out a plan to release a WMD, or to participate in a WMD incident.

International Terrorism

The unlawful use of force or violence committed by a group or individual who has some connection to a foreign power, or whose activities transcend national boundaries against persons or property to intimidate or coerce a government, the civilian population, or any segment thereof, in furtherance of political or social objectives.

Investigator In Charge

The official responsible for the crime scene investigation.

J

Jane's Chem-Bio Handbook

A spiral-bound handbook that includes quick-reference tabs to easily look up and identify chemical and biological agents, delivery mechanisms, their effects, and how to respond.

L

Latent Print

A print impression not readily visible, made by contact of the hands or feet with a surface resulting in the transfer of materials from the skin to that surface.

Life Safety

The joint consideration of both the life and physical well being of individuals.

M

Measurement Scale

An object showing standard units of length, such as a ruler, used in photographic documentation of an item of evidence.

Military Designation/Symbol

Each agent has a symbol; it is not a chemical symbol or formula, but rather a shorthand way of designating the agent. Learn these symbols.

Mobilization	The process and procedures used by all organizations—federal, state and local—for activating, assembling, and transporting all resources that have been requested to respond to or support an incident.
Mobilization Center	An off-incident location at which emergency service personnel and equipment are temporarily located pending assignment, release, or reassignment.
Multiple Scenes	Two or more physical locations of evidence associated with a crime (e.g. glass jars or metal cans).

N

Nerve Agents	Military agents including tabun, sarin, soman, and VX.
Nonporous Container	Packaging through which liquids or vapors cannot pass (e.g., glass jars or metal cans).
Neutron	A type of radiation with a range of hundreds of feet. Neutron radiation is an internal and external hazard, requiring several feet of dirt or water, or a foot of concrete, for adequate shielding.

O

Other Responders	Individuals involved in an aspect of the crime scene, such as perimeter security, traffic control, media management, scene processing and technical support, as well as prosecutors, medical personnel, medical examiners, coroners, forensic examiners, evidence technicians, and fire and rescue officers.
Overpack	(1): A package used to contain one or more packages to facilitate handling and protection of the inner packages; (2): a term used to describe the placement of damaged or leaking packages in a recovery drum or an overpack; (3): the outer packaging for radioactive materials.

P

Patient

A victim (see victim) who is awaiting or is under medical care or treatment.

Personal Protective Equipment (PPE)

Articles such as disposable gloves, masks, and eye protection utilized to provide a barrier to keep biological or chemical hazards from contacting the skin, eyes, and mucous membranes, and to avoid contamination of the crime scene.

Phosgene

A commercially available, non-persistent chemical agent, usually disseminated in liquid or gas form. Has an odor of newly mown hay.

Potassium Chlorate

A common ingredient in some fireworks, potassium chlorate is an explosive with 83% of the power of TNT.

Potential Threat Element (PTE)

Any group or individual with which there are allegations or information indicating a possibility of the unlawful use of force or violence, specifically the utilization of a Weapon of Mass Destruction, against persons or property to intimidate or coerce a government, the civilian population, or any segment thereof, in furtherance of a specific agenda.

Porous Container

Packaging through which liquids or vapors may pass (e.g., paper bags, cloth bags).

Propellants

Also referred to as low explosives, propellants are designed to provide a controlled release of gas to perform useful work.

Pyrotechnics

Explosive type used to create smoke, light, heat, and sound; not typically used in suicide bombings, but in other types of bombings and arson.

R

Radiological Threat

The pending exposure to radiation energy. (This energy can be produced by short-wave x-rays or through unstable isotopes.)

Radiological Dispersal Device (RDD)

A conventional explosive or bomb containing radioactive material.

RAIN	Acronym. **R**ecognition, **A**voidance, **I**solation and Notification (RAIN) is used by individuals to quickly gather and process information and to synthesize the information in order to facilitate life safety actions in a WMD incident.
Rate of Action/ Onset Time	The period of time that elapses before a victim begins to show or feel the symptoms of a particular agent. With some agents, this time will be just a few seconds, in other cases it could be minutes to hours. Knowing the onset time is important because it indicates how much time is left.
Route of Entry	How the agent gets into the body. Most of the agents will enter through the respiratory (inhalation). Some of the agents can also enter through skin and eyes.

S

Sarin	A military, non-persistent chemical nerve agent, usually disseminated in liquid or gas form. Has a faintly sweet smell.
Smallpox	A viral biological agent. It is naturally occurring, and passes from person to person most readily during the cool, dry winter months.
Soman	A military, non-persistent chemical nerve agent, usually disseminated in liquid or gas form. Has a camphor smell.
Standard/Reference	Material of a verifiable/documented source which, when compared to evidence of an unknown source, shows an association or linkage between an offender, crime scene, and/or victim.
Symptoms	Each of the agents will cause the victim to exhibit symptoms. In many cases these symptoms can be recognized and provide an indicator of the type of agent.

T

Tabun

A military, non-persistent chemical nerve agent, usually disseminated in liquid or gas form. Has a slightly fruity smell.

Toxic Industrial Chemical/Materials (TIC/TIM)

Commercially available chemical agents including ammonia, chlorine, and hydrogen cyanide.

Toxicity

Toxicity is the term used to indicate how much of a substance (in this case, one of the agents) is needed to cause a specified effect such as incapacitation or death. The amount of agent needed to cause an effect is also referred to as a dose. Respiratory lethality or toxicity is expressed in parts per million (ppm). PPM is an expression of concentration (C) or how many parts of a given substance are mixed in a million parts of air. If an individual is exposed to this concentration over time (T), usually expressed in one minute, then he or she will receive a Dosage. The exact PPM concentration required to cause lethality is a variable, depending on breathing rate, health, etc. Taking into consideration these variables, the term LCt50 is the expression used to indicate a given PPM concentration expected to be lethal to 50 percent of those exposed for one minute. ICt50 would express the same, except I is the incapacitating dosage. Skin lethality is expressed as LD50 and will normally be expressed in grams or milligrams per individual. How much (or how little) is 1 part per Million Example: 1 drop of liquid from an eye dropper is 1 millionth of a tank of gas in an average compact car (13 gallon tank), or 1/8 inch is 1 millionth of a mile. A milligram is 1/1000 of a gram and there are 28.3 grams in an ounce.

Toxins

Potent poisons produced by almost every known major category of organism. Fungi, flowering plants, and bacteria produce many of the most deadly toxins.

Trace Evidence	Physical evidence that results from the transfer of small quantities of materials (e.g., hair, textile fibers, paint chips, glass fragments, gunshot residue particles).
Transient Evidence	Evidence that, by its very nature or the conditions at the scene, will lose its evidentiary value if not preserved and protected (e.g., blood in the rain).
Tularemia	A bacterial biological agent. It is naturally occurring and can be transmitted to humans by the bite of an infected tick, deerfly or other insect.

V

Venezuelan Equine Encephalomyelitis (VEE)	A viral biological agent. It is naturally occurring and not transmittable through human contact.
Victim	One whose injuries are the result of WMD exposure and has not yet received medical evaluation.
Viruses	Smaller than bacteria and uses the reproductive mechanism of host cells to create more viruses.
Volatility/Persistency	Volatility is important because it provides an indication of how rapidly an agent will evaporate. The more volatile an agent is, the more rapidly it will evaporate. Evaporation will cause the agent to become a true gas or vapor and reduce the liquid hazard. Temperature, wind speed, and humidity at the incident site influence how rapidly an agent will evaporate. This evaporation process is also referred to as persistency (the amount of time an agent will remain a threat in the incident site). A nonpersistent agent will not remain at the incident site as a persistent agent. Obviously, if an agent is released inside an enclosed space, weather will not play a role, and the persistency will normally increase.
VX	A military, persistent chemical nerve agent, usually disseminated in liquid or gas form. VX is odorless.

W

Warm Zone   The area where personnel, equipment decon-
                             tamination, and hot zone support takes place.

Weapon(s) of Mass   A weapon of mass destruction is any device that
Destruction (WMD)   is designed or intended intended to cause mass
                             destruction and/or death. (Refer to Title 18 USC,
                             Section 2332a for an in-depth definition).

INDEX

REFERENCE LIST

Center for Disease Control and Prevention. <http://emergency.cdc.gov/az/a.asp>

Center for Disease Control and Prevention. <http://www.cdc.gov/ncidod/dvbid/plague/>

Center for Disease Control and Prevention. <http://www.bt.cdc.gov/agent/plague/factsheet.asp>

Federal Bureau of Investigation. <http://www.fbi.gov/about-us/history/famous-cases/anthrax-amerithrax/amerithrax-investigation>

Hyper Physics. <http://hyperphysics.phy-astr.gsu.edu/hbase/hframe.html>

Semp BioQuickies: The VHS Virus. <http://www.semp.us/_media/securitas_9b.pdf>

World Health Organization. <http://www.who.int/mediacentre/factsheets/smallpox/en/>

Barrie, Allison. *"Tang Bomb: Liquid Explosives are the New Weapon of Choice."* http://www.foxnews.com/story/0,2933,356491,00.html

Francis. J., (1992). *The Complete Security Officer's Manual and Career Guide*. Orlando: Security digest publication.

Green, G., & Fischer, R. J. (1992). *Introduction to Security* (5th ed.) Boston: Butterworth-Heinemann.

Iannone, N. F., (1994). *Supervision of Police Personnel* (5th ed.) Englewood Cliffs: Prentis-Hall Career & Technology

Hoffman, T. W., (2010). *New York State Criminal Law for Security Professionals* New York: Looseleaf Law Publications, Inc.

New York State Criminal Procedure Law (current year). New York: Looseleaf Law Publications, Inc.

New York State Eight Hour In-Service Training Curriculum (2010). Albany: Division of Criminal Justice Services, Bureau of Municipal Police.

New York State Eight Hour Security Guard Pre-Service Training Curriculum (2010). Albany: Division of Criminal Justices Services, Bureau of Municipal Police.

New York State Law Extracts (current year). New York: Looseleaf Law Publications, Inc.

New York State Penal Law (current year). New York: Looseleaf Law Publications, Inc.

New York State Sixteen-hour On-The-Job Training Curriculum (2010). Albany: Division of Criminal Justice Services, Bureau of Municipal Police.

O'Hara, C. E., & O'Hara G. L., (1988). *Fundamentals of Criminal Investigation* (revised 5th ed.) Springfield: Charles C Thomas

A Note on Counter-Terrorism
Training and Additional Resources

When *Duties and Responsibilities for Security Officers in NYS* was first compiled, the threat of domestic terrorism had not yet reached the dangerously elevated levels we currently face. Looseleaf Law recognizes, however, that in today's pressurized atmosphere of terror threats, this type of training is crucial for every professional who accepts the challenge of protecting the safety of U.S. citizens and property.

In light of that, we strongly recommend that all security professionals read the following resources: